Concrete®

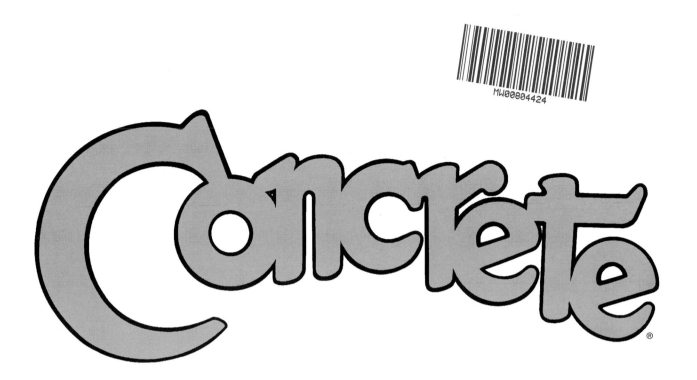

SHORT STORIES
1990-1995

PAUL
CHADWICK

With an introduction by
Mark Verheiden

DARK HORSE COMICS®

Jed Hotchkiss • *art assistance (selected stories)*
Bill Spicer • *lettering*
Lynn Adair • *collection editor*
Brian Gogolin • *collection design manager*

Mike Richardson • publisher
Neil Hankerson • executive vice president
David Scroggy • vice president of publishing
Lou Bank • vice president of sales & marketing
Andy Karabatsos • vice president of finance
Mark Anderson • general counsel
Randy Stradley • creative director
Cindy Marks • director of production & design
Mark Cox • art director
Sean Tierney • computer graphics director
Chris Creviston • director of accounting
Michael Martens • marketing director
Tod Borleske • sales & licensing director
Mark Ellington • director of operations
Dale LaFountain • director of m.i.s.

**Published by
Dark Horse Comics, Inc.
10956 SE Main Street
Milwaukie, OR 97222**

CONCRETE ®: SHORT STORIES 1990-1995
© 1990-1995, 1996 by Paul Chadwick.
Compilation © 1996 by Dark Horse Comics, Inc.
Cover image © 1995 by Paul Chadwick.

January 1996
First edition
ISBN: 1-56971-099-6

Printed in Canada

2 4 6 8 10 9 7 5 3 1

CONTENTS

INTRODUCTION

When Paul Chadwick first asked me to write the introduction to this collection of *Concrete* short stories, I was stumped. I mean, what more can be said about *Concrete*, one of the most original and highly praised comic-book series of the '80s and '90s? The walls of Paul's office are already buckling from the weight of awards received, and if good reviews were gold, Paul would be kicking Bill Gates out of the pole position on the *Forbes* "Most Wealthy" list. Bottom line: if you're the type of informed consumer who reads introductions to validate a book-buying decision, you can stop right now. This puppy has a pedigree.

Still, never one to shrink from a challenge, I reread the short stories in this volume to see if there was wiggle room for some trenchant revisionist analysis — a re-examination, if you will, of the Chadwickian oeuvre, complete with footnotes, words like "oeuvre," and the peculiar, comma-strewn sentence structure so common to academic review.[1]

Three problems with that approach: 1) You're going to read the stories yourself; you don't need me to tell you how good they are; 2) I slept through the critical dissertation lectures during my collegiate English lit. days (though, as I recall, Hemingway hated his mother); and 3) you're hardly dealing with an unbiased, dispassionate observer of Chadwick's work. You see, ladies and gentlemen, I slept on Paul Chadwick's couch — every sprung, metal-joint jabbing inch of the upholstered S.O.B. — and lived to tell the tale.

I've been lucky enough to call Paul Chadwick a friend since the mid-'70s, when we were both kids, struggling with this crazy, burning desire to write and draw comic books.[2] Separated by Pacific Northwest geography — Paul lived near Seattle while I dodged raindrops in the suburbs of Portland — we met through the mail not long after I'd organized an amateur press association called APA-FIVE.[3] Paul joined the group early on, writing and drawing hundreds of pages of material and quickly distinguishing himself as one of the good guys. Whether he actually owned any furniture at this point, I'm not entirely sure.

Most people require a certain "ramping up" period before their skills mature, but Paul's talent was evident from day one. This preternatural, early ability was the source of great competitive anguish among those of us still trying to figure out why "i" went before "e" except after "c." I'm not trying to suggest Paul hasn't advanced artistically since those early days; only noting that the careful, deliberate subject matter you'll find in many of these *Concrete* tales is hardly the work of some "Johnny-Come-Trendoid" hopping on the latest fad. You're getting the real article, carefully considered, which is one reason the stories tend to linger in the brain-pan long after you've finished reading them.

Sometime in the late '70s/early '80s[4], Paul moved to Los Angeles to attend art school. After graduation, he toiled for a time in the vineyard known as Hollywood, stomping celluloid grapes while simultaneously working on the initial sketches and concepts that would become *Concrete*. It was around this time that Paul invited me to move to L.A. — so I might try my hand at the picture business — offering to share his apartment until I could get on my feet. And so I made my first acquaintance with Paul's torturous couch. Aye, matey, I can see it now — green it was, the scabrous nightmare, like some medieval torture, torn from the pages of Poe and resurrected into plush-pillow life —

— Wait a minute. Did I just turn into a pirate to talk about a couch? Sorry.

Concrete is ostensibly about a political speech writer who finds himself trapped in a miraculous body of living stone, but the character's origin is virtually the only fantastic element in the series. In mainstream comic-book terms, Concrete is an anomaly. Despite the character's physical appearance and great strength, he really isn't a "hero" in the cape-and-costume sense. If you're coming aboard expecting the conventions of a superhero book, you're in for rough sailing. Nobody grits their teeth[5], nobody punches anyone else through walls, and the characters are driven by human emotions considerably more complicated than rage and revenge and sleeping on an extremely uncomfortable couch.[6] If you're looking for "Concrete-Man," make a U-turn and move along.

Of course, this non-hero modus operandi violates every commercial imperative of mainstream comics, but dammit, ice cream can be more than vanilla (though I draw the line at "Peanut Butter and Jelly"), television can be more than sitcoms, and comics can be more — much more — than wall-to-wall punch-outs.[7]

And this collection of *Concrete* stories proves the point. The tales herein are less high-powered rock 'em sock 'em drama than meditations on our world — on our devastated ecology, on art, loneliness, and the casual caprice of fate — all filtered through the sensibilities of Concrete, whose grotesque condition at once distances him from the world of men (and more importantly for Concrete, women) while perversely bringing him closer to hidden worlds in the sky, the earth, and the sea.

Concrete's exquisite torment is the emotional core of these stories, and the great miracle of this book is that his torment doesn't have the whine of self-pity. More often than not, Concrete overcomes what others might perceive as adversity to take joy from his condition. And so, stories that in other hands might sink into despair become celebrations of the wonder of intellectual curiosity and the fulfillment of dreams.

Paul Chadwick's a good friend, superb writer, and extraordinary artist — if it weren't for that damn couch, he'd be too wonderful for words — and *Concrete* is one of the best comics of the last ten years. But don't take my word for it. Turn to story one, page one, panel one, and read on.

—Mark Verheiden
Pasadena, CA
September 1995

---

1. Ignore this footnote.
2. If there are any ageist movie executives reading this, please note that Paul and I swapped high fives across our delivery room incubators moments after we were born.
3. Other early members included Mark Badger, Chris Warner, Frank Miller, Randy Stradley, and Mike Richardson, but unfortunately, no one's heard from any of these people since.
4. Sorry about the broad range in dates, but you don't expect me to actually research this, do you?
5. In fact, I don't think Concrete HAS any teeth. But don't take anything I say for granite. (At least I kept the gratuitous rock puns in the footnotes!)
6. Despite this, you're not going to find me leveling a broad stroke, absolutist tirade against mainstream comics. By the way, is Superman still dead?
7. Have I mentioned that goddamn couch yet?

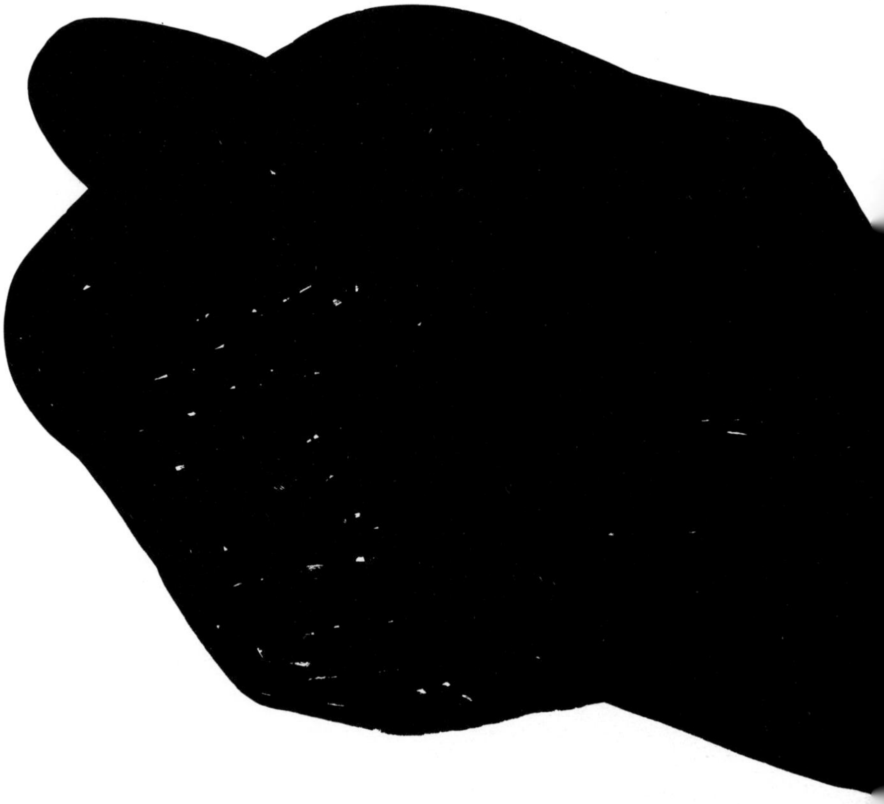

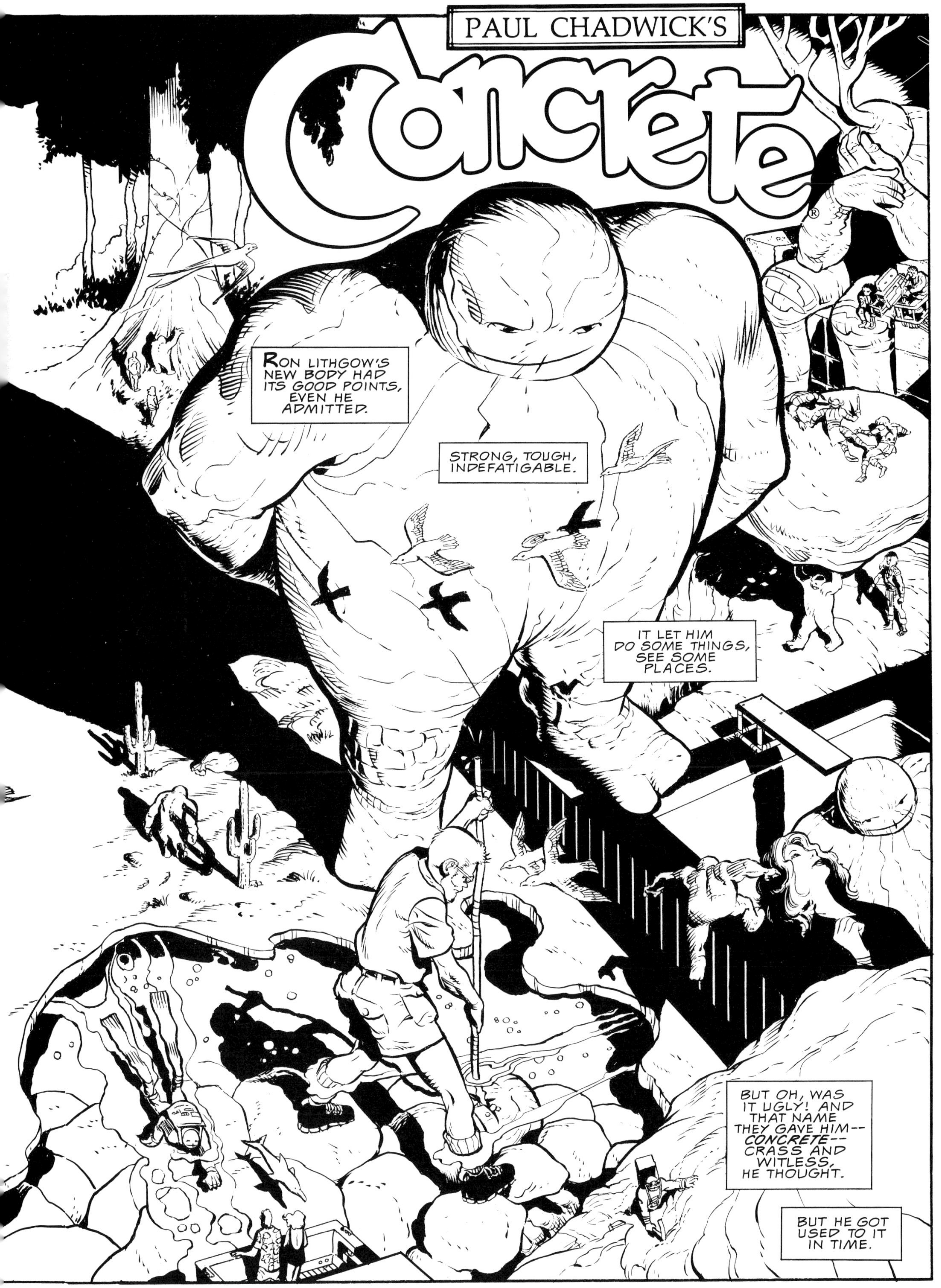
PAUL CHADWICK'S
Concrete®
RON LITHGOW'S NEW BODY HAD ITS GOOD POINTS, EVEN HE ADMITTED.
STRONG, TOUGH, INDEFATIGABLE.
IT LET HIM DO SOME THINGS, SEE SOME PLACES.
BUT OH, WAS IT UGLY! AND THAT NAME THEY GAVE HIM-- CONCRETE-- CRASS AND WITLESS, HE THOUGHT.
BUT HE GOT USED TO IT IN TIME.

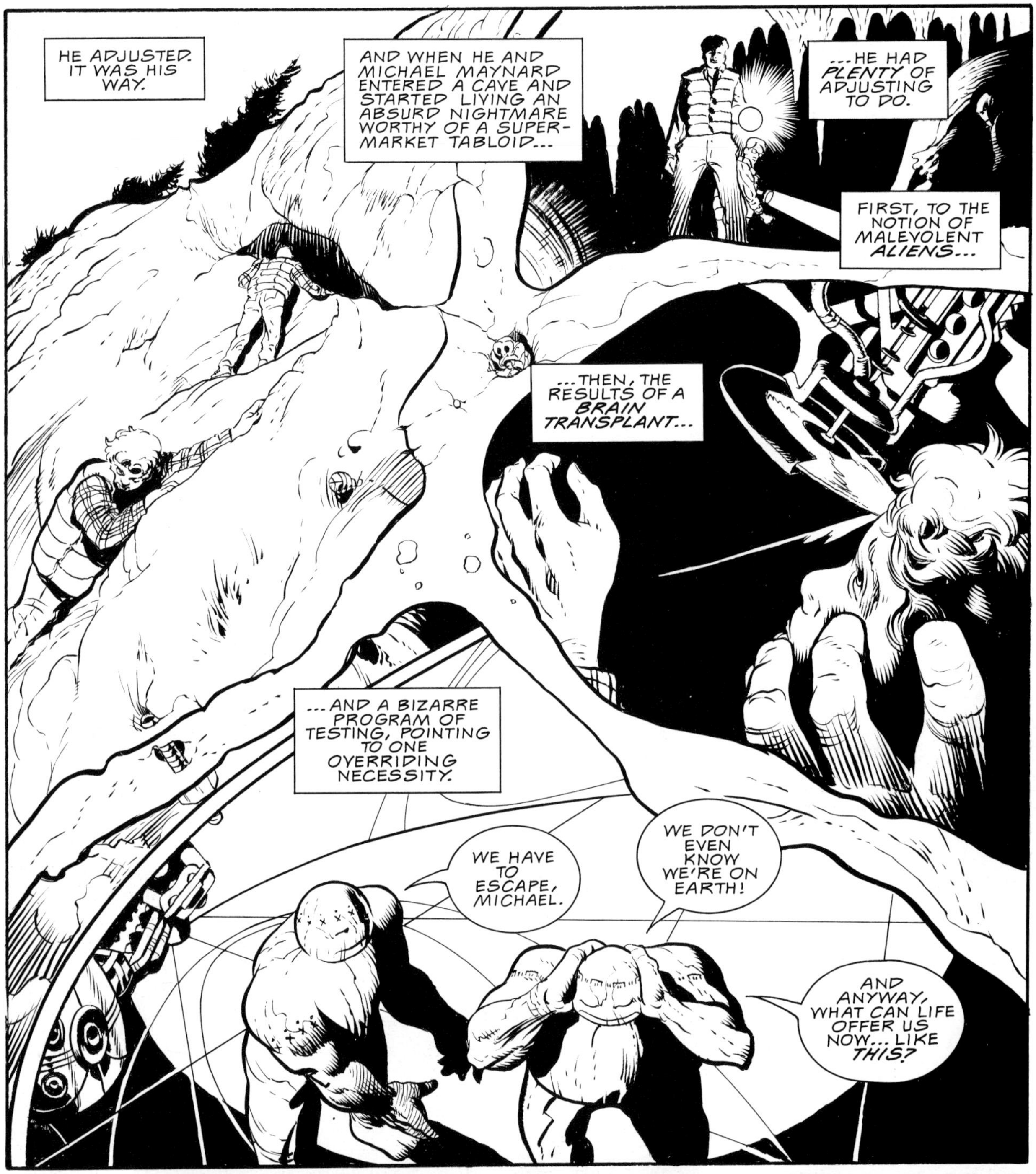
HE ADJUSTED. IT WAS HIS WAY.
AND WHEN HE AND MICHAEL MAYNARD ENTERED A CAVE AND STARTED LIVING AN ABSURD NIGHTMARE WORTHY OF A SUPER-MARKET TABLOID...
...HE HAD PLENTY OF ADJUSTING TO DO.
FIRST, TO THE NOTION OF MALEVOLENT ALIENS...
...THEN, THE RESULTS OF A BRAIN TRANSPLANT...
...AND A BIZARRE PROGRAM OF TESTING, POINTING TO ONE OVERRIDING NECESSITY.
WE HAVE TO ESCAPE, MICHAEL.
WE DON'T EVEN KNOW WE'RE ON EARTH!
AND ANYWAY, WHAT CAN LIFE OFFER US NOW... LIKE THIS?
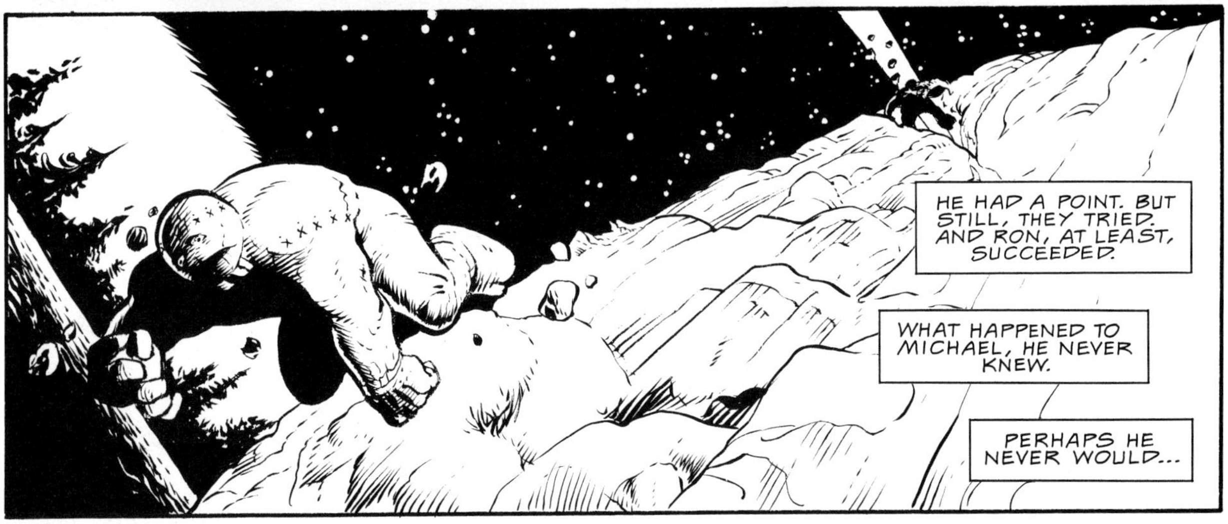
HE HAD A POINT. BUT STILL, THEY TRIED. AND RON, AT LEAST, SUCCEEDED.
WHAT HAPPENED TO MICHAEL, HE NEVER KNEW.
PERHAPS HE NEVER WOULD...

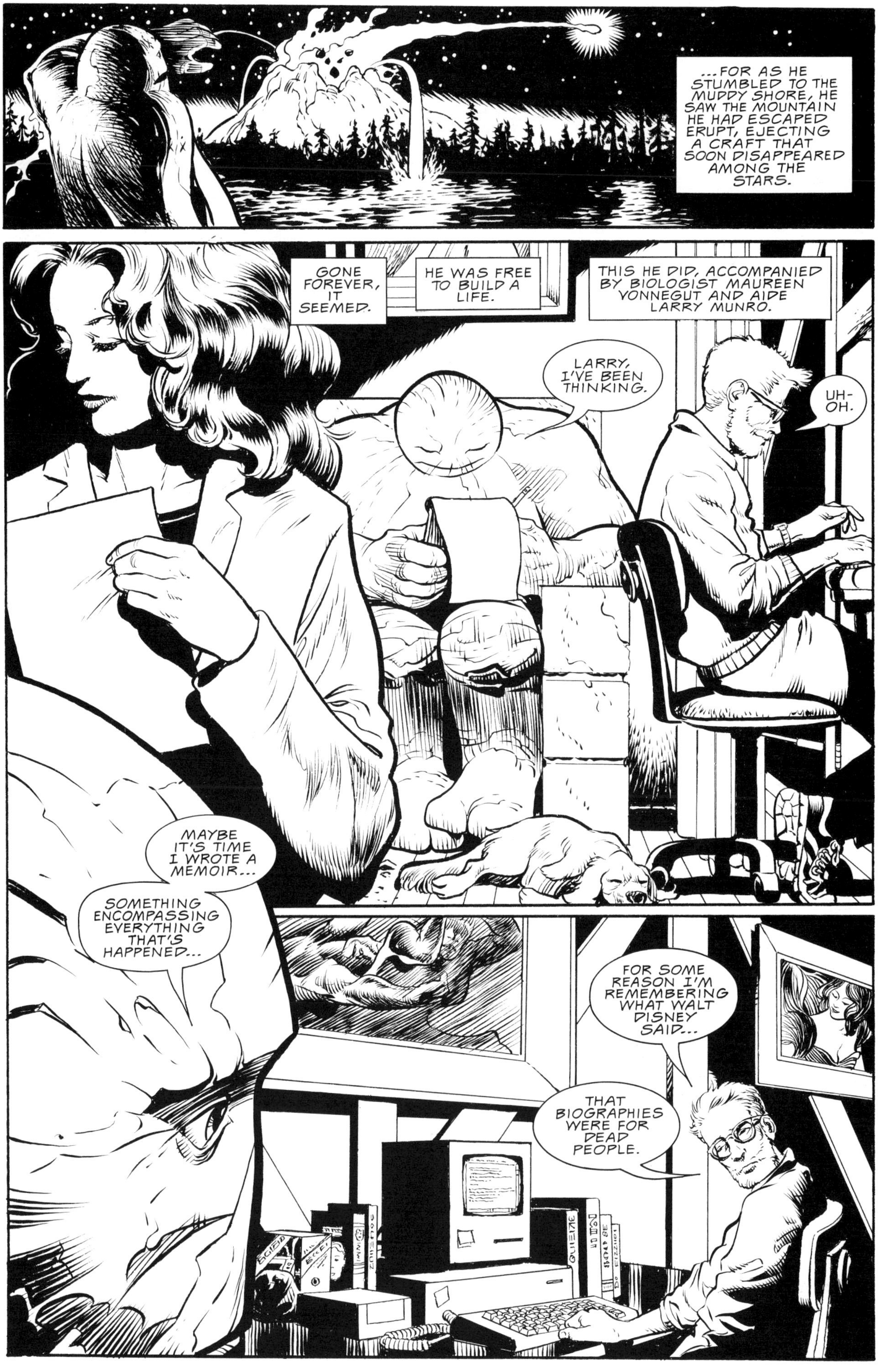
...FOR AS HE STUMBLED TO THE MUDDY SHORE, HE SAW THE MOUNTAIN HE HAD ESCAPED ERUPT, EJECTING A CRAFT THAT SOON DISAPPEARED AMONG THE STARS.
GONE FOREVER, IT SEEMED.
HE WAS FREE TO BUILD A LIFE.
THIS HE DID, ACCOMPANIED BY BIOLOGIST MAUREEN VONNEGUT AND AIDE LARRY MUNRO.
LARRY, I'VE BEEN THINKING.
UH-OH.
MAYBE IT'S TIME I WROTE A MEMOIR...
SOMETHING ENCOMPASSING EVERYTHING THAT'S HAPPENED...
FOR SOME REASON I'M REMEMBERING WHAT WALT DISNEY SAID...
THAT BIOGRAPHIES WERE FOR DEAD PEOPLE.

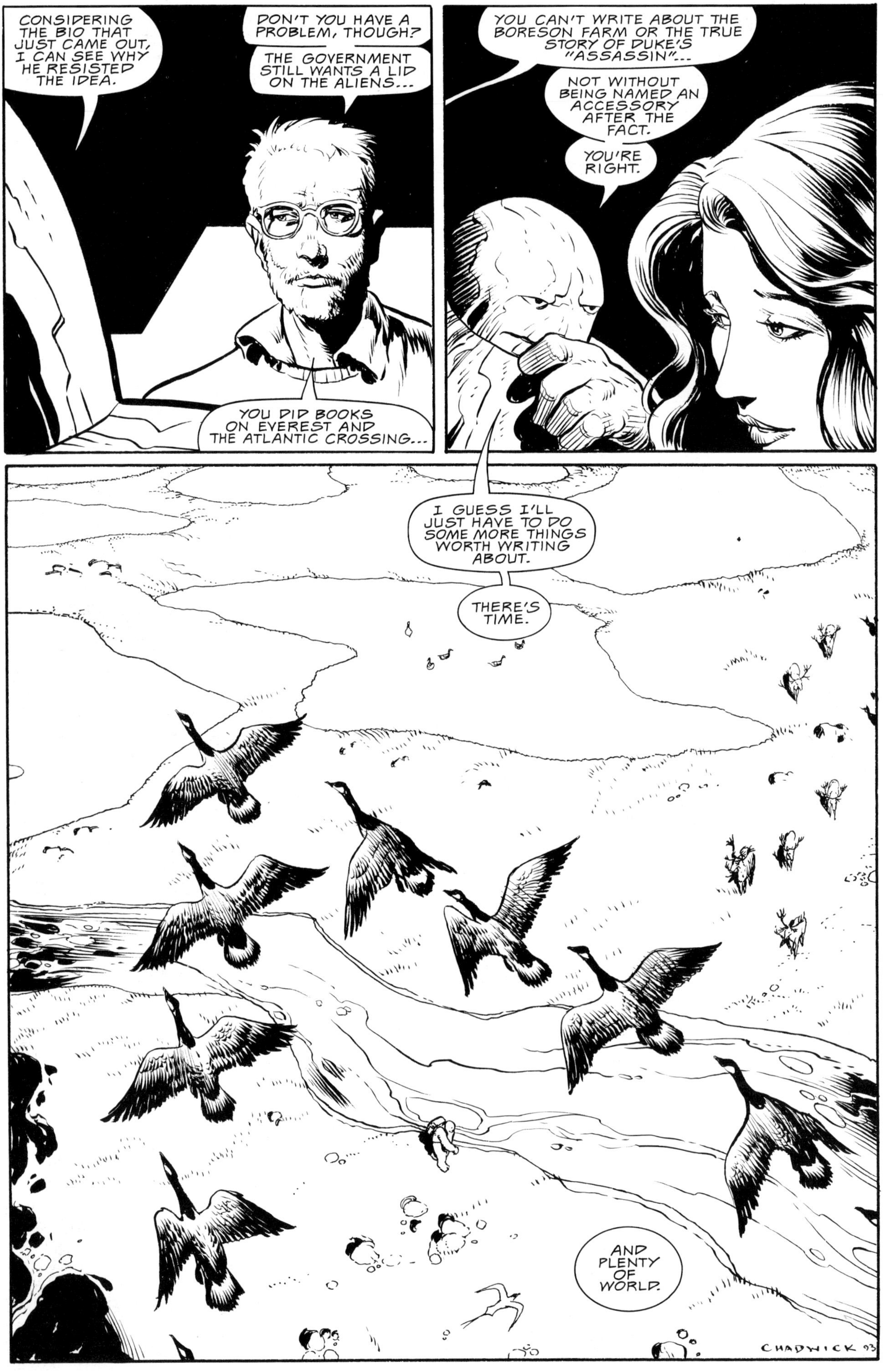
CONSIDERING THE BIO THAT JUST CAME OUT, I CAN SEE WHY HE RESISTED THE IDEA.
DON'T YOU HAVE A PROBLEM, THOUGH?
THE GOVERNMENT STILL WANTS A LID ON THE ALIENS...
YOU DID BOOKS ON EVEREST AND THE ATLANTIC CROSSING...
YOU CAN'T WRITE ABOUT THE BORESON FARM OR THE TRUE STORY OF DUKE'S "ASSASSIN"...
NOT WITHOUT BEING NAMED AN ACCESSORY AFTER THE FACT.
YOU'RE RIGHT.
I GUESS I'LL JUST HAVE TO DO SOME MORE THINGS WORTH WRITING ABOUT.
THERE'S TIME.
AND PLENTY OF WORLD.
CHADWICK 93

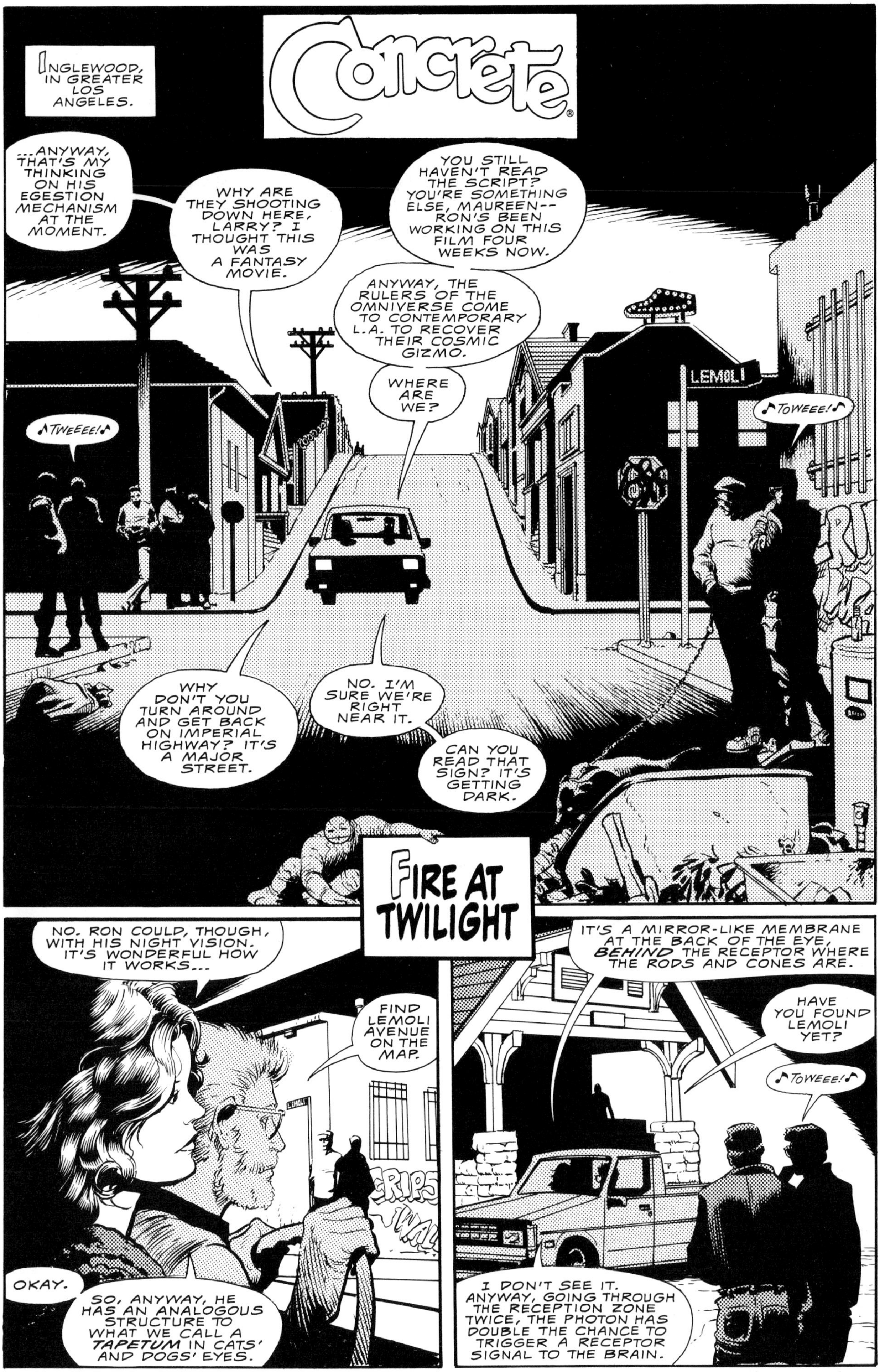
Concrete®
INGLEWOOD, IN GREATER LOS ANGELES.
...ANYWAY, THAT'S MY THINKING ON HIS EGESTION MECHANISM AT THE MOMENT.
WHY ARE THEY SHOOTING DOWN HERE, LARRY? I THOUGHT THIS WAS A FANTASY MOVIE.
YOU STILL HAVEN'T READ THE SCRIPT? YOU'RE SOMETHING ELSE, MAUREEN-- RON'S BEEN WORKING ON THIS FILM FOUR WEEKS NOW.
ANYWAY, THE RULERS OF THE OMNIVERSE COME TO CONTEMPORARY L.A. TO RECOVER THEIR COSMIC GIZMO.
WHERE ARE WE?
LEMOLI
♪TWEEEE!♪
♪TOWEEE!♪
WHY DON'T YOU TURN AROUND AND GET BACK ON IMPERIAL HIGHWAY? IT'S A MAJOR STREET.
NO. I'M SURE WE'RE RIGHT NEAR IT.
CAN YOU READ THAT SIGN? IT'S GETTING DARK.
FIRE AT TWILIGHT
NO. RON COULD, THOUGH, WITH HIS NIGHT VISION. IT'S WONDERFUL HOW IT WORKS...
FIND LEMOLI AVENUE ON THE MAP.
CRIPS
OKAY.
SO, ANYWAY, HE HAS AN ANALOGOUS STRUCTURE TO WHAT WE CALL A TAPETUM IN CATS' AND DOGS' EYES.
IT'S A MIRROR-LIKE MEMBRANE AT THE BACK OF THE EYE, BEHIND THE RECEPTOR WHERE THE RODS AND CONES ARE.
HAVE YOU FOUND LEMOLI YET?
♪TOWEEE!♪
I DON'T SEE IT. ANYWAY, GOING THROUGH THE RECEPTION ZONE TWICE, THE PHOTON HAS DOUBLE THE CHANCE TO TRIGGER A RECEPTOR SIGNAL TO THE BRAIN.

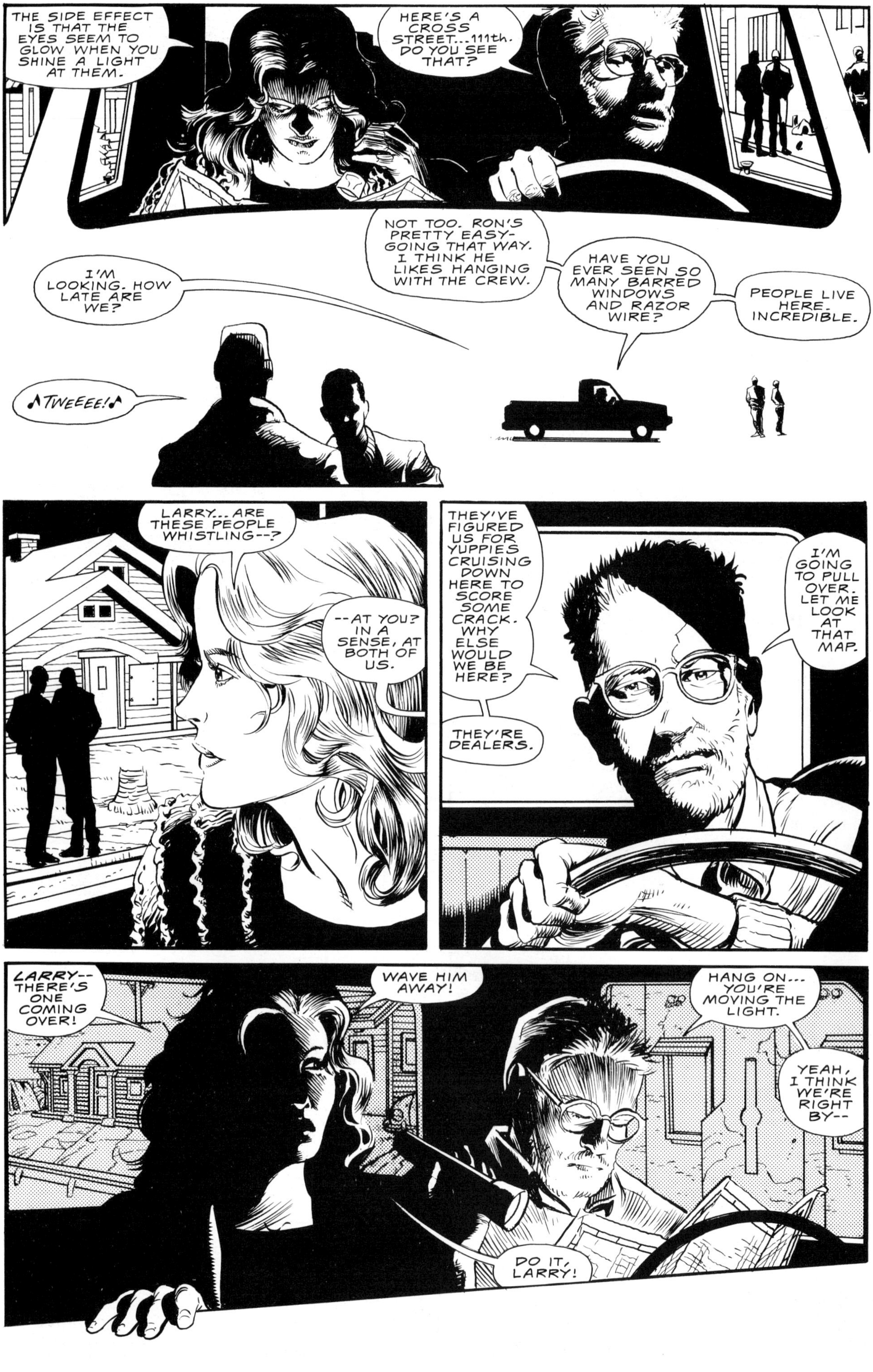
THE SIDE EFFECT IS THAT THE EYES SEEM TO GLOW WHEN YOU SHINE A LIGHT AT THEM.
HERE'S A CROSS STREET...111th. DO YOU SEE THAT?
I'M LOOKING. HOW LATE ARE WE?
NOT TOO. RON'S PRETTY EASY-GOING THAT WAY. I THINK HE LIKES HANGING WITH THE CREW.
HAVE YOU EVER SEEN SO MANY BARRED WINDOWS AND RAZOR WIRE?
PEOPLE LIVE HERE. INCREDIBLE.
♪TWEEEE!♪
LARRY... ARE THESE PEOPLE WHISTLING--?
--AT YOU? IN A SENSE, AT BOTH OF US.
THEY'VE FIGURED US FOR YUPPIES CRUISING DOWN HERE TO SCORE SOME CRACK. WHY ELSE WOULD WE BE HERE?
THEY'RE DEALERS.
I'M GOING TO PULL OVER. LET ME LOOK AT THAT MAP.
LARRY-- THERE'S ONE COMING OVER!
WAVE HIM AWAY!
HANG ON... YOU'RE MOVING THE LIGHT.
YEAH, I THINK WE'RE RIGHT BY--
DO IT, LARRY!

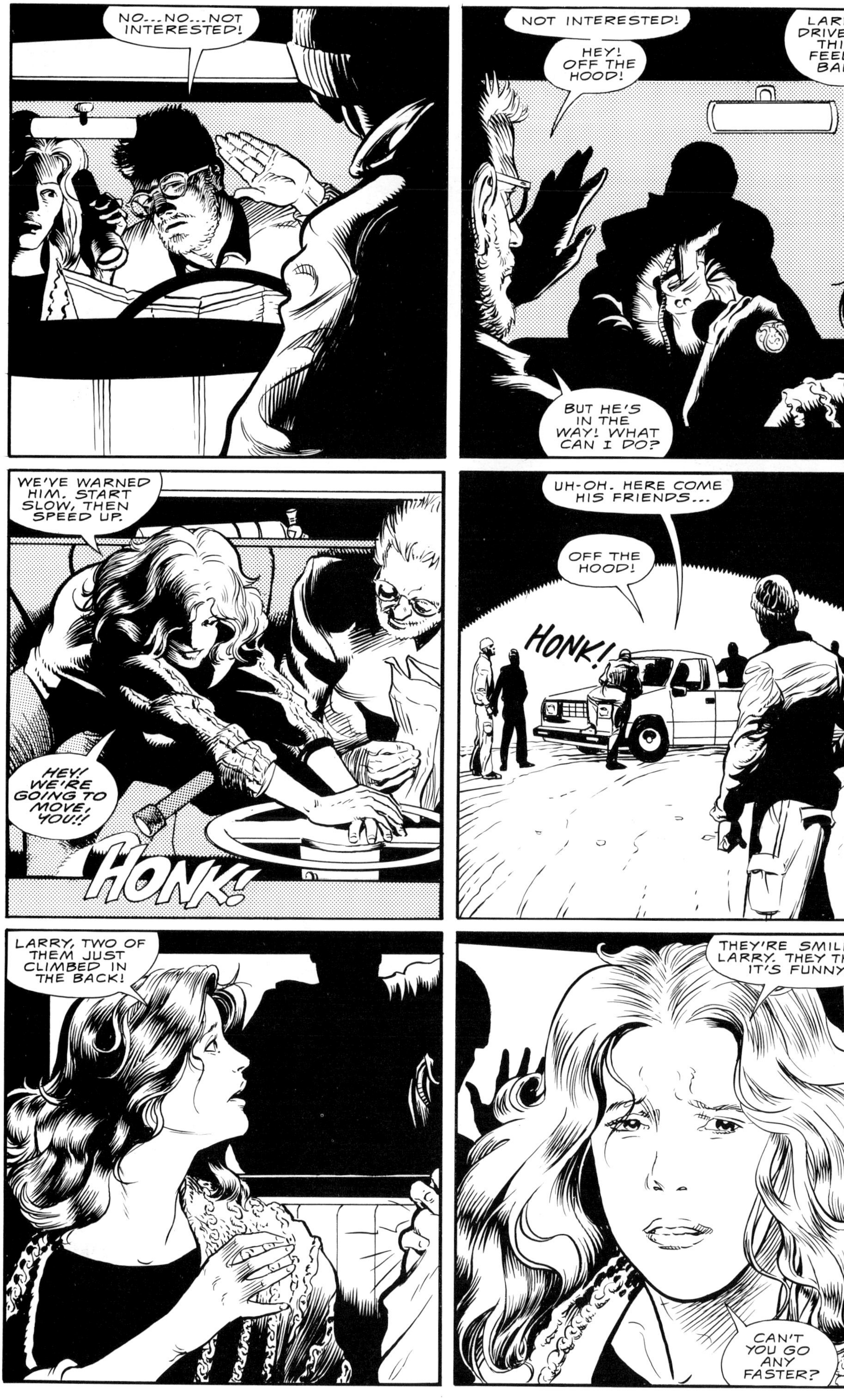
NO...NO...NOT INTERESTED!
NOT INTERESTED!
HEY! OFF THE HOOD!
LARRY, DRIVE ON. THIS FEELS BAD...
BUT HE'S IN THE WAY! WHAT CAN I DO?
WE'VE WARNED HIM. START SLOW, THEN SPEED UP.
HEY! WE'RE GOING TO MOVE, YOU!!
HONK!
UH-OH. HERE COME HIS FRIENDS...
OFF THE HOOD!
HONK!
LARRY, TWO OF THEM JUST CLIMBED IN THE BACK!
THEY'RE SMILING, LARRY. THEY THINK IT'S FUNNY.
CAN'T YOU GO ANY FASTER?

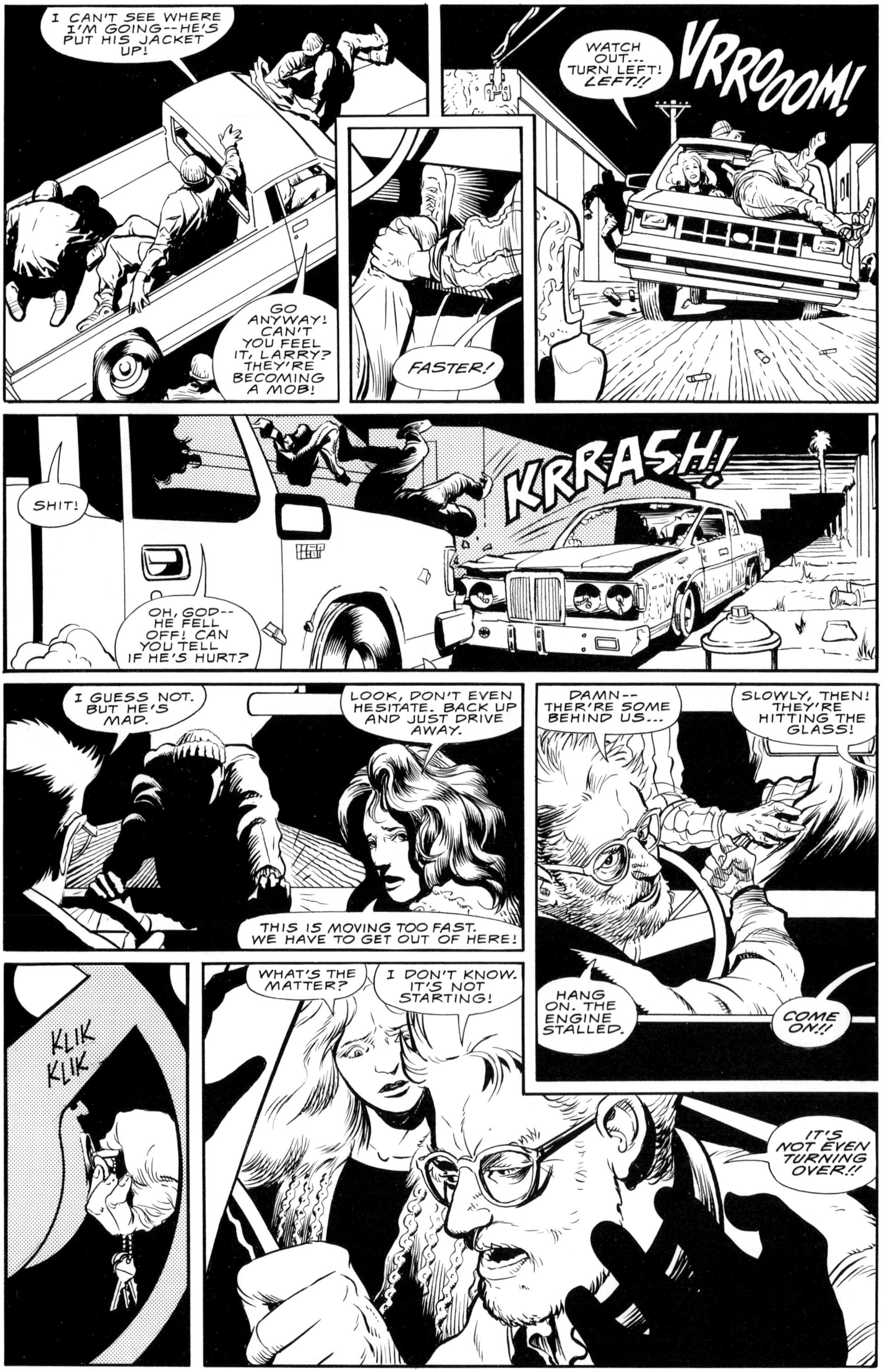
I CAN'T SEE WHERE I'M GOING--HE'S PUT HIS JACKET UP!
GO ANYWAY! CAN'T YOU FEEL IT, LARRY? THEY'RE BECOMING A MOB!
FASTER!
WATCH OUT... TURN LEFT! LEFT!!
VRROOOM!
SHIT!
KRRASH!
OH, GOD-- HE FELL OFF! CAN YOU TELL IF HE'S HURT?
I GUESS NOT. BUT HE'S MAD.
LOOK, DON'T EVEN HESITATE. BACK UP AND JUST DRIVE AWAY.
THIS IS MOVING TOO FAST. WE HAVE TO GET OUT OF HERE!
DAMN-- THER'RE SOME BEHIND US...
SLOWLY, THEN! THEY'RE HITTING THE GLASS!
HANG ON. THE ENGINE STALLED.
COME ON!!
KLIK KLIK
WHAT'S THE MATTER?
I DON'T KNOW. IT'S NOT STARTING!
IT'S NOT EVEN TURNING OVER!!

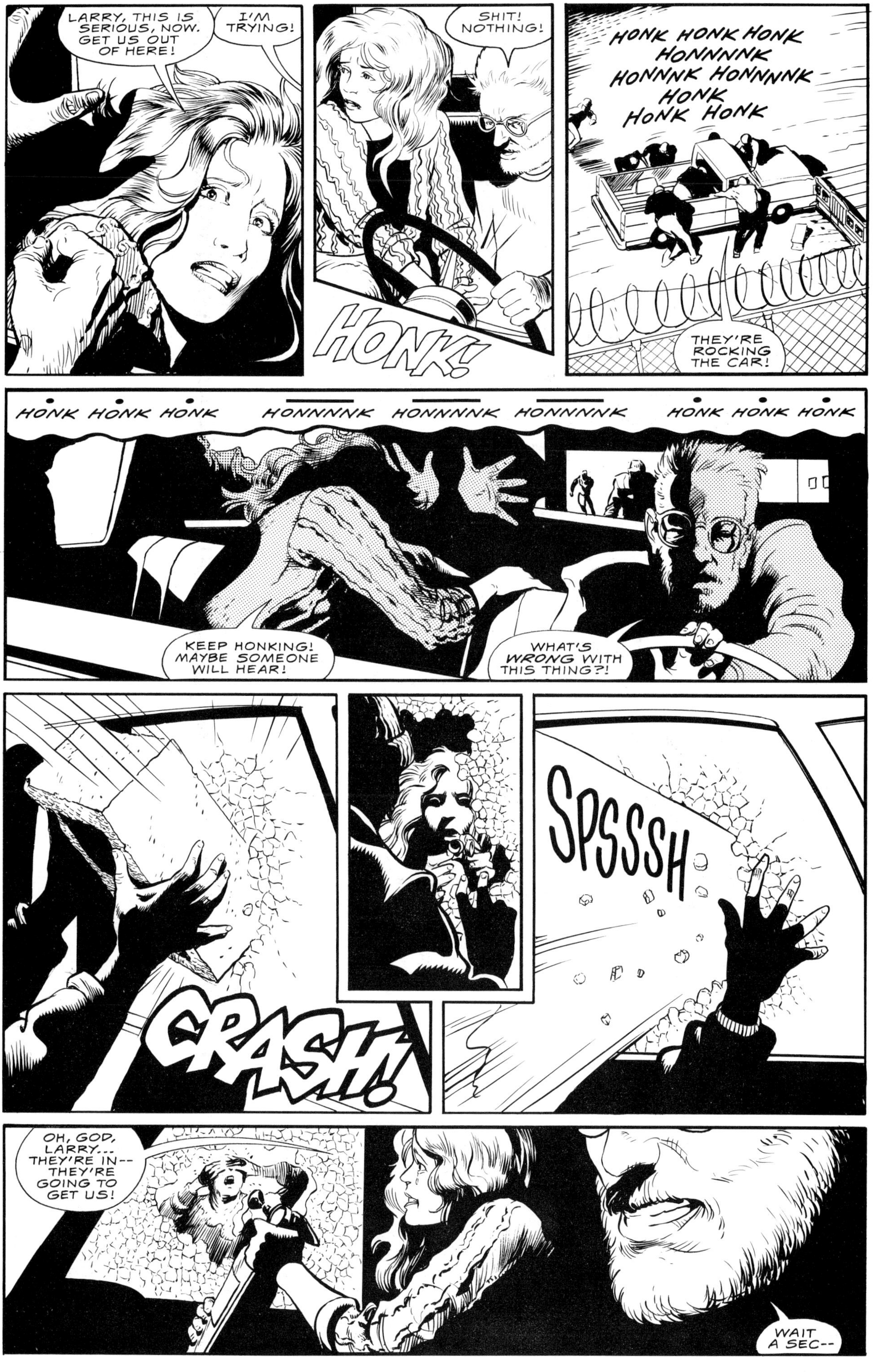

LARRY, THIS IS SERIOUS, NOW. GET US OUT OF HERE!
I'M TRYING!
SHIT! NOTHING!
HONK!
HONK HONK HONK HONNNNK HONNNK HONNNNK HONK HONK HONK
THEY'RE ROCKING THE CAR!
HONK HONK HONK HONNNNK HONNNNK HONNNNK HONK HONK HONK
KEEP HONKING! MAYBE SOMEONE WILL HEAR!
WHAT'S WRONG WITH THIS THING?!
CRASH!
SPSSSH
OH, GOD, LARRY... THEY'RE IN-- THEY'RE GOING TO GET US!
WAIT A SEC--

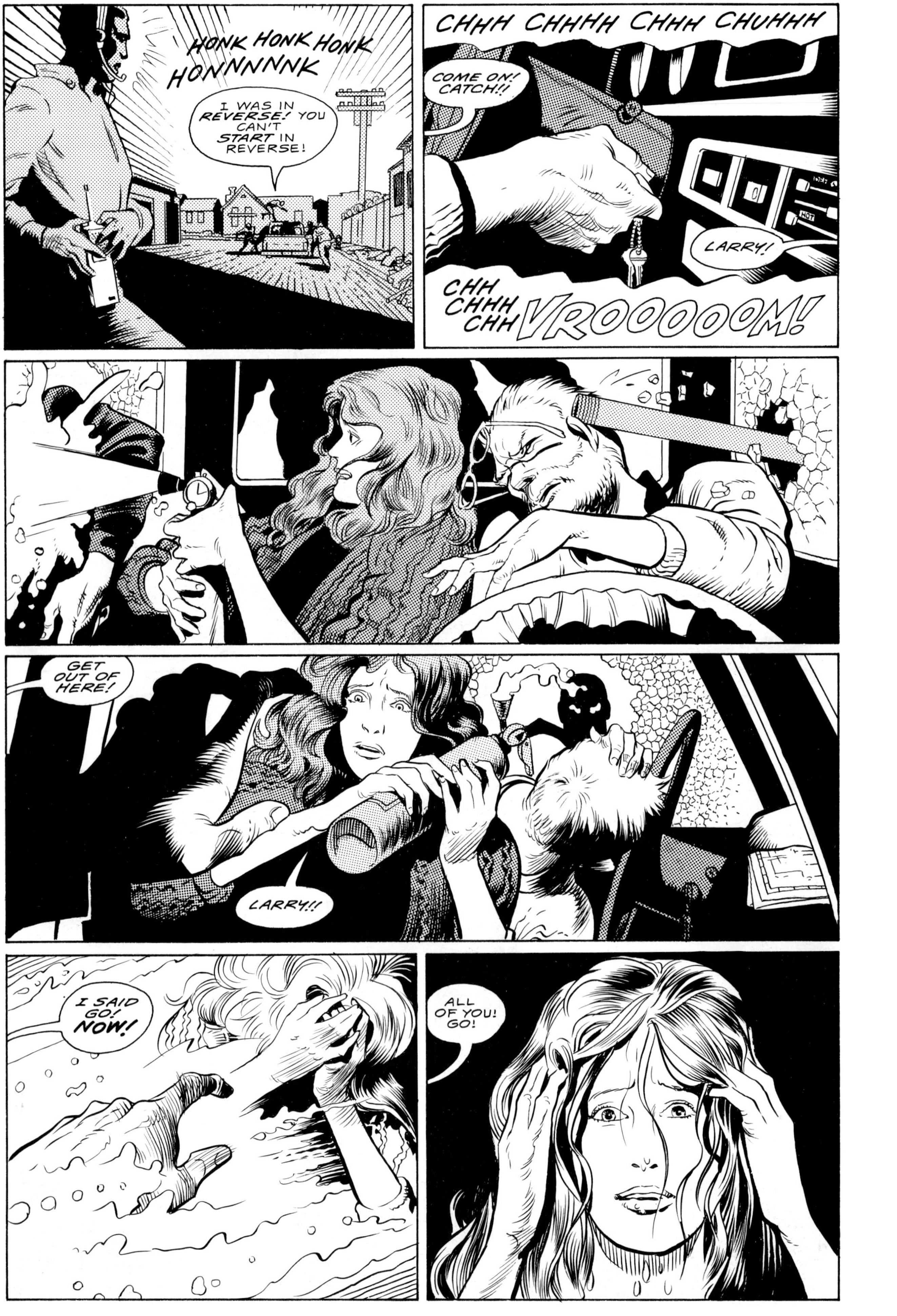
HONK HONK HONK
HONNNNNK
I WAS IN REVERSE! YOU CAN'T START IN REVERSE!
CHHH CHHHH CHHH CHUHHH
COME ON! CATCH!!
LARRY!
CHH CHHH CHH VROOOOOM!
GET OUT OF HERE!
LARRY!!
I SAID GO! NOW!
ALL OF YOU! GO!

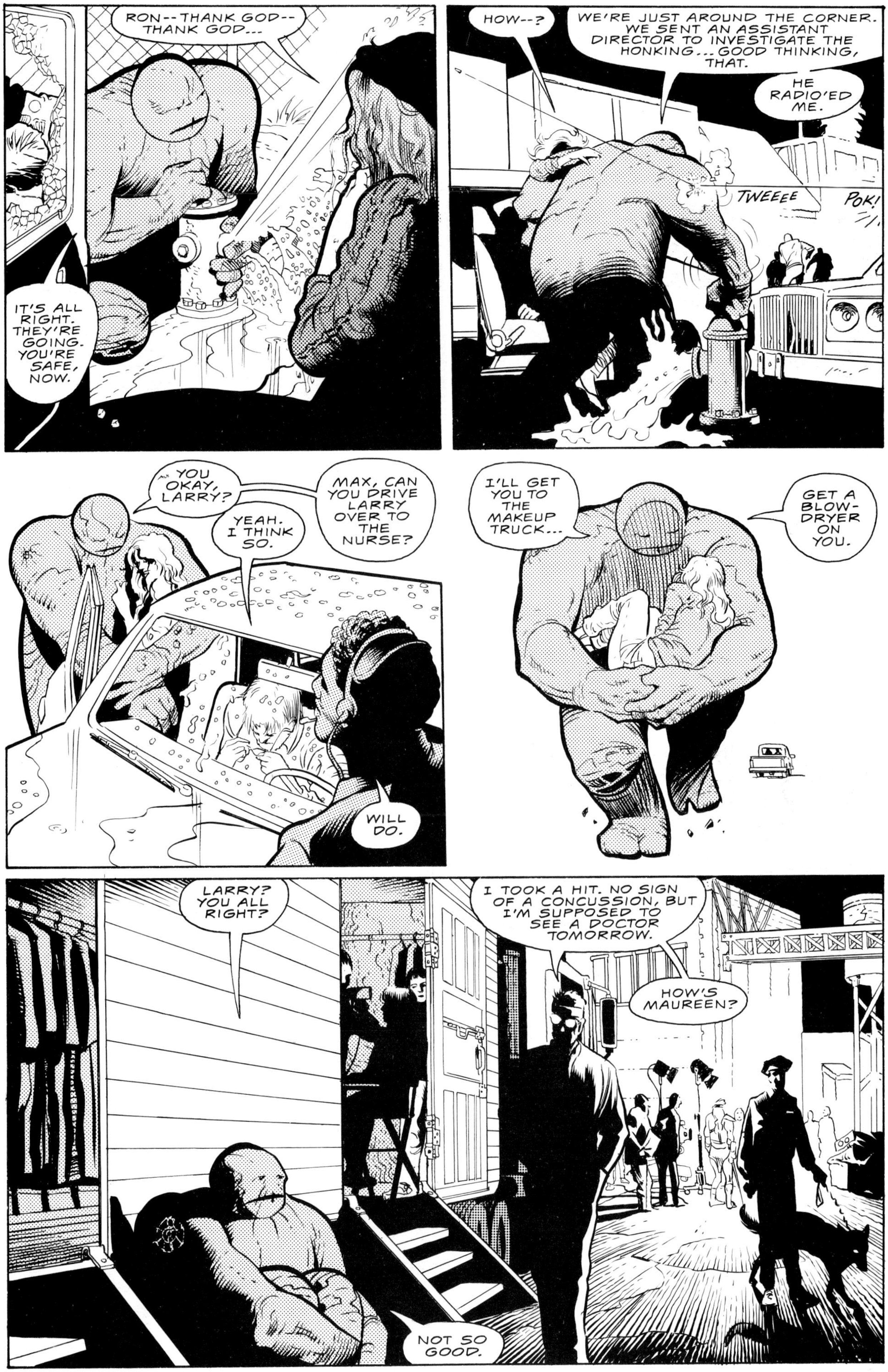

RON--THANK GOD--THANK GOD...
IT'S ALL RIGHT. THEY'RE GOING. YOU'RE SAFE, NOW.
HOW--?
WE'RE JUST AROUND THE CORNER. WE SENT AN ASSISTANT DIRECTOR TO INVESTIGATE THE HONKING... GOOD THINKING, THAT.
HE RADIO'ED ME.
TWEEEE
POK!
YOU OKAY, LARRY?
YEAH. I THINK SO.
MAX, CAN YOU DRIVE LARRY OVER TO THE NURSE?
WILL DO.
I'LL GET YOU TO THE MAKEUP TRUCK...
GET A BLOW-DRYER ON YOU.
LARRY? YOU ALL RIGHT?
I TOOK A HIT. NO SIGN OF A CONCUSSION, BUT I'M SUPPOSED TO SEE A DOCTOR TOMORROW.
HOW'S MAUREEN?
NOT SO GOOD.

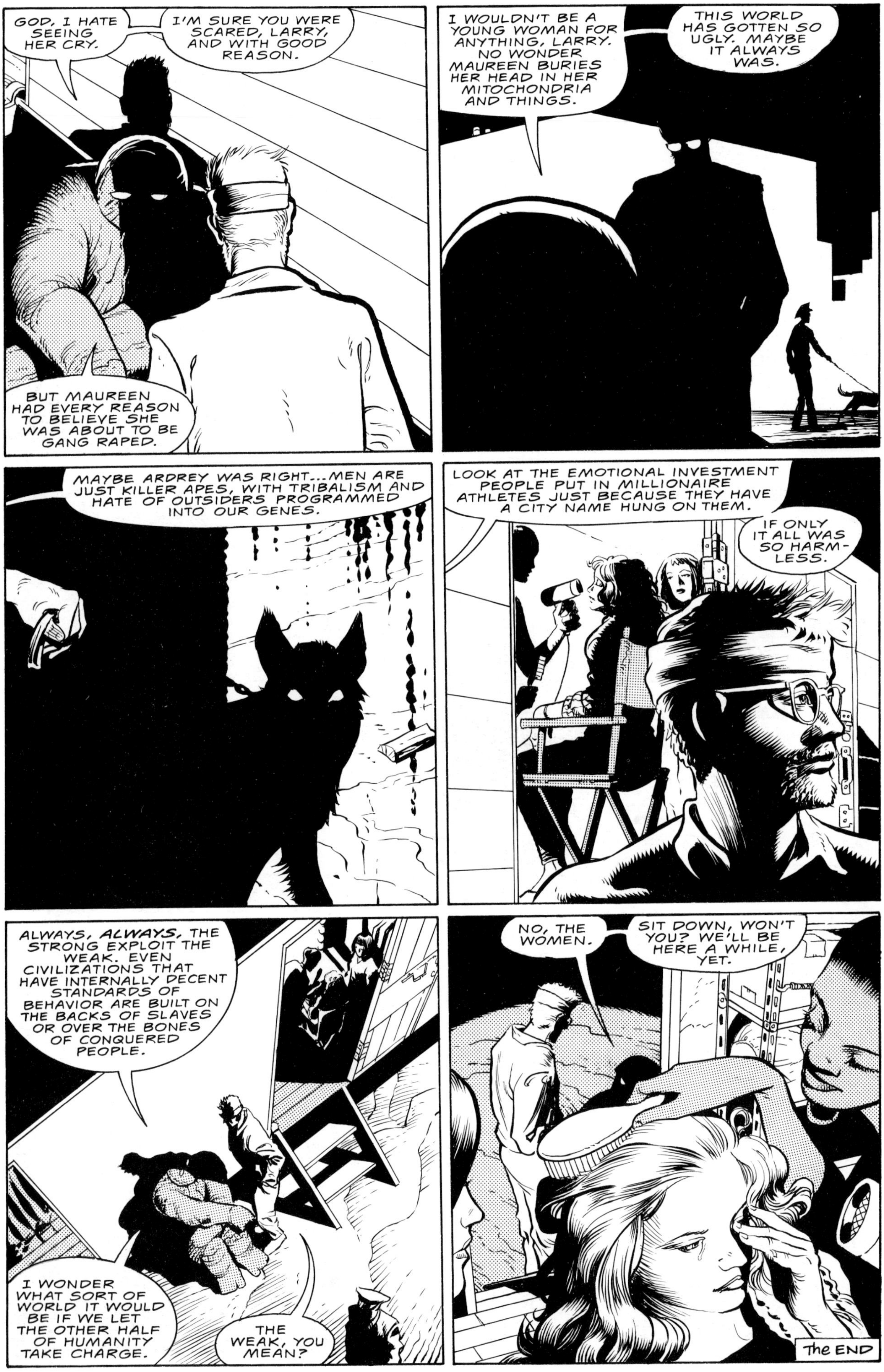
GOD, I HATE SEEING HER CRY.
I'M SURE YOU WERE SCARED, LARRY, AND WITH GOOD REASON.
BUT MAUREEN HAD EVERY REASON TO BELIEVE SHE WAS ABOUT TO BE GANG RAPED.
I WOULDN'T BE A YOUNG WOMAN FOR ANYTHING, LARRY. NO WONDER MAUREEN BURIES HER HEAD IN HER MITOCHONDRIA AND THINGS.
THIS WORLD HAS GOTTEN SO UGLY. MAYBE IT ALWAYS WAS.
MAYBE ARDREY WAS RIGHT...MEN ARE JUST KILLER APES, WITH TRIBALISM AND HATE OF OUTSIDERS PROGRAMMED INTO OUR GENES.
LOOK AT THE EMOTIONAL INVESTMENT PEOPLE PUT IN MILLIONAIRE ATHLETES JUST BECAUSE THEY HAVE A CITY NAME HUNG ON THEM.
IF ONLY IT ALL WAS SO HARMLESS.
ALWAYS, ALWAYS, THE STRONG EXPLOIT THE WEAK. EVEN CIVILIZATIONS THAT HAVE INTERNALLY DECENT STANDARDS OF BEHAVIOR ARE BUILT ON THE BACKS OF SLAVES OR OVER THE BONES OF CONQUERED PEOPLE.
I WONDER WHAT SORT OF WORLD IT WOULD BE IF WE LET THE OTHER HALF OF HUMANITY TAKE CHARGE.
THE WEAK, YOU MEAN?
NO, THE WOMEN.
SIT DOWN, WON'T YOU? WE'LL BE HERE A WHILE, YET.
The END

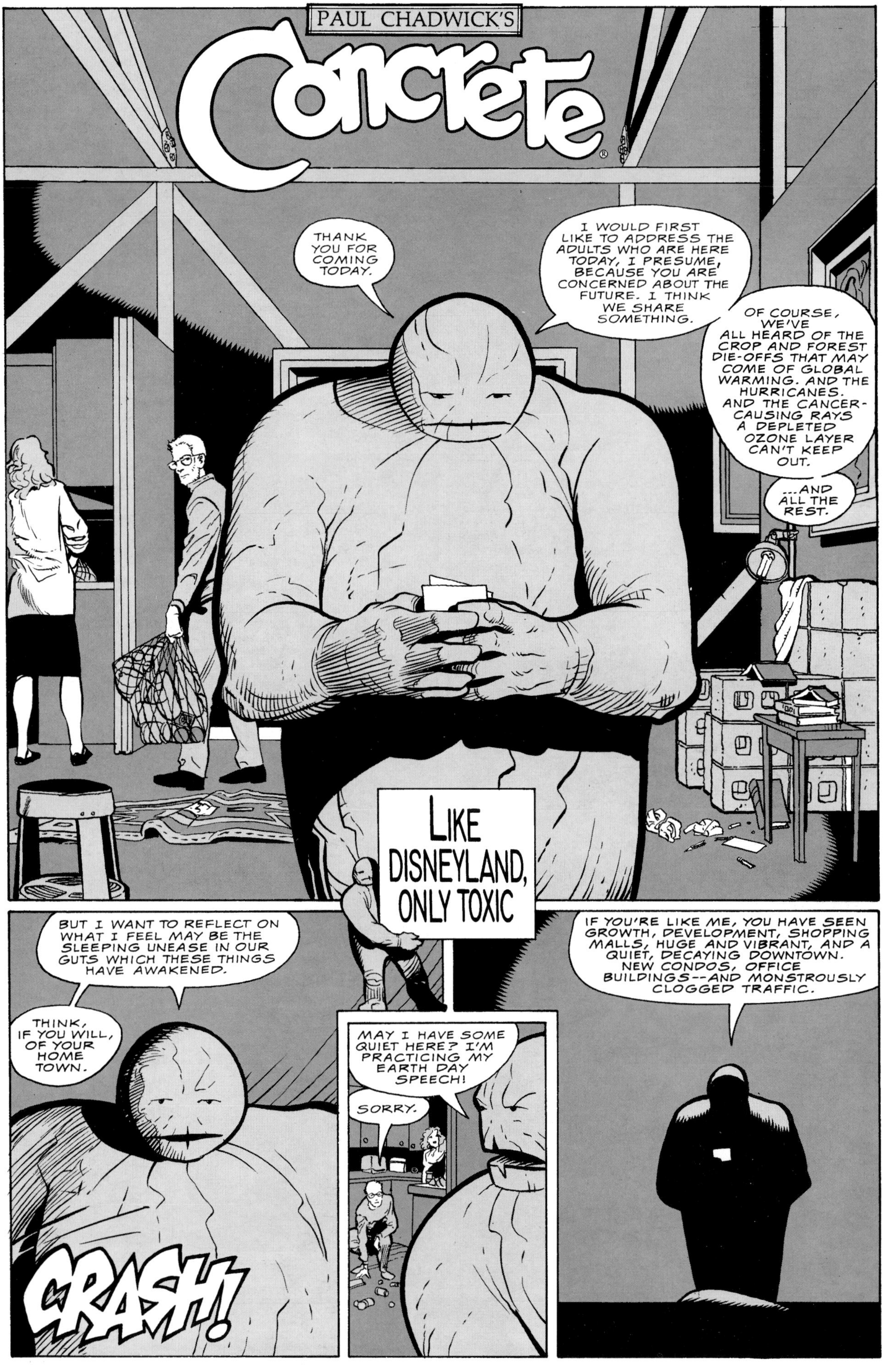
PAUL CHADWICK'S
Concrete
THANK YOU FOR COMING TODAY.
I WOULD FIRST LIKE TO ADDRESS THE ADULTS WHO ARE HERE TODAY, I PRESUME, BECAUSE YOU ARE CONCERNED ABOUT THE FUTURE. I THINK WE SHARE SOMETHING.
OF COURSE, WE'VE ALL HEARD OF THE CROP AND FOREST DIE-OFFS THAT MAY COME OF GLOBAL WARMING. AND THE HURRICANES. AND THE CANCER-CAUSING RAYS A DEPLETED OZONE LAYER CAN'T KEEP OUT.
...AND ALL THE REST.
LIKE DISNEYLAND, ONLY TOXIC
BUT I WANT TO REFLECT ON WHAT I FEEL MAY BE THE SLEEPING UNEASE IN OUR GUTS WHICH THESE THINGS HAVE AWAKENED.
THINK, IF YOU WILL, OF YOUR HOME TOWN.
CRASH!
MAY I HAVE SOME QUIET HERE? I'M PRACTICING MY EARTH DAY SPEECH!
SORRY.
IF YOU'RE LIKE ME, YOU HAVE SEEN GROWTH, DEVELOPMENT, SHOPPING MALLS, HUGE AND VIBRANT, AND A QUIET, DECAYING DOWNTOWN. NEW CONDOS, OFFICE BUILDINGS--AND MONSTROUSLY CLOGGED TRAFFIC.

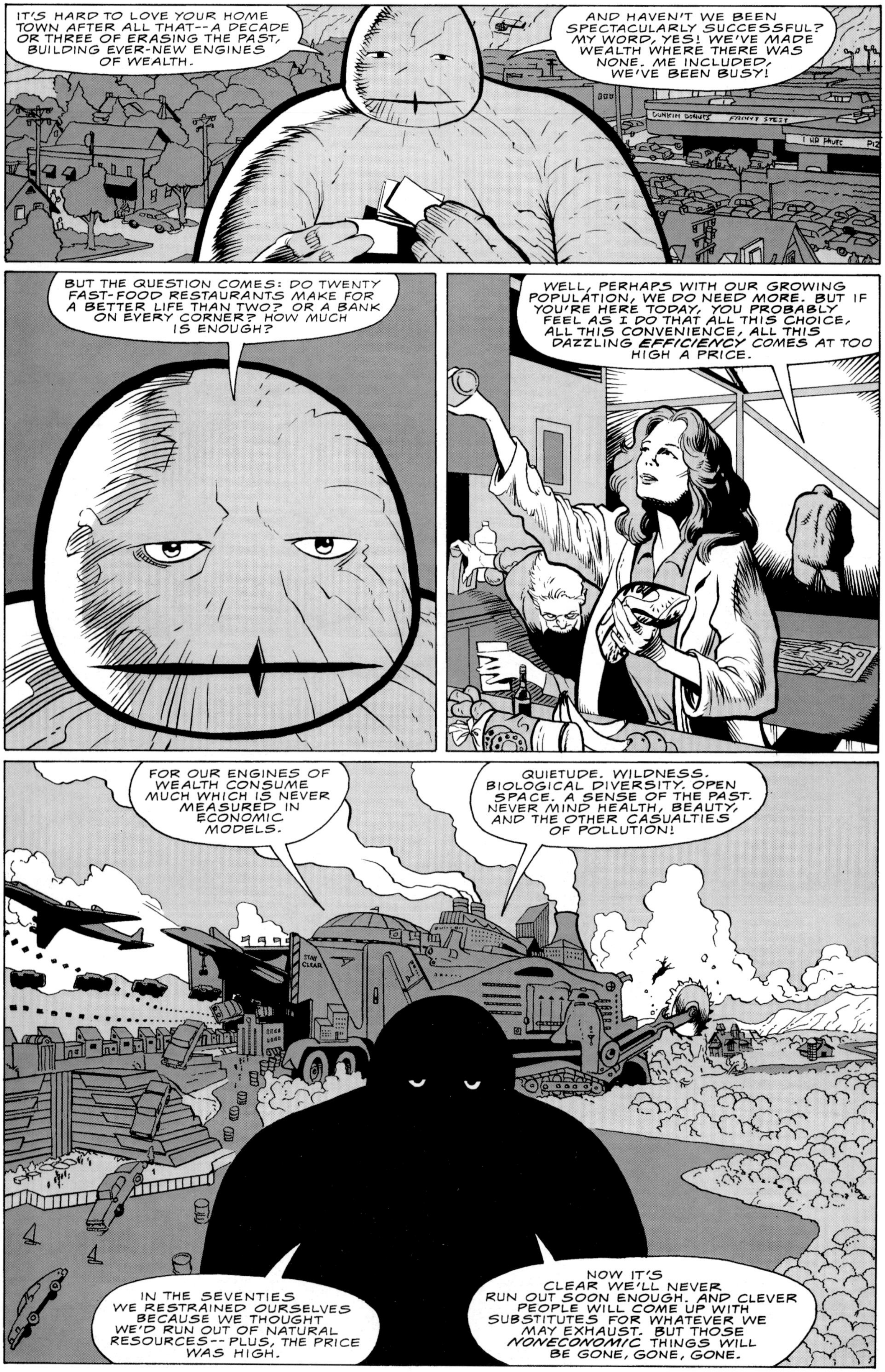
IT'S HARD TO LOVE YOUR HOME TOWN AFTER ALL THAT--A DECADE OR THREE OF ERASING THE PAST, BUILDING EVER-NEW ENGINES OF WEALTH.
AND HAVEN'T WE BEEN SPECTACULARLY SUCCESSFUL? MY WORD, YES! WE'VE MADE WEALTH WHERE THERE WAS NONE. ME INCLUDED, WE'VE BEEN BUSY!
BUT THE QUESTION COMES: DO TWENTY FAST-FOOD RESTAURANTS MAKE FOR A BETTER LIFE THAN TWO? OR A BANK ON EVERY CORNER? HOW MUCH IS ENOUGH?
WELL, PERHAPS WITH OUR GROWING POPULATION, WE DO NEED MORE. BUT IF YOU'RE HERE TODAY, YOU PROBABLY FEEL AS I DO THAT ALL THIS CHOICE, ALL THIS CONVENIENCE, ALL THIS DAZZLING *EFFICIENCY* COMES AT TOO HIGH A PRICE.
FOR OUR ENGINES OF WEALTH CONSUME MUCH WHICH IS NEVER MEASURED IN ECONOMIC MODELS.
QUIETUDE. WILDNESS. BIOLOGICAL DIVERSITY. OPEN SPACE. A SENSE OF THE PAST. NEVER MIND HEALTH, BEAUTY, AND THE OTHER CASUALTIES OF POLLUTION!
STAY CLEAR
IN THE SEVENTIES WE RESTRAINED OURSELVES BECAUSE WE THOUGHT WE'D RUN OUT OF NATURAL RESOURCES--PLUS, THE PRICE WAS HIGH.
NOW IT'S CLEAR WE'LL NEVER RUN OUT SOON ENOUGH. AND CLEVER PEOPLE WILL COME UP WITH SUBSTITUTES FOR WHATEVER WE MAY EXHAUST. BUT THOSE *NONECONOMIC* THINGS WILL BE GONE, GONE, GONE.

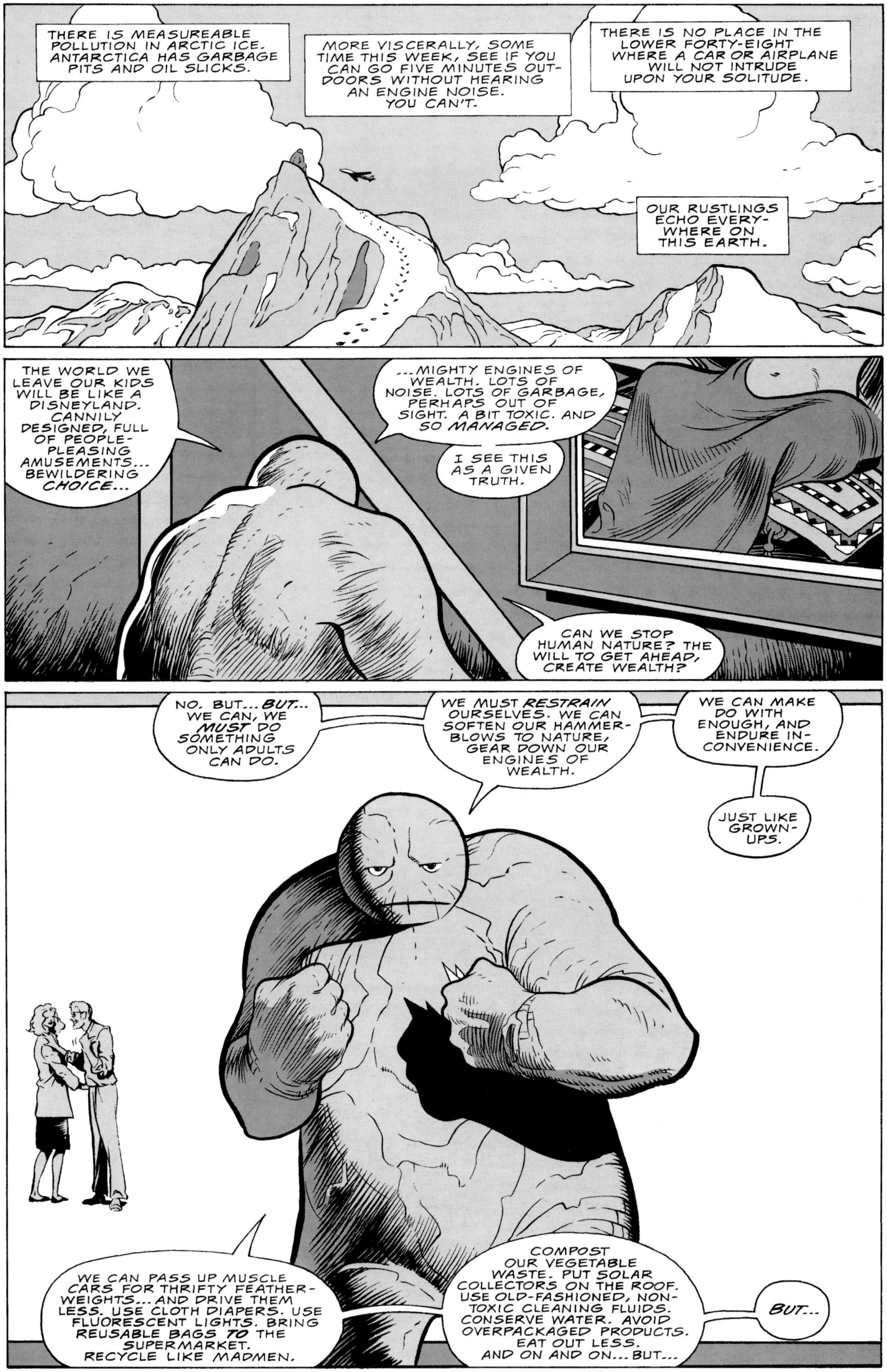
THERE IS MEASUREABLE POLLUTION IN ARCTIC ICE. ANTARCTICA HAS GARBAGE PITS AND OIL SLICKS.
MORE VISCERALLY, SOME TIME THIS WEEK, SEE IF YOU CAN GO FIVE MINUTES OUT-DOORS WITHOUT HEARING AN ENGINE NOISE. YOU CAN'T.
THERE IS NO PLACE IN THE LOWER FORTY-EIGHT WHERE A CAR OR AIRPLANE WILL NOT INTRUDE UPON YOUR SOLITUDE.
OUR RUSTLINGS ECHO EVERY-WHERE ON THIS EARTH.
THE WORLD WE LEAVE OUR KIDS WILL BE LIKE A DISNEYLAND. CANNILY DESIGNED, FULL OF PEOPLE-PLEASING AMUSEMENTS... BEWILDERING CHOICE...
...MIGHTY ENGINES OF WEALTH. LOTS OF NOISE. LOTS OF GARBAGE, PERHAPS OUT OF SIGHT. A BIT TOXIC. AND SO MANAGED.
I SEE THIS AS A GIVEN TRUTH.
CAN WE STOP HUMAN NATURE? THE WILL TO GET AHEAD, CREATE WEALTH?
NO. BUT... BUT... WE CAN, WE MUST DO SOMETHING ONLY ADULTS CAN DO.
WE MUST RESTRAIN OURSELVES. WE CAN SOFTEN OUR HAMMER-BLOWS TO NATURE, GEAR DOWN OUR ENGINES OF WEALTH.
WE CAN MAKE DO WITH ENOUGH, AND ENDURE IN-CONVENIENCE.
JUST LIKE GROWN-UPS.
WE CAN PASS UP MUSCLE CARS FOR THRIFTY FEATHER-WEIGHTS... AND DRIVE THEM LESS. USE CLOTH DIAPERS. USE FLUORESCENT LIGHTS. BRING REUSABLE BAGS TO THE SUPERMARKET. RECYCLE LIKE MADMEN.
COMPOST OUR VEGETABLE WASTE. PUT SOLAR COLLECTORS ON THE ROOF. USE OLD-FASHIONED, NON-TOXIC CLEANING FLUIDS. CONSERVE WATER. AVOID OVERPACKAGED PRODUCTS. EAT OUT LESS. AND ON AND ON... BUT...
BUT...

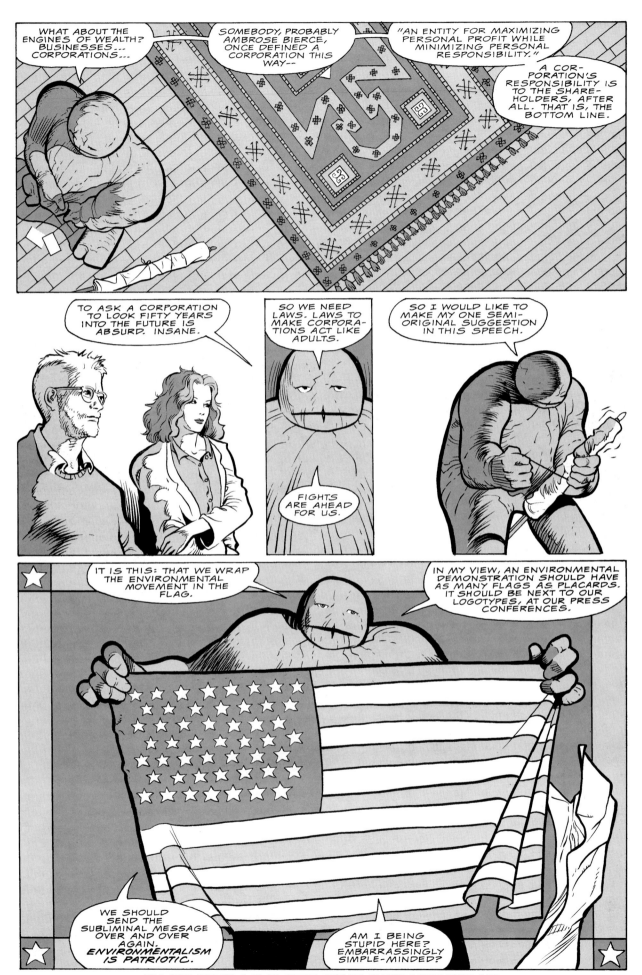

WHAT ABOUT THE ENGINES OF WEALTH? BUSINESSES... CORPORATIONS...

SOMEBODY, PROBABLY AMBROSE BIERCE, ONCE DEFINED A CORPORATION THIS WAY--

"AN ENTITY FOR MAXIMIZING PERSONAL PROFIT WHILE MINIMIZING PERSONAL RESPONSIBILITY."

A CORPORATION'S RESPONSIBILITY IS TO THE SHAREHOLDERS, AFTER ALL. THAT IS, THE BOTTOM LINE.

TO ASK A CORPORATION TO LOOK FIFTY YEARS INTO THE FUTURE IS ABSURD. INSANE.

SO WE NEED LAWS. LAWS TO MAKE CORPORATIONS ACT LIKE ADULTS.

SO I WOULD LIKE TO MAKE MY ONE SEMI-ORIGINAL SUGGESTION IN THIS SPEECH.

FIGHTS ARE AHEAD FOR US.

IT IS THIS: THAT WE WRAP THE ENVIRONMENTAL MOVEMENT IN THE FLAG.

IN MY VIEW, AN ENVIRONMENTAL DEMONSTRATION SHOULD HAVE AS MANY FLAGS AS PLACARDS. IT SHOULD BE NEXT TO OUR LOGOTYPES, AT OUR PRESS CONFERENCES.

WE SHOULD SEND THE SUBLIMINAL MESSAGE OVER AND OVER AGAIN. *ENVIRONMENTALISM IS PATRIOTIC.*

AM I BEING STUPID HERE? EMBARRASSINGLY SIMPLE-MINDED?

YOU CAN ORDER A FLAG FROM SEARS IF YOU CAN'T FIND ONE AT YOUR NEAREST DISCOUNT STORE.

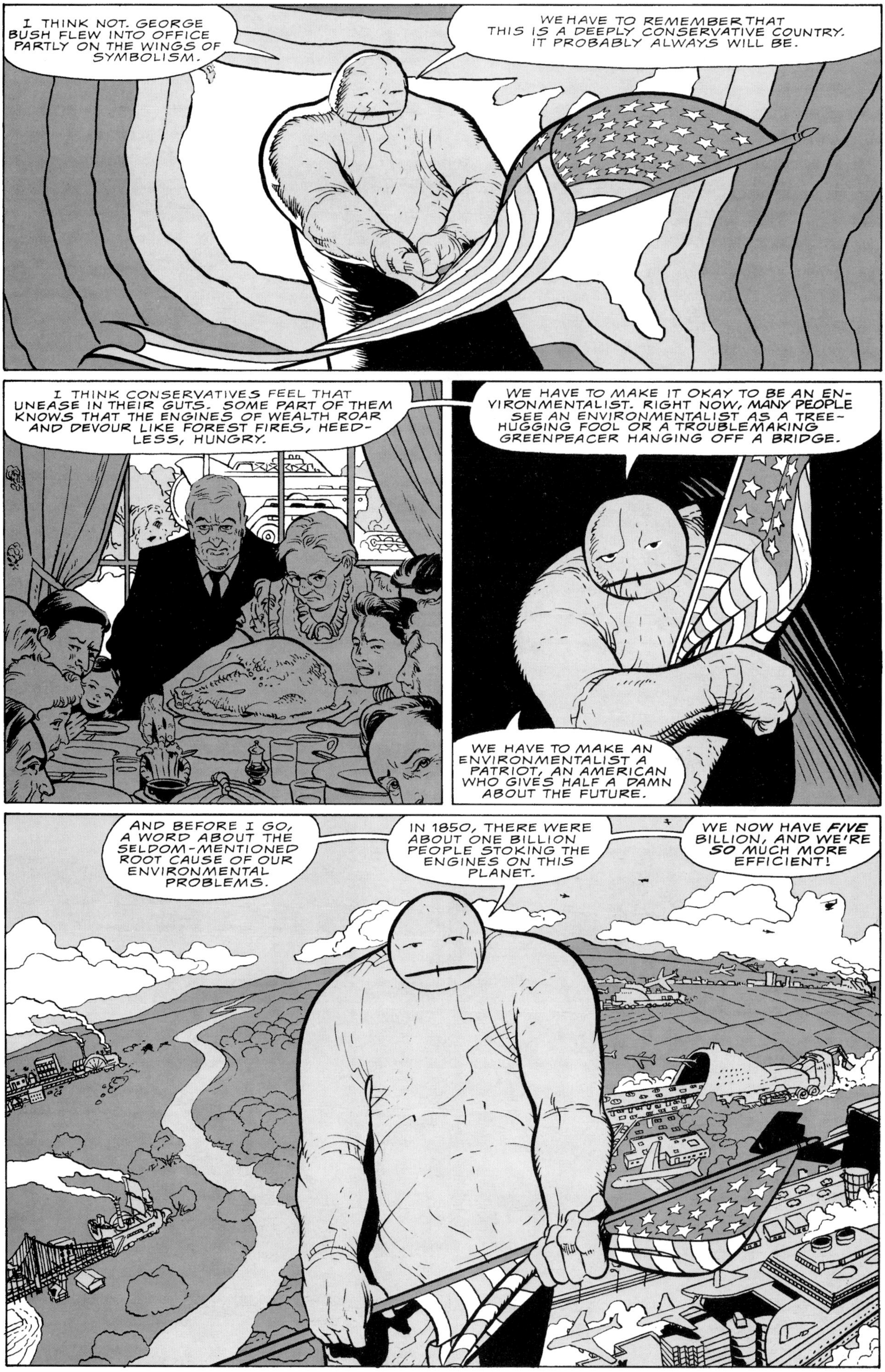
I THINK NOT. GEORGE BUSH FLEW INTO OFFICE PARTLY ON THE WINGS OF SYMBOLISM.
WE HAVE TO REMEMBER THAT THIS IS A DEEPLY CONSERVATIVE COUNTRY. IT PROBABLY ALWAYS WILL BE.
I THINK CONSERVATIVES FEEL THAT UNEASE IN THEIR GUTS. SOME PART OF THEM KNOWS THAT THE ENGINES OF WEALTH ROAR AND DEVOUR LIKE FOREST FIRES, HEEDLESS, HUNGRY.
WE HAVE TO MAKE IT OKAY TO BE AN ENVIRONMENTALIST. RIGHT NOW, MANY PEOPLE SEE AN ENVIRONMENTALIST AS A TREE-HUGGING FOOL OR A TROUBLEMAKING GREENPEACER HANGING OFF A BRIDGE.
WE HAVE TO MAKE AN ENVIRONMENTALIST A PATRIOT, AN AMERICAN WHO GIVES HALF A DAMN ABOUT THE FUTURE.
AND BEFORE I GO, A WORD ABOUT THE SELDOM-MENTIONED ROOT CAUSE OF OUR ENVIRONMENTAL PROBLEMS.
IN 1850, THERE WERE ABOUT ONE BILLION PEOPLE STOKING THE ENGINES ON THIS PLANET.
WE NOW HAVE *FIVE* BILLION, AND WE'RE *SO* MUCH MORE EFFICIENT!

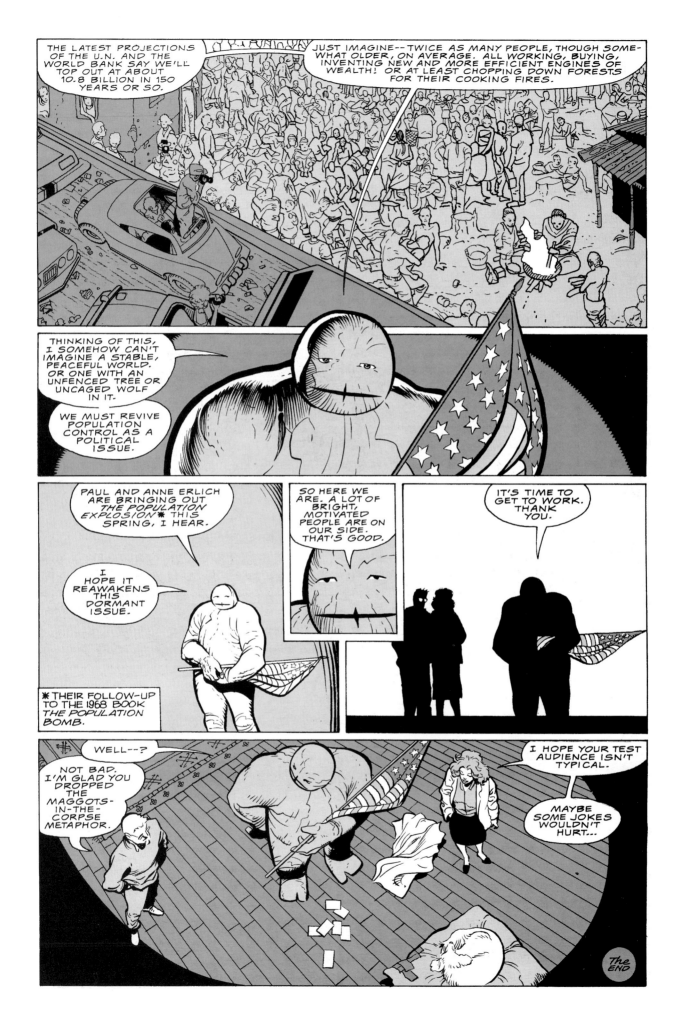

THE LATEST PROJECTIONS OF THE U.N. AND THE WORLD BANK SAY WE'LL TOP OUT AT ABOUT 10.8 BILLION IN 150 YEARS OR SO.

JUST IMAGINE-- TWICE AS MANY PEOPLE, THOUGH SOMEWHAT OLDER, ON AVERAGE. ALL WORKING, BUYING, INVENTING NEW AND MORE EFFICIENT ENGINES OF WEALTH! OR AT LEAST CHOPPING DOWN FORESTS FOR THEIR COOKING FIRES.

THINKING OF THIS, I SOMEHOW CAN'T IMAGINE A STABLE, PEACEFUL WORLD. OR ONE WITH AN UNFENCED TREE OR UNCAGED WOLF IN IT.

WE MUST REVIVE POPULATION CONTROL AS A POLITICAL ISSUE.

PAUL AND ANNE ERLICH ARE BRINGING OUT THE POPULATION EXPLOSION* THIS SPRING, I HEAR.

I HOPE IT REAWAKENS THIS DORMANT ISSUE.

*THEIR FOLLOW-UP TO THE 1968 BOOK THE POPULATION BOMB.

SO HERE WE ARE. A LOT OF BRIGHT, MOTIVATED PEOPLE ARE ON OUR SIDE. THAT'S GOOD.

IT'S TIME TO GET TO WORK. THANK YOU.

WELL--?

NOT BAD. I'M GLAD YOU DROPPED THE MAGGOTS- IN-THE- CORPSE METAPHOR.

I HOPE YOUR TEST AUDIENCE ISN'T TYPICAL.

MAYBE SOME JOKES WOULDN'T HURT...

The END

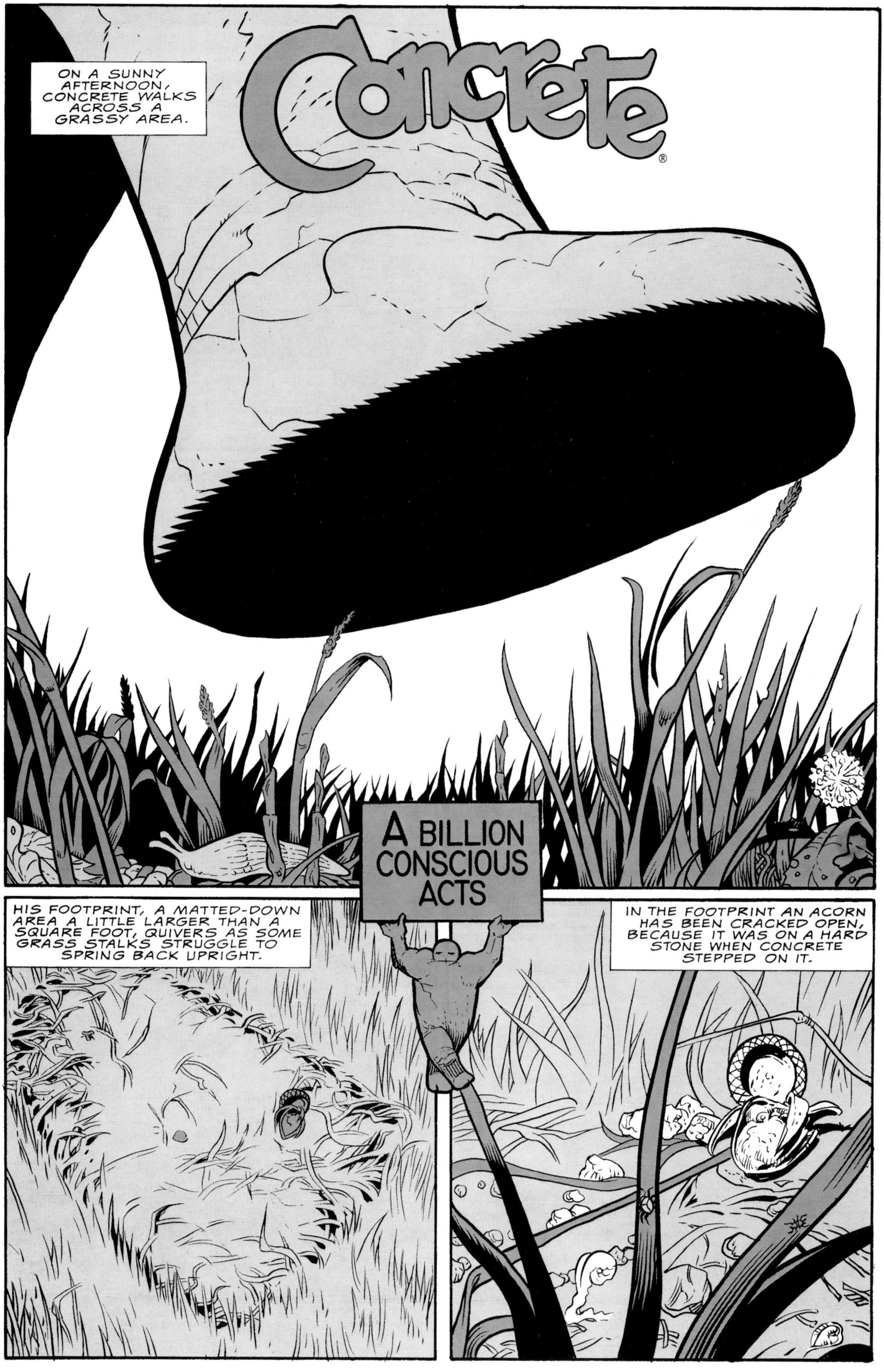
ON A SUNNY AFTERNOON, CONCRETE WALKS ACROSS A GRASSY AREA.
Concrete®
A BILLION CONSCIOUS ACTS
HIS FOOTPRINT, A MATTED-DOWN AREA A LITTLE LARGER THAN A SQUARE FOOT, QUIVERS AS SOME GRASS STALKS STRUGGLE TO SPRING BACK UPRIGHT.
IN THE FOOTPRINT AN ACORN HAS BEEN CRACKED OPEN, BECAUSE IT WAS ON A HARD STONE WHEN CONCRETE STEPPED ON IT.

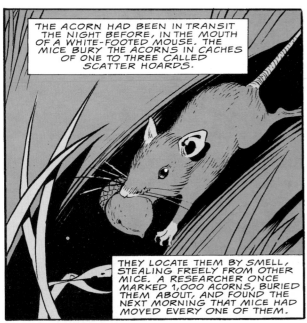

THE ACORN HAD BEEN IN TRANSIT THE NIGHT BEFORE, IN THE MOUTH OF A WHITE-FOOTED MOUSE. THE MICE BURY THE ACORNS IN CACHES OF ONE TO THREE CALLED SCATTER HOARDS.

THEY LOCATE THEM BY SMELL, STEALING FREELY FROM OTHER MICE. A RESEARCHER ONCE MARKED 1,000 ACORNS, BURIED THEM ABOUT, AND FOUND THE NEXT MORNING THAT MICE HAD MOVED EVERY ONE OF THEM.

THE MOUSE HAD BEEN RUSHING, KNOWING HE WAS VULNERABLE IN THIS OPEN AREA...

...TO NO AVAIL. A BARRED OWL HAD SNATCHED HIM UP AND EATEN HIM. OWLS HAVE UNUSUAL, RAGGED, FLUFFY EDGES TO THEIR WING FEATHERS THAT MAKES THEIR FLIGHT NEARLY SILENT.

INCIDENTALLY, THERE'S A SUPPOSEDLY TRUE STORY ABOUT A YOUNG BOY BEING SO STARTLED BY COMING ACROSS AN OWL FACE-TO-FACE IN THE DAYTIME THAT HE THREW IT TO THE GROUND AND STAMPED IT TO DEATH.

THE BOY'S NAME: WALT DISNEY.

THE MOUSE, HAD HE LIVED, MIGHT HAVE BEEN PLEASED AT THE DELICACIES IN THE ACORN.

IT HAS BEEN WELL COLONIZED.

IT HAD FIRST BEEN BROACHED BY AN ACORN WEEVIL. USING TINY TEETH AT THE END OF A LONG SNOUT, IT CUTS INTO THE HARD SHELL.

IT THEN DRILLS INTO THE MEAT BY ROTATING ITS HEAD SIDE-TO-SIDE UNTIL ITS SNOUT IS COMPLETELY BURIED.

A FEMALE MAY LAY AN EGG IN EACH CHANNEL SHE DRILLS. IN DAYS THE LARVAE HATCH, EATING THEIR WAY OUT FROM INSIDE.

THE JOLT OF THE ACORN'S FALL TO THE GROUND CUES THE LARVA TO EXIT THE ACORN. OUT OF A TINY OPENING, HE SQUEEZES OUT, A BAG OF JELLO OOZING THROUGH A KEYHOLE.

BUT OTHERS OCCUPY THE ACORN. A FILBERT WORM GROWS WITHIN, THOUGH IT WILL NEVER BE A MOTH.

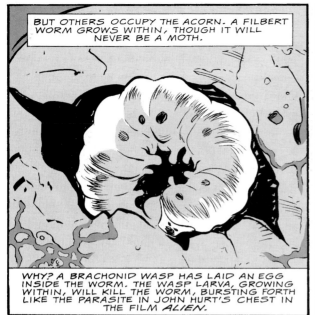

WHY? A BRACHONID WASP HAS LAID AN EGG INSIDE THE WORM. THE WASP LARVA, GROWING WITHIN, WILL KILL THE WORM, BURSTING FORTH LIKE THE PARASITE IN JOHN HURT'S CHEST IN THE FILM *ALIEN*.

HORROR ABOUNDS IN THIS MICROVERSE; CENTIPEDES AND FUNGUS GNAT GRUBS WOLF DOWN MAGGOTS AND LARVAE, LIKE LIONS ROAMING AND KILLING IN A MATERNITY WARD.

BUT SOME ESCAPE. THE ACORN WEEVIL LARVA BURROWS INTO THE EARTH, WHERE IT WILL LIE DORMANT FOR ONE TO FIVE YEARS. WAITING.

AND NOW THAT THE ACORN IS BROKEN, SOME OF THE SPRINGTAILS IN IT WILL LIKELY SURVIVE. AS SMALL AS THE CROSSBAR OF THE "H" IN THIS LINE, YOU WILL PROBABLY NEVER SEE SPRINGTAILS, EXCEPT ON THE SNOW, WHERE THEY CAN SWARM HALF A MILLION STRONG, LOOKING LIKE A SPRINKLING OF PEPPER.

THEY'RE EVERYWHERE, FROM ARCTIC TO ANTARCTIC, WHEREVER THERE IS AT LEAST LICHEN, ALGAE, POLLEN AND FUNGAL SPORES. ANY DECAYING FOLIAGE WILL DO, THOUGH.

A LITTLE FORKED ORGAN ON THEIR ABDOMEN ALLOWS THEM TO COCK THEMSELVES LIKE MOUSETRAPS. WHEN THEY GO, THEY CAN FLIP A HUNDRED MILLIMETERS INTO THE AIR.

THIS ACORN IS A LOSS, BUT ANOTHER, BURIED AND SPROUTING BENEATH THE FOOTPRINT, MAY GROW TO THE PROVERBIAL "MIGHTY OAK".

A SIZABLE OAK TREE, DURING A TYPICAL GROWING SEASON, GIVES OFF 28,000 GALLONS OF MOISTURE. IMAGINE LIFTING SO MUCH WATER IN BUCKETS TO THIRTY FEET.

LORD BYRON ONCE PLANTED AN OAK TREE AS A BOY. "AS THIS TREE GROWS, SO SHALL I PROSPER," HE SAID.

HE RETURNED A FEW YEARS LATER TO FIND IT DEAD OR NEARLY SO. BUT HE WAS JUST FINE.

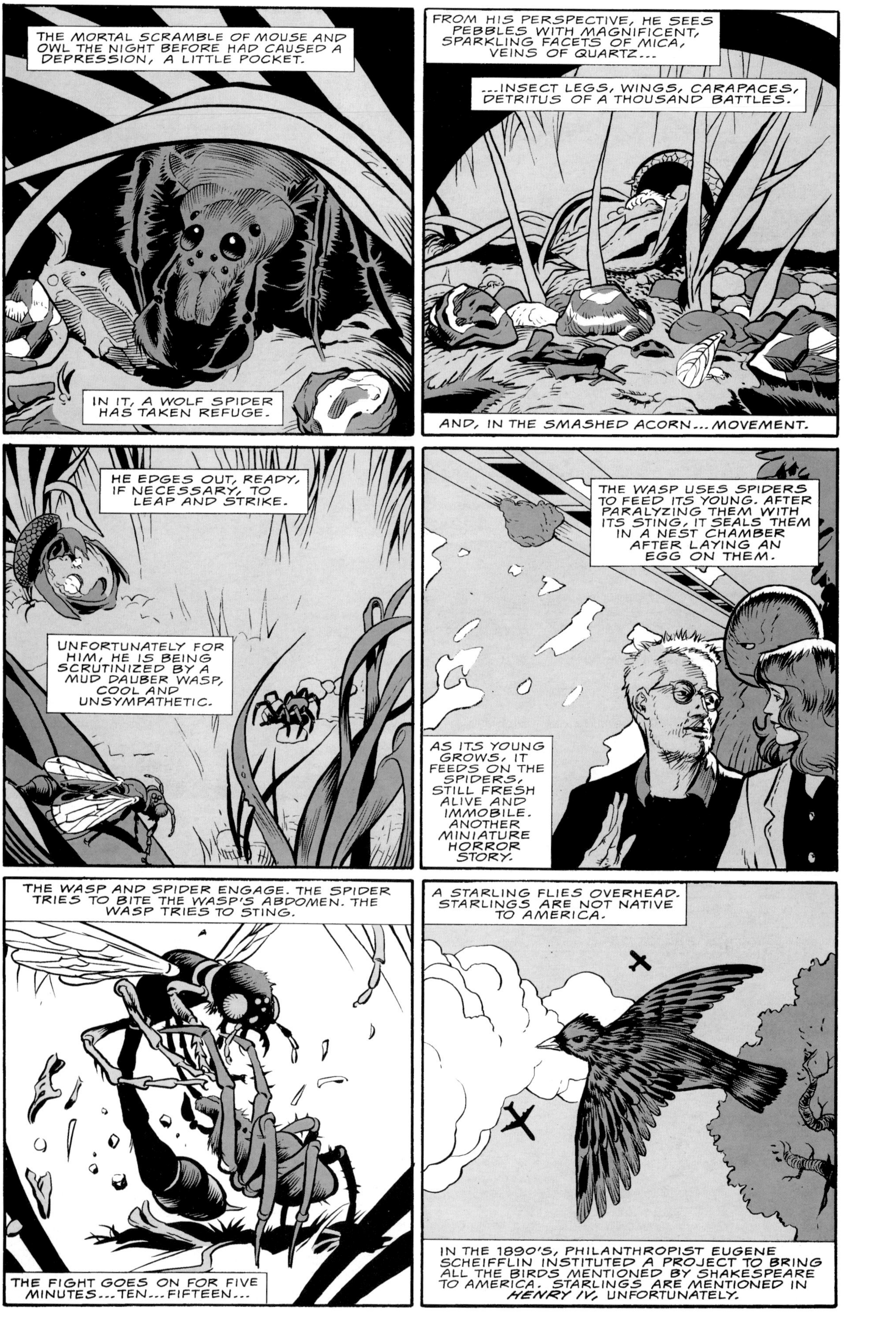
THE MORTAL SCRAMBLE OF MOUSE AND OWL THE NIGHT BEFORE HAD CAUSED A DEPRESSION, A LITTLE POCKET.
IN IT, A WOLF SPIDER HAS TAKEN REFUGE.
FROM HIS PERSPECTIVE, HE SEES PEBBLES WITH MAGNIFICENT, SPARKLING FACETS OF MICA, VEINS OF QUARTZ...
...INSECT LEGS, WINGS, CARAPACES, DETRITUS OF A THOUSAND BATTLES.
AND, IN THE SMASHED ACORN... MOVEMENT.
HE EDGES OUT, READY, IF NECESSARY, TO LEAP AND STRIKE.
UNFORTUNATELY FOR HIM, HE IS BEING SCRUTINIZED BY A MUD DAUBER WASP, COOL AND UNSYMPATHETIC.
THE WASP USES SPIDERS TO FEED ITS YOUNG. AFTER PARALYZING THEM WITH ITS STING, IT SEALS THEM IN A NEST CHAMBER AFTER LAYING AN EGG ON THEM.
AS ITS YOUNG GROWS, IT FEEDS ON THE SPIDERS, STILL FRESH ALIVE AND IMMOBILE. ANOTHER MINIATURE HORROR STORY.
THE WASP AND SPIDER ENGAGE. THE SPIDER TRIES TO BITE THE WASP'S ABDOMEN. THE WASP TRIES TO STING.
THE FIGHT GOES ON FOR FIVE MINUTES... TEN... FIFTEEN...
A STARLING FLIES OVERHEAD. STARLINGS ARE NOT NATIVE TO AMERICA.
IN THE 1890'S, PHILANTHROPIST EUGENE SCHEIFFLIN INSTITUTED A PROJECT TO BRING ALL THE BIRDS MENTIONED BY SHAKESPEARE TO AMERICA. STARLINGS ARE MENTIONED IN HENRY IV, UNFORTUNATELY.

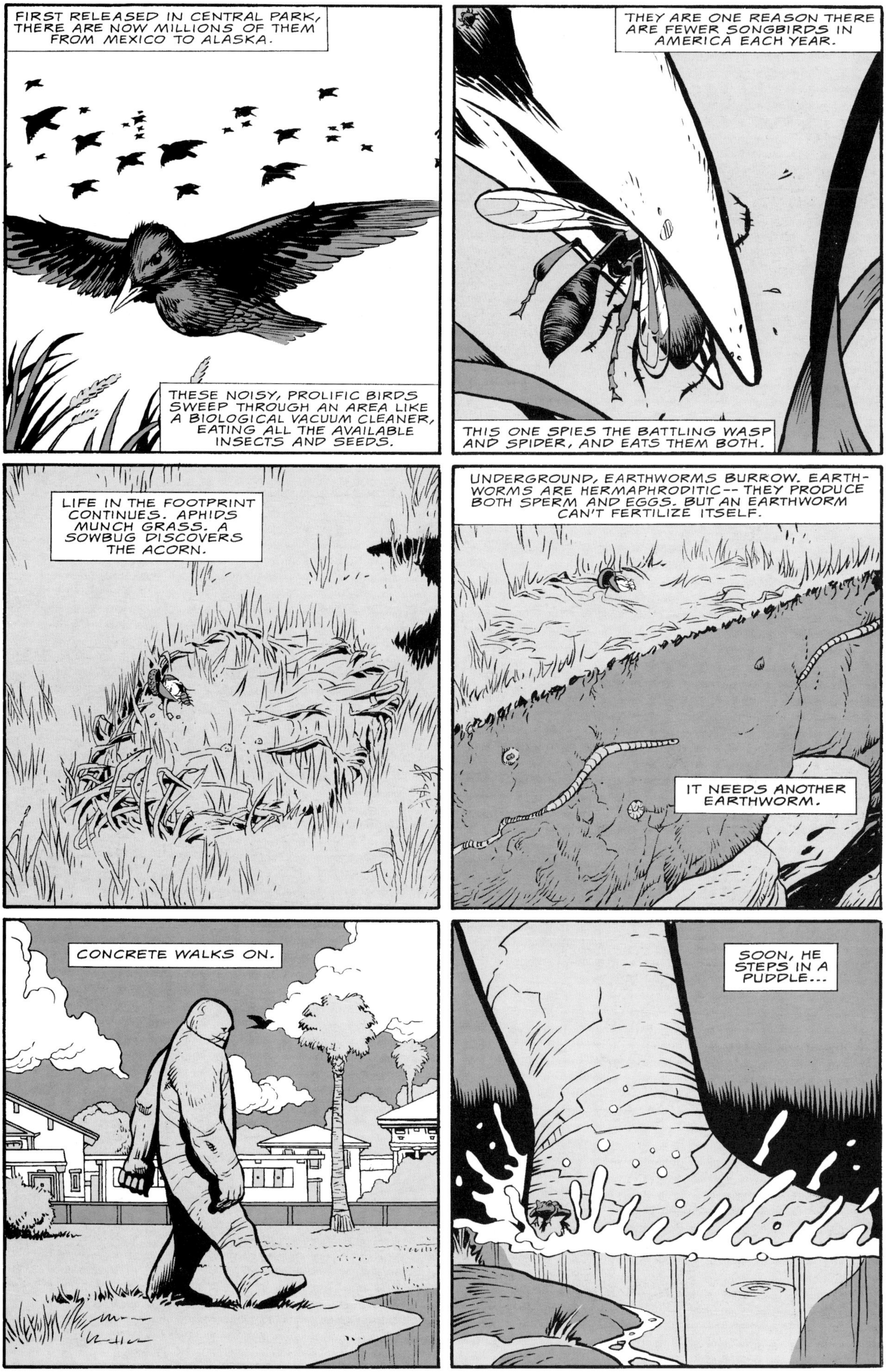
FIRST RELEASED IN CENTRAL PARK, THERE ARE NOW MILLIONS OF THEM FROM MEXICO TO ALASKA.
THESE NOISY, PROLIFIC BIRDS SWEEP THROUGH AN AREA LIKE A BIOLOGICAL VACUUM CLEANER, EATING ALL THE AVAILABLE INSECTS AND SEEDS.
THEY ARE ONE REASON THERE ARE FEWER SONGBIRDS IN AMERICA EACH YEAR.
THIS ONE SPIES THE BATTLING WASP AND SPIDER, AND EATS THEM BOTH.
LIFE IN THE FOOTPRINT CONTINUES. APHIDS MUNCH GRASS. A SOWBUG DISCOVERS THE ACORN.
UNDERGROUND, EARTHWORMS BURROW. EARTHWORMS ARE HERMAPHRODITIC -- THEY PRODUCE BOTH SPERM AND EGGS. BUT AN EARTHWORM CAN'T FERTILIZE ITSELF.
IT NEEDS ANOTHER EARTHWORM.
CONCRETE WALKS ON.
SOON, HE STEPS IN A PUDDLE...

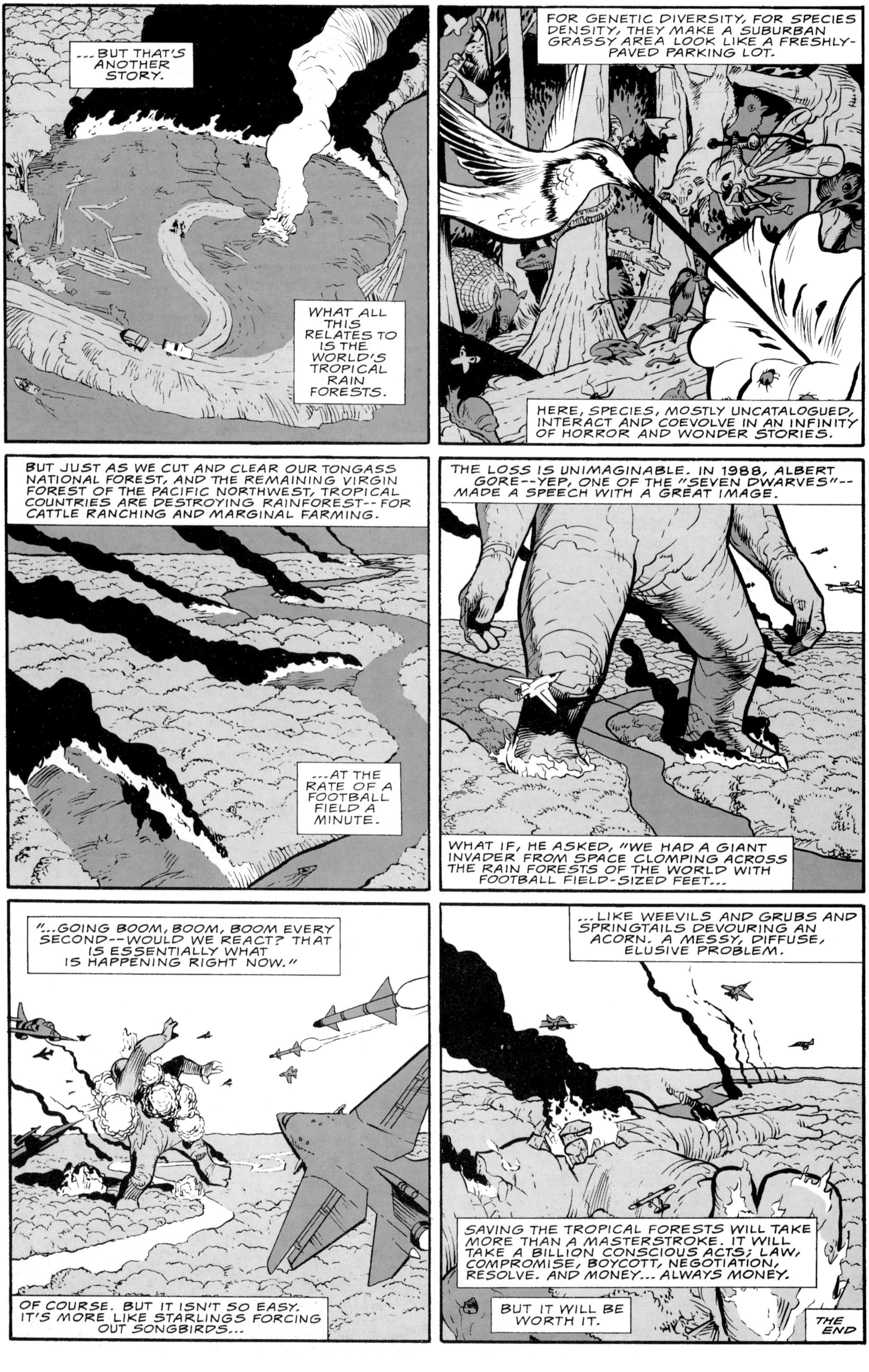
...BUT THAT'S ANOTHER STORY.
WHAT ALL THIS RELATES TO IS THE WORLD'S TROPICAL RAIN FORESTS.
FOR GENETIC DIVERSITY, FOR SPECIES DENSITY, THEY MAKE A SUBURBAN GRASSY AREA LOOK LIKE A FRESHLY-PAVED PARKING LOT.
HERE, SPECIES, MOSTLY UNCATALOGUED, INTERACT AND COEVOLVE IN AN INFINITY OF HORROR AND WONDER STORIES.
BUT JUST AS WE CUT AND CLEAR OUR TONGASS NATIONAL FOREST, AND THE REMAINING VIRGIN FOREST OF THE PACIFIC NORTHWEST, TROPICAL COUNTRIES ARE DESTROYING RAINFOREST--FOR CATTLE RANCHING AND MARGINAL FARMING.
...AT THE RATE OF A FOOTBALL FIELD A MINUTE.
THE LOSS IS UNIMAGINABLE. IN 1988, ALBERT GORE--YEP, ONE OF THE "SEVEN DWARVES"--MADE A SPEECH WITH A GREAT IMAGE.
WHAT IF, HE ASKED, "WE HAD A GIANT INVADER FROM SPACE CLOMPING ACROSS THE RAIN FORESTS OF THE WORLD WITH FOOTBALL FIELD-SIZED FEET...
"...GOING BOOM, BOOM, BOOM EVERY SECOND--WOULD WE REACT? THAT IS ESSENTIALLY WHAT IS HAPPENING RIGHT NOW."
OF COURSE. BUT IT ISN'T SO EASY. IT'S MORE LIKE STARLINGS FORCING OUT SONGBIRDS...
...LIKE WEEVILS AND GRUBS AND SPRINGTAILS DEVOURING AN ACORN. A MESSY, DIFFUSE, ELUSIVE PROBLEM.
SAVING THE TROPICAL FORESTS WILL TAKE MORE THAN A MASTERSTROKE. IT WILL TAKE A BILLION CONSCIOUS ACTS; LAW, COMPROMISE, BOYCOTT, NEGOTIATION, RESOLVE. AND MONEY... ALWAYS MONEY.
BUT IT WILL BE WORTH IT.
THE END

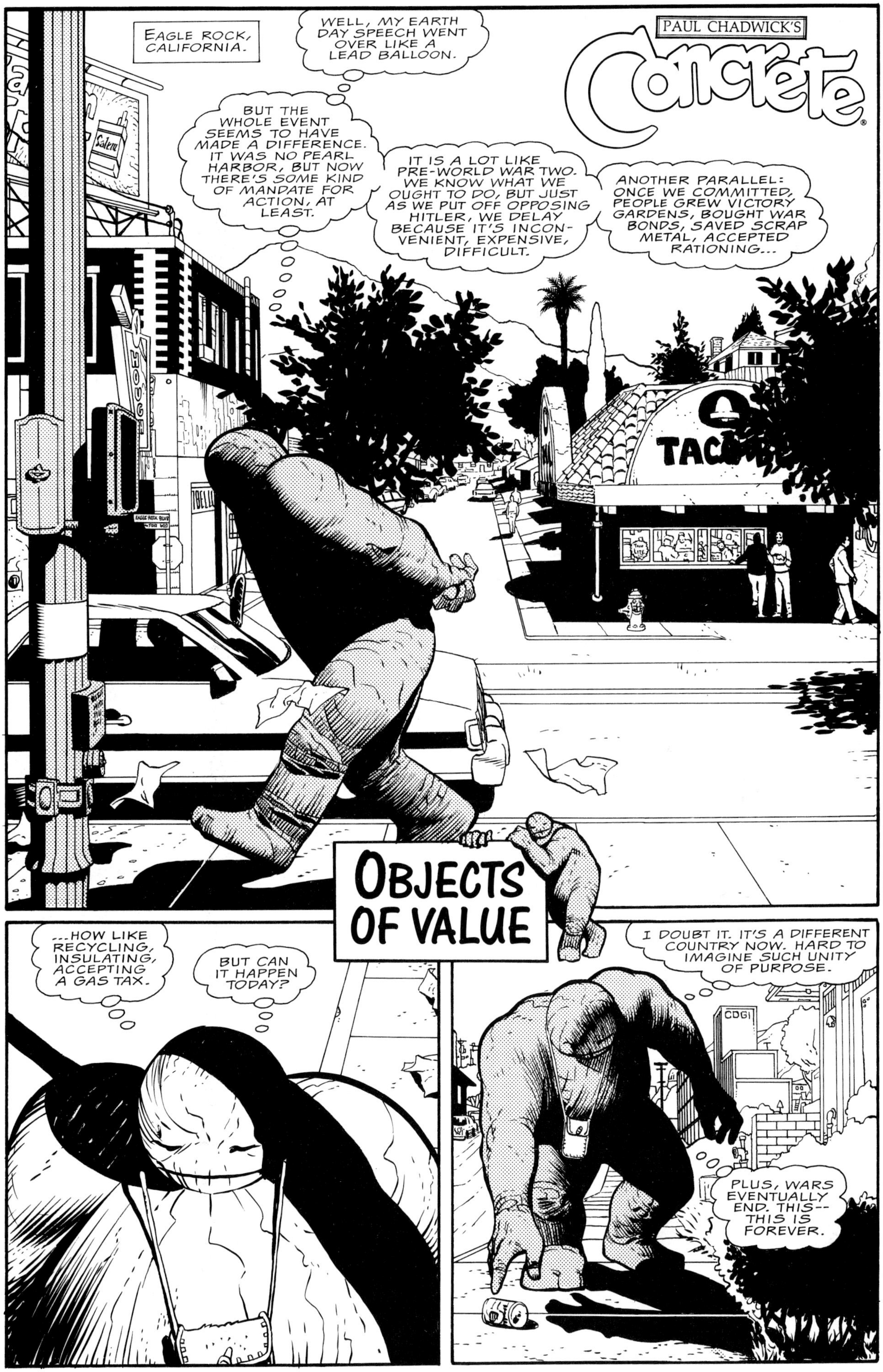
PAUL CHADWICK'S
Concrete
EAGLE ROCK, CALIFORNIA.
WELL, MY EARTH DAY SPEECH WENT OVER LIKE A LEAD BALLOON.
BUT THE WHOLE EVENT SEEMS TO HAVE MADE A DIFFERENCE. IT WAS NO PEARL HARBOR, BUT NOW THERE'S SOME KIND OF MANDATE FOR ACTION, AT LEAST.
IT IS A LOT LIKE PRE-WORLD WAR TWO. WE KNOW WHAT WE OUGHT TO DO, BUT JUST AS WE PUT OFF OPPOSING HITLER, WE DELAY BECAUSE IT'S INCON-VENIENT, EXPENSIVE, DIFFICULT.
ANOTHER PARALLEL: ONCE WE COMMITTED, PEOPLE GREW VICTORY GARDENS, BOUGHT WAR BONDS, SAVED SCRAP METAL, ACCEPTED RATIONING...
TACO
OBJECTS OF VALUE
...HOW LIKE RECYCLING, INSULATING, ACCEPTING A GAS TAX.
BUT CAN IT HAPPEN TODAY?
I DOUBT IT. IT'S A DIFFERENT COUNTRY NOW. HARD TO IMAGINE SUCH UNITY OF PURPOSE.
PLUS, WARS EVENTUALLY END. THIS-- THIS IS FOREVER.

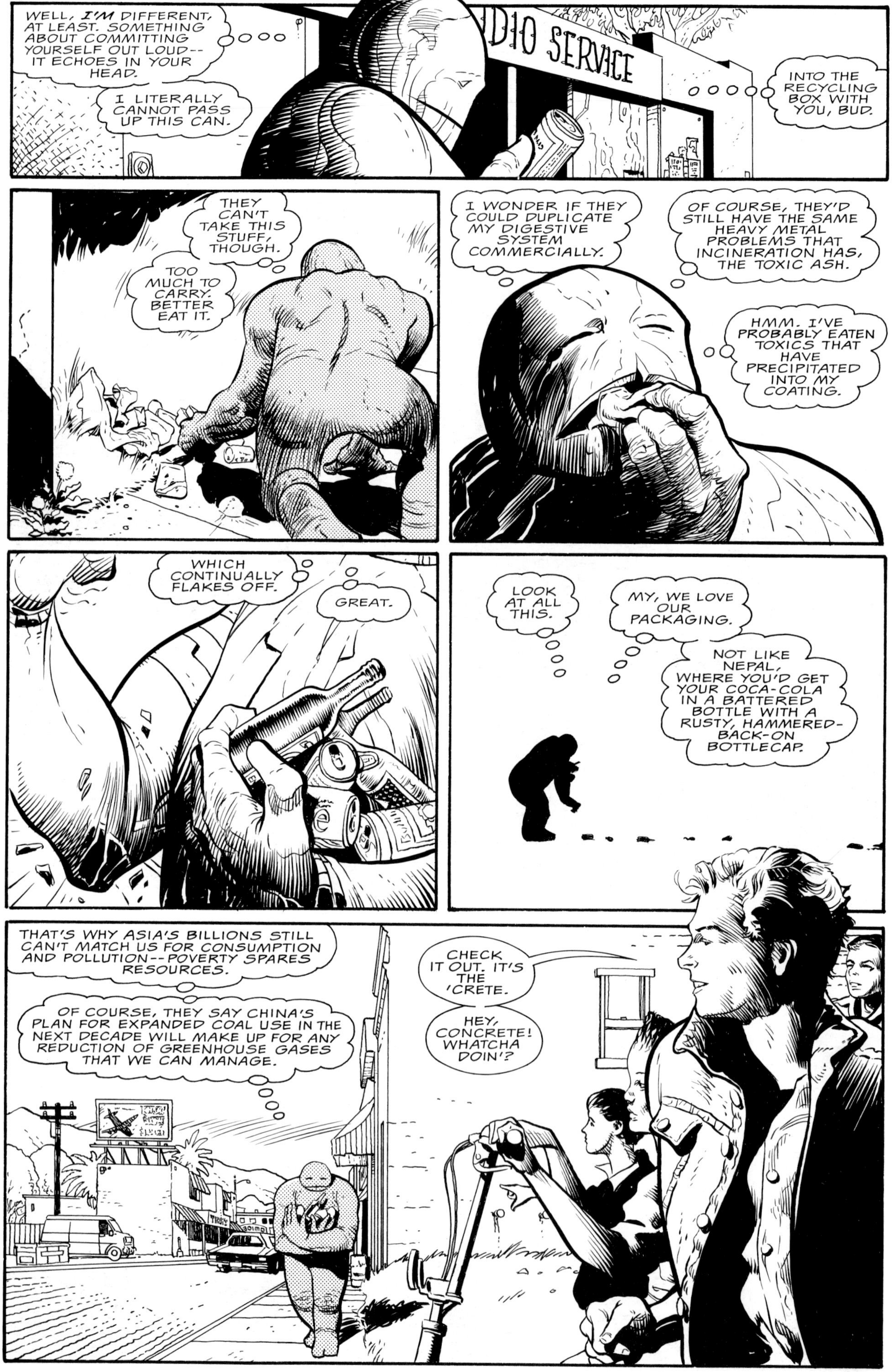

WELL, I'M DIFFERENT, AT LEAST. SOMETHING ABOUT COMMITTING YOURSELF OUT LOUD-- IT ECHOES IN YOUR HEAD.
I LITERALLY CANNOT PASS UP THIS CAN.
INTO THE RECYCLING BOX WITH YOU, BUD.
THEY CAN'T TAKE THIS STUFF, THOUGH.
TOO MUCH TO CARRY. BETTER EAT IT.
I WONDER IF THEY COULD DUPLICATE MY DIGESTIVE SYSTEM COMMERCIALLY.
OF COURSE, THEY'D STILL HAVE THE SAME HEAVY METAL PROBLEMS THAT INCINERATION HAS, THE TOXIC ASH.
HMM. I'VE PROBABLY EATEN TOXICS THAT HAVE PRECIPITATED INTO MY COATING.
WHICH CONTINUALLY FLAKES OFF.
GREAT.
LOOK AT ALL THIS.
MY, WE LOVE OUR PACKAGING.
NOT LIKE NEPAL, WHERE YOU'D GET YOUR COCA-COLA IN A BATTERED BOTTLE WITH A RUSTY, HAMMERED-BACK-ON BOTTLECAP.
THAT'S WHY ASIA'S BILLIONS STILL CAN'T MATCH US FOR CONSUMPTION AND POLLUTION--POVERTY SPARES RESOURCES.
OF COURSE, THEY SAY CHINA'S PLAN FOR EXPANDED COAL USE IN THE NEXT DECADE WILL MAKE UP FOR ANY REDUCTION OF GREENHOUSE GASES THAT WE CAN MANAGE.
CHECK IT OUT. IT'S THE 'CRETE.
HEY, CONCRETE! WHATCHA DOIN'?

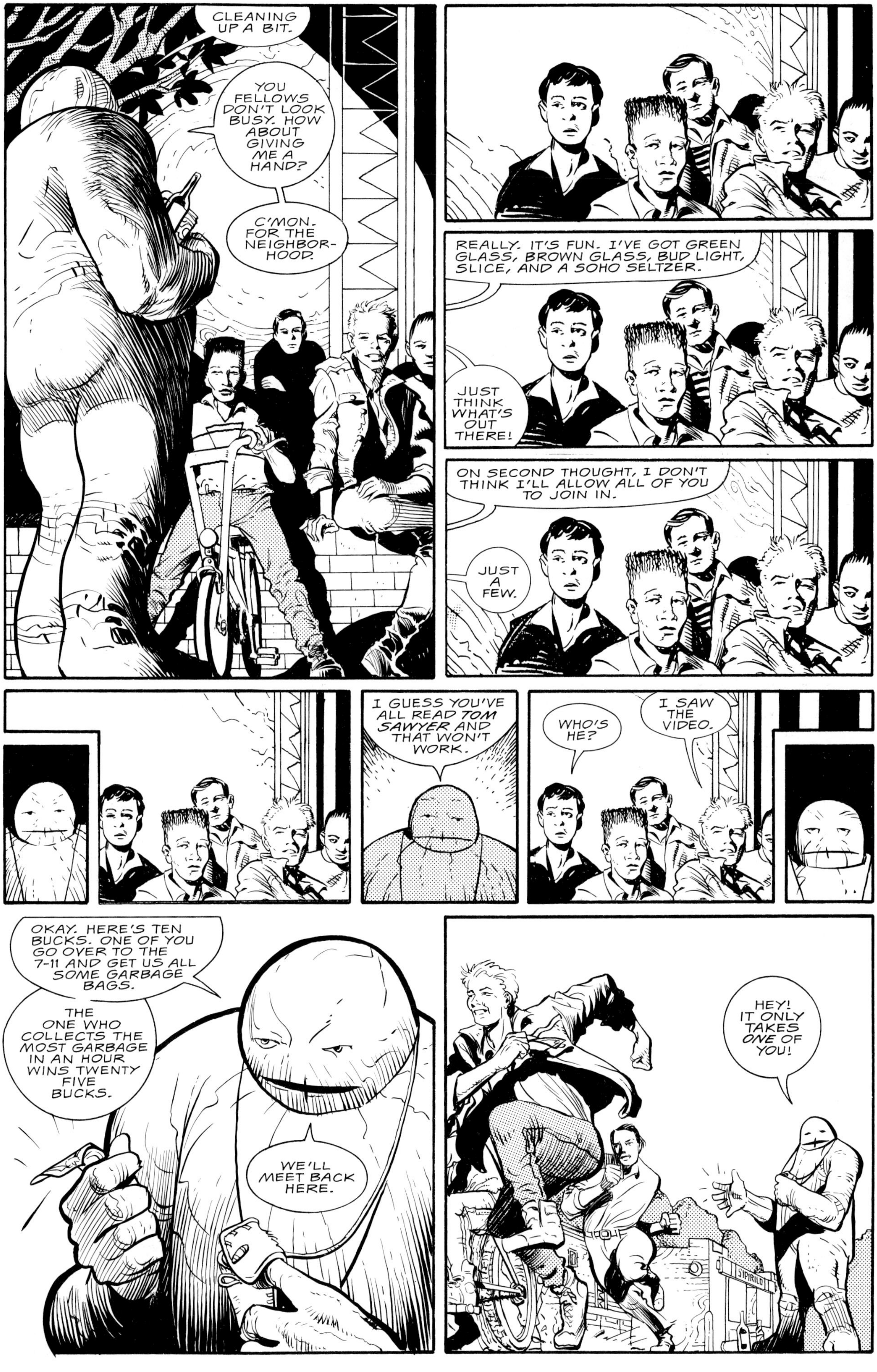
CLEANING UP A BIT.
YOU FELLOWS DON'T LOOK BUSY. HOW ABOUT GIVING ME A HAND?
C'MON. FOR THE NEIGHBOR-HOOD.
REALLY. IT'S FUN. I'VE GOT GREEN GLASS, BROWN GLASS, BUD LIGHT, SLICE, AND A SOHO SELTZER.
JUST THINK WHAT'S OUT THERE!
ON SECOND THOUGHT, I DON'T THINK I'LL ALLOW ALL OF YOU TO JOIN IN.
JUST A FEW.
I GUESS YOU'VE ALL READ *TOM SAWYER* AND THAT WON'T WORK.
WHO'S HE?
I SAW THE VIDEO.
OKAY. HERE'S TEN BUCKS. ONE OF YOU GO OVER TO THE 7-11 AND GET US ALL SOME GARBAGE BAGS.
THE ONE WHO COLLECTS THE MOST GARBAGE IN AN HOUR WINS TWENTY FIVE BUCKS.
WE'LL MEET BACK HERE.
HEY! IT ONLY TAKES *ONE* OF YOU!
SPIRITO

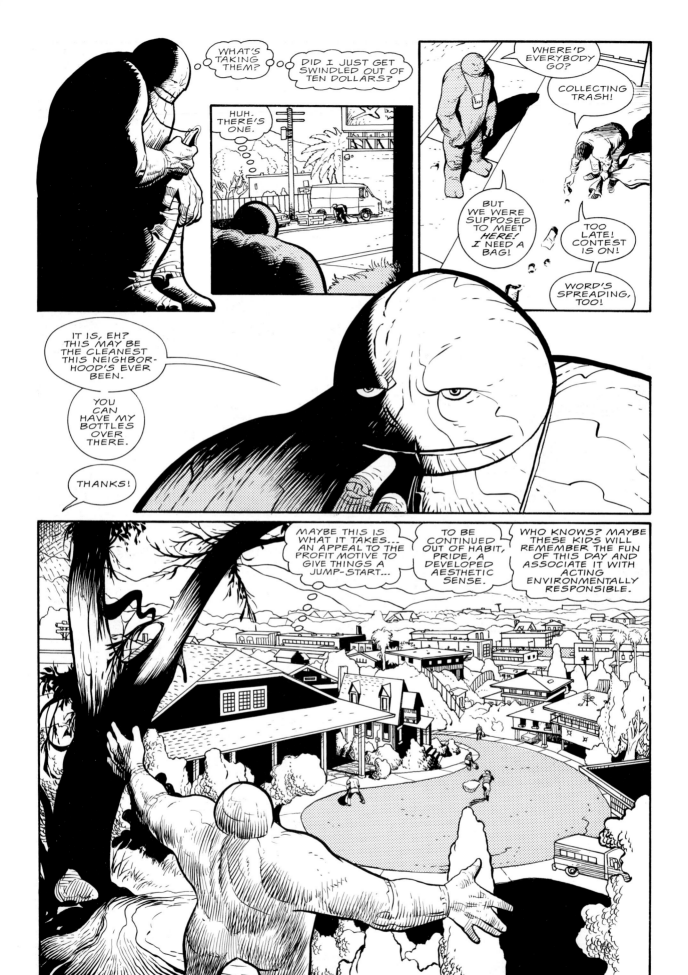

WHAT'S TAKING THEM?

DID I JUST GET SWINDLED OUT OF TEN DOLLARS?

HUH. THERE'S ONE.

WHERE'D EVERYBODY GO?

COLLECTING TRASH!

BUT WE WERE SUPPOSED TO MEET *HERE!* I NEED A BAG!

TOO LATE! CONTEST IS ON!

WORD'S SPREADING, TOO!

IT IS, EH? THIS MAY BE THE CLEANEST THIS NEIGHBORHOOD'S EVER BEEN.

YOU CAN HAVE MY BOTTLES OVER THERE.

THANKS!

MAYBE THIS IS WHAT IT TAKES... AN APPEAL TO THE PROFIT MOTIVE TO GIVE THINGS A JUMP-START...

TO BE CONTINUED OUT OF HABIT, PRIDE, A DEVELOPED AESTHETIC SENSE.

WHO KNOWS? MAYBE THESE KIDS WILL REMEMBER THE FUN OF THIS DAY AND ASSOCIATE IT WITH ACTING ENVIRONMENTALLY RESPONSIBLE.

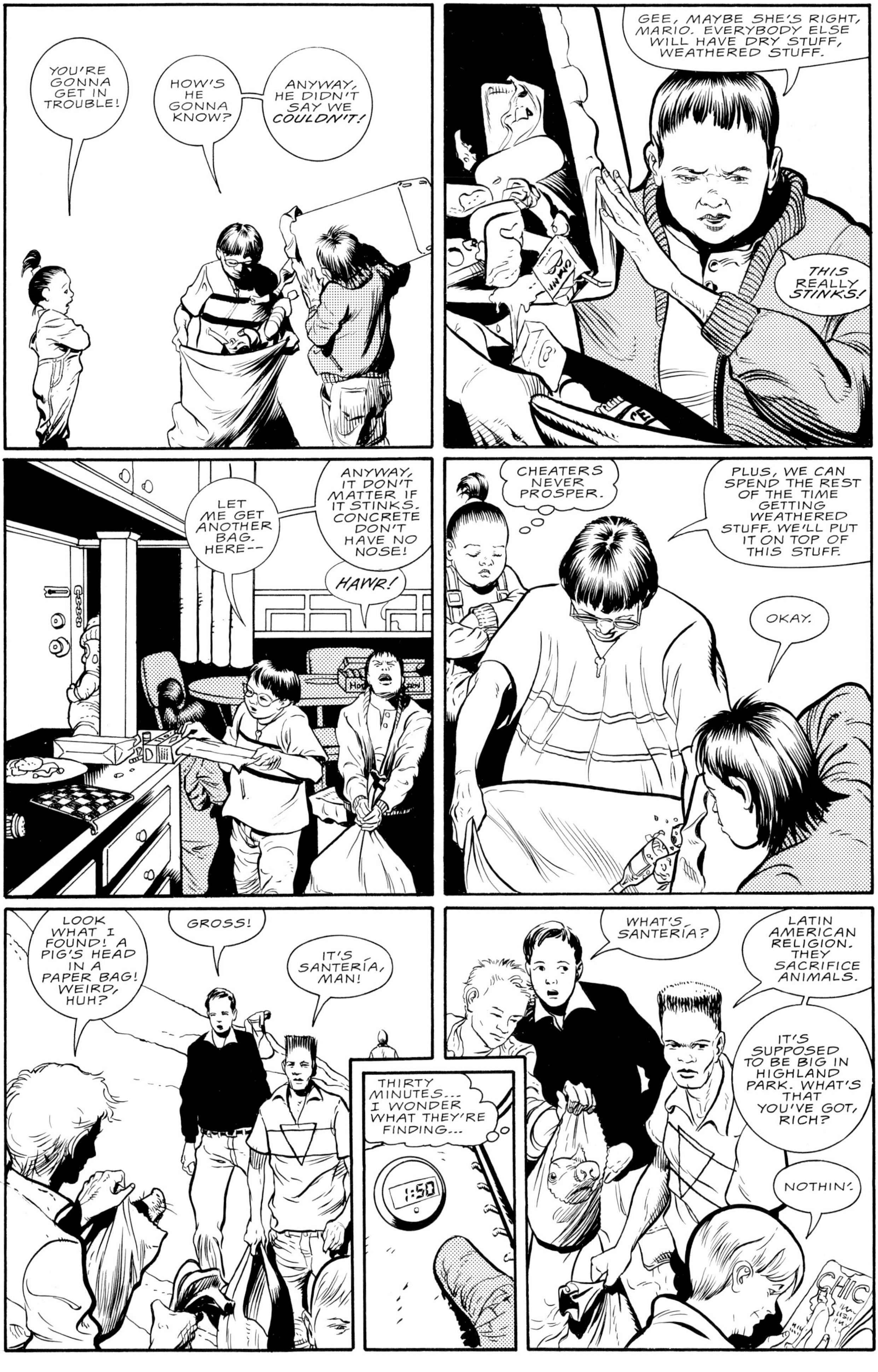
YOU'RE GONNA GET IN TROUBLE!
HOW'S HE GONNA KNOW?
ANYWAY, HE DIDN'T SAY WE *COULDN'T!*
GEE, MAYBE SHE'S RIGHT, MARIO. EVERYBODY ELSE WILL HAVE DRY STUFF, WEATHERED STUFF.
THIS REALLY *STINKS!*
LET ME GET ANOTHER BAG. HERE--
ANYWAY, IT DON'T MATTER IF IT STINKS. CONCRETE DON'T HAVE NO NOSE!
HAWR!
CHEATERS NEVER PROSPER.
PLUS, WE CAN SPEND THE REST OF THE TIME GETTING WEATHERED STUFF. WE'LL PUT IT ON TOP OF THIS STUFF.
OKAY.
LOOK WHAT I FOUND! A PIG'S HEAD IN A PAPER BAG! WEIRD, HUH?
GROSS!
IT'S SANTERÍA, MAN!
THIRTY MINUTES... I WONDER WHAT THEY'RE FINDING...
1:50
WHAT'S SANTERÍA?
LATIN AMERICAN RELIGION. THEY SACRIFICE ANIMALS.
IT'S SUPPOSED TO BE BIG IN HIGHLAND PARK. WHAT'S THAT YOU'VE GOT, RICH?
NOTHIN'.
CHIC

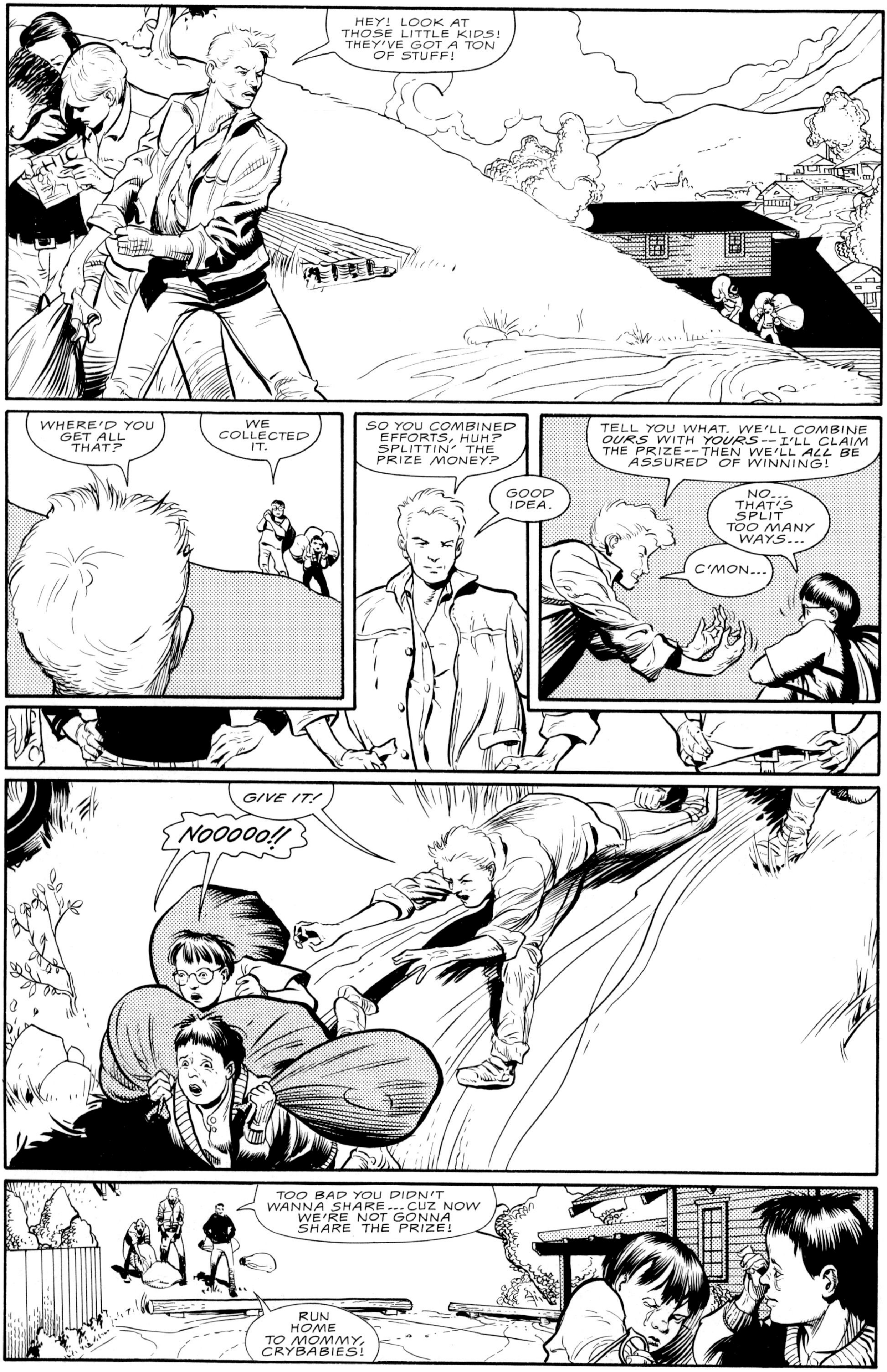
HEY! LOOK AT THOSE LITTLE KIDS! THEY'VE GOT A TON OF STUFF!
WHERE'D YOU GET ALL THAT?
WE COLLECTED IT.
SO YOU COMBINED EFFORTS, HUH? SPLITTIN' THE PRIZE MONEY?
GOOD IDEA.
TELL YOU WHAT. WE'LL COMBINE OURS WITH YOURS--I'LL CLAIM THE PRIZE--THEN WE'LL ALL BE ASSURED OF WINNING!
NO... THAT'S SPLIT TOO MANY WAYS...
C'MON...
GIVE IT!
NOOOOO!!
TOO BAD YOU DIDN'T WANNA SHARE... CUZ NOW WE'RE NOT GONNA SHARE THE PRIZE!
RUN HOME TO MOMMY, CRYBABIES!

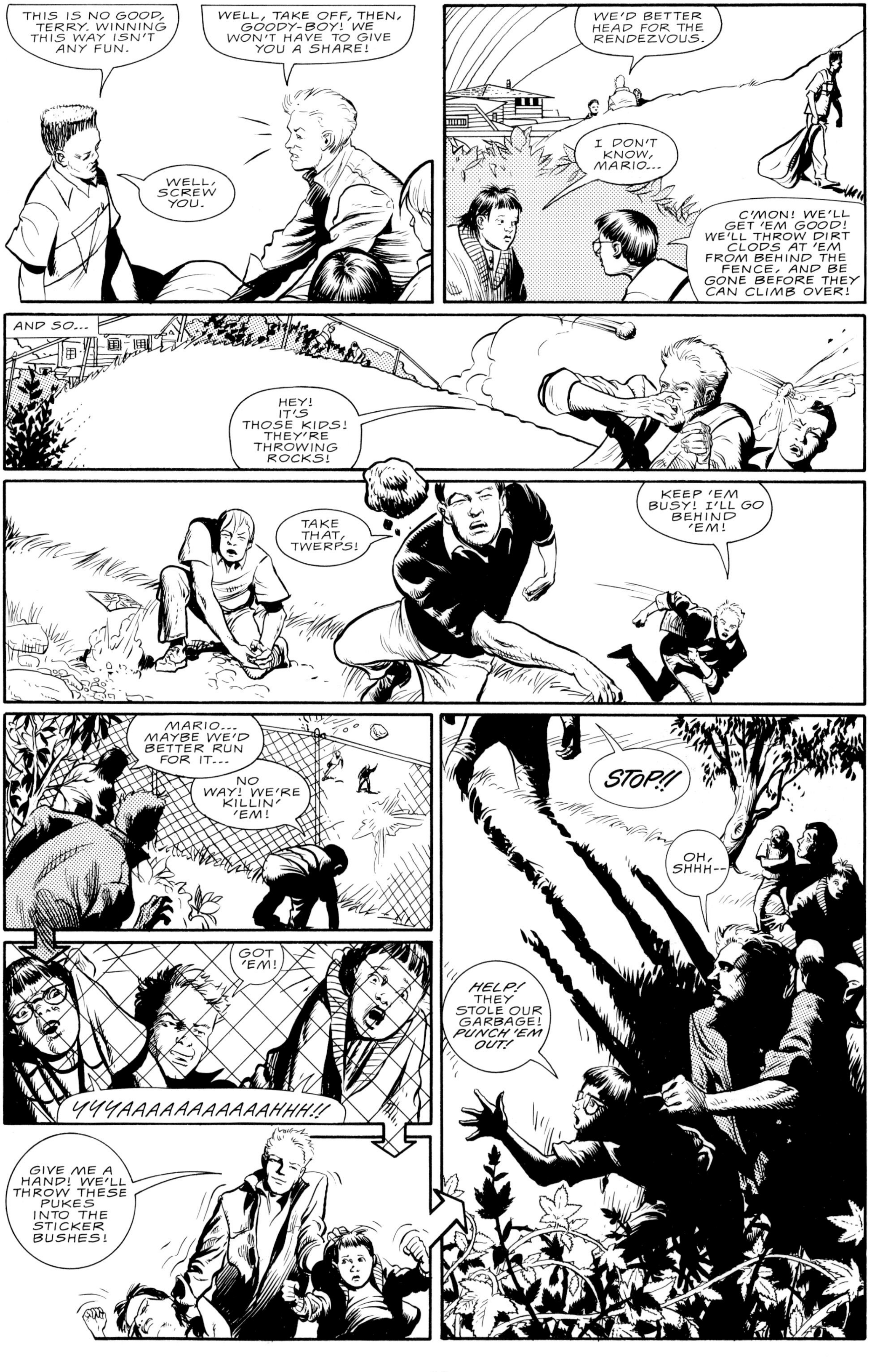

THIS IS NO GOOD, TERRY. WINNING THIS WAY ISN'T ANY FUN.
WELL, TAKE OFF, THEN, GOODY-BOY! WE WON'T HAVE TO GIVE YOU A SHARE!
WELL, SCREW YOU.
WE'D BETTER HEAD FOR THE RENDEZVOUS.
I DON'T KNOW, MARIO...
C'MON! WE'LL GET 'EM GOOD! WE'LL THROW DIRT CLODS AT 'EM FROM BEHIND THE FENCE, AND BE GONE BEFORE THEY CAN CLIMB OVER!
AND SO...
HEY! IT'S THOSE KIDS! THEY'RE THROWING ROCKS!
TAKE THAT, TWERPS!
KEEP 'EM BUSY! I'LL GO BEHIND 'EM!
MARIO... MAYBE WE'D BETTER RUN FOR IT...
NO WAY! WE'RE KILLIN' 'EM!
GOT 'EM!
YYYAAAAAAAAAAAAHHH!!
GIVE ME A HAND! WE'LL THROW THESE PUKES INTO THE STICKER BUSHES!
STOP!!
OH, SHHH--
HELP! THEY STOLE OUR GARBAGE! PUNCH 'EM OUT!

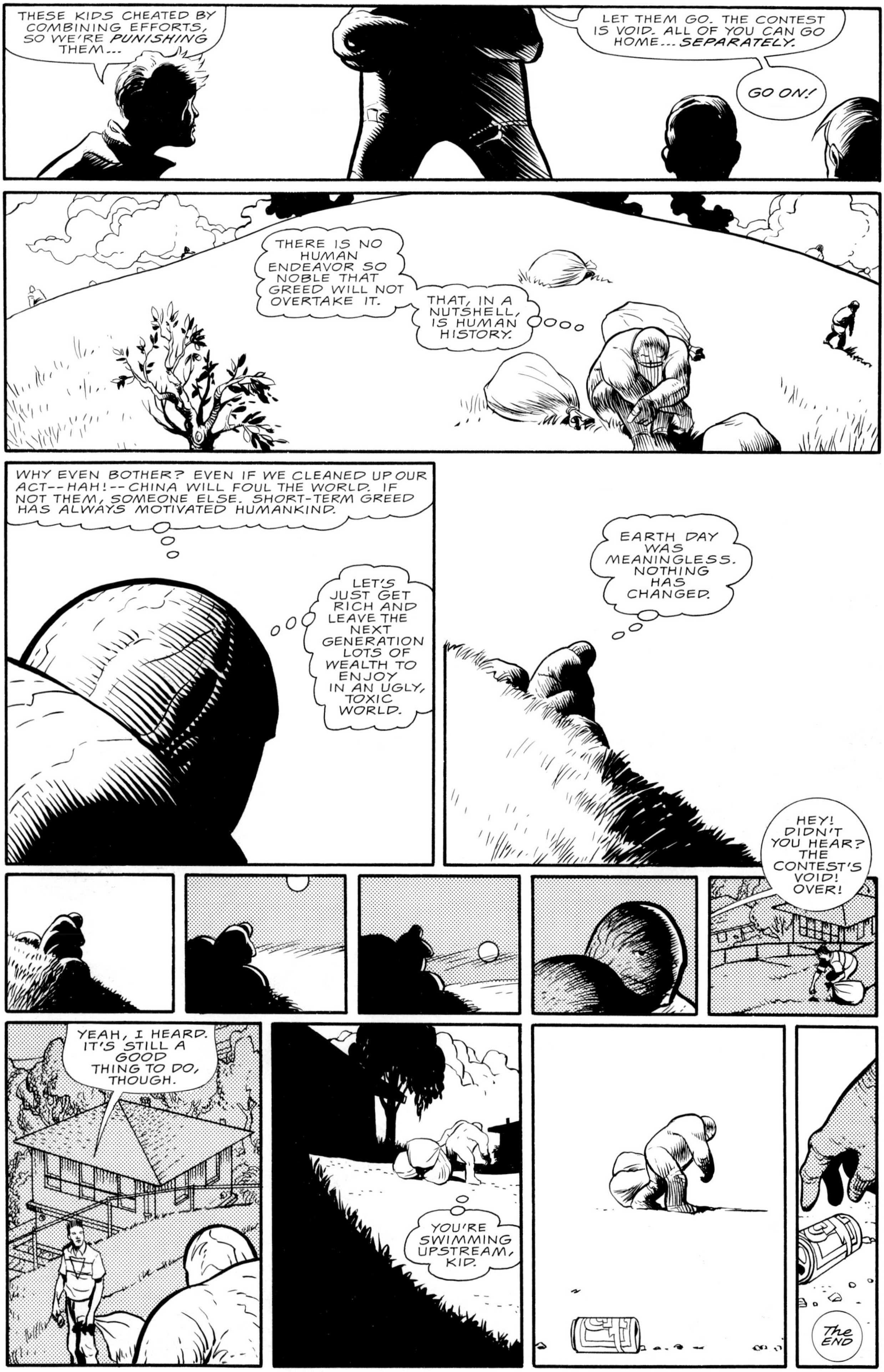
THESE KIDS CHEATED BY COMBINING EFFORTS, SO WE'RE PUNISHING THEM...
LET THEM GO. THE CONTEST IS VOID. ALL OF YOU CAN GO HOME... SEPARATELY.
GO ON!
THERE IS NO HUMAN ENDEAVOR SO NOBLE THAT GREED WILL NOT OVERTAKE IT.
THAT, IN A NUTSHELL, IS HUMAN HISTORY.
WHY EVEN BOTHER? EVEN IF WE CLEANED UP OUR ACT--HAH!--CHINA WILL FOUL THE WORLD. IF NOT THEM, SOMEONE ELSE. SHORT-TERM GREED HAS ALWAYS MOTIVATED HUMANKIND.
LET'S JUST GET RICH AND LEAVE THE NEXT GENERATION LOTS OF WEALTH TO ENJOY IN AN UGLY, TOXIC WORLD.
EARTH DAY WAS MEANINGLESS. NOTHING HAS CHANGED.
HEY! DIDN'T YOU HEAR? THE CONTEST'S VOID! OVER!
YEAH, I HEARD. IT'S STILL A GOOD THING TO DO, THOUGH.
YOU'RE SWIMMING UPSTREAM, KID.
The END

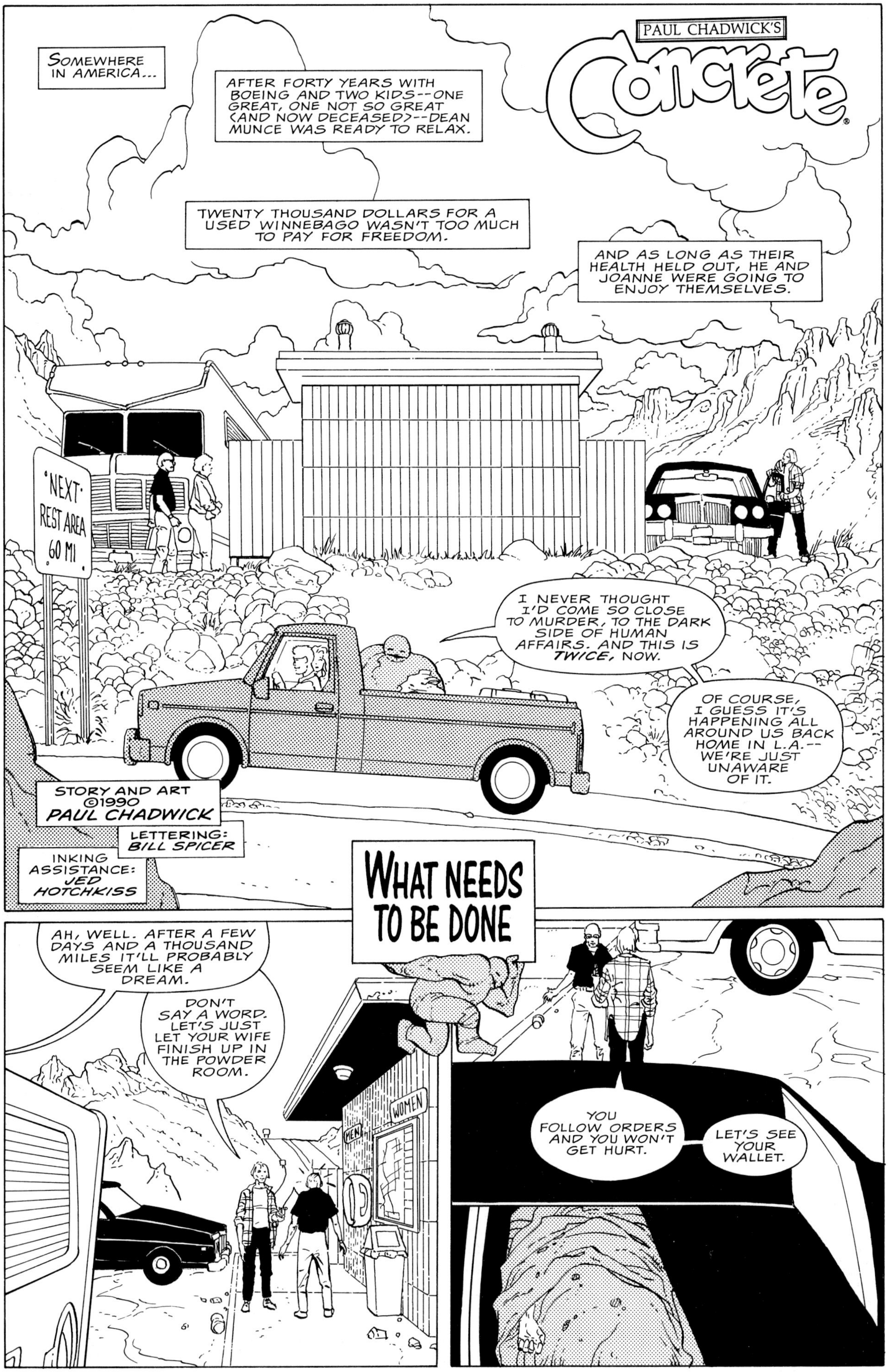
PAUL CHADWICK'S
Concrete
SOMEWHERE IN AMERICA...
AFTER FORTY YEARS WITH BOEING AND TWO KIDS--ONE GREAT, ONE NOT SO GREAT (AND NOW DECEASED)--DEAN MUNCE WAS READY TO RELAX.
TWENTY THOUSAND DOLLARS FOR A USED WINNEBAGO WASN'T TOO MUCH TO PAY FOR FREEDOM.
AND AS LONG AS THEIR HEALTH HELD OUT, HE AND JOANNE WERE GOING TO ENJOY THEMSELVES.
"NEXT" REST AREA 60 MI
I NEVER THOUGHT I'D COME SO CLOSE TO MURDER, TO THE DARK SIDE OF HUMAN AFFAIRS. AND THIS IS TWICE, NOW.
OF COURSE, I GUESS IT'S HAPPENING ALL AROUND US BACK HOME IN L.A.--WE'RE JUST UNAWARE OF IT.
STORY AND ART ©1990 PAUL CHADWICK
LETTERING: BILL SPICER
INKING ASSISTANCE: JED HOTCHKISS
WHAT NEEDS TO BE DONE
AH, WELL. AFTER A FEW DAYS AND A THOUSAND MILES IT'LL PROBABLY SEEM LIKE A DREAM.
DON'T SAY A WORD. LET'S JUST LET YOUR WIFE FINISH UP IN THE POWDER ROOM.
MEN
WOMEN
YOU FOLLOW ORDERS AND YOU WON'T GET HURT.
LET'S SEE YOUR WALLET.

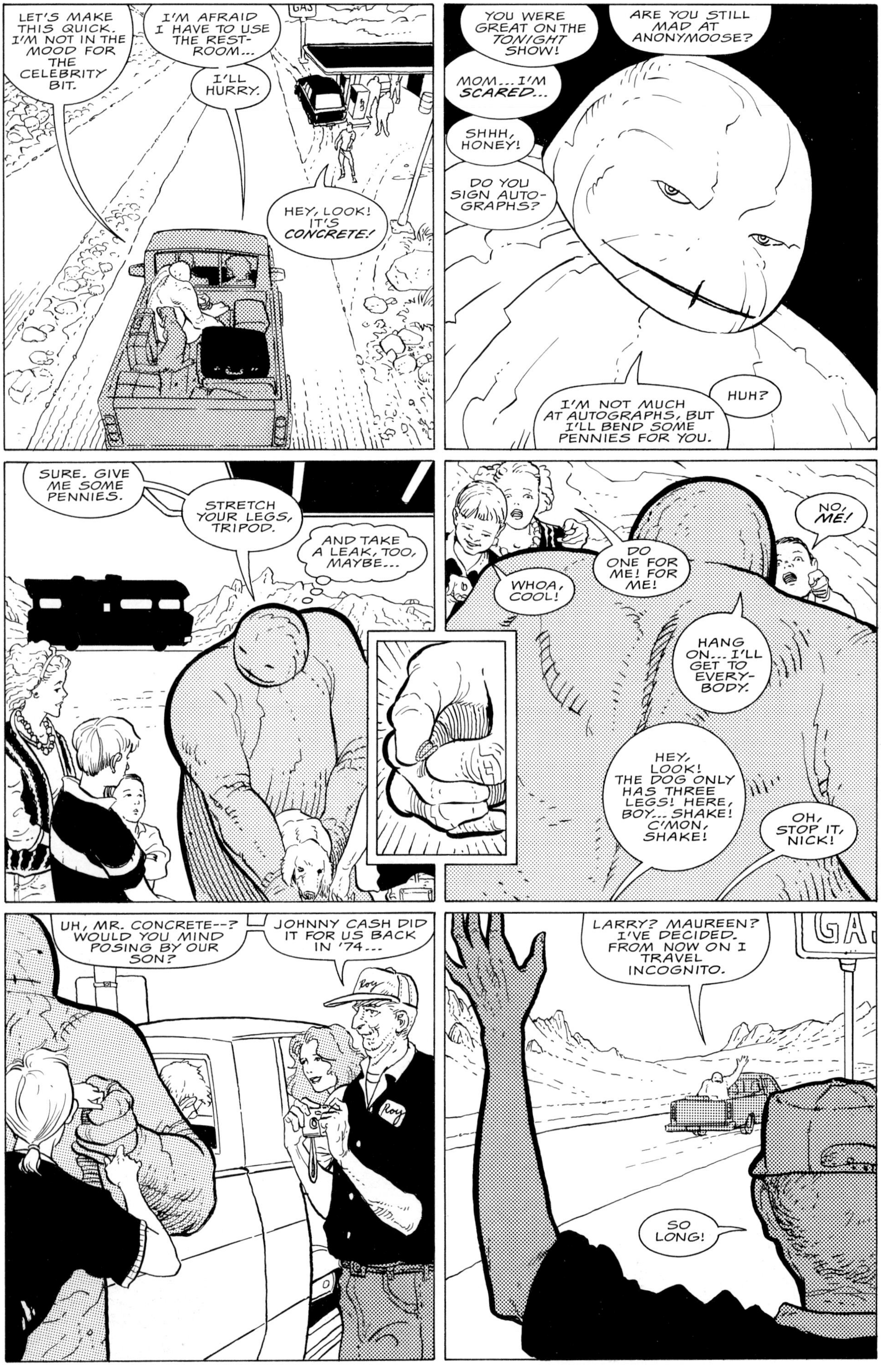
LET'S MAKE THIS QUICK. I'M NOT IN THE MOOD FOR THE CELEBRITY BIT.
I'M AFRAID I HAVE TO USE THE REST-ROOM...
I'LL HURRY.
GAS
HEY, LOOK! IT'S CONCRETE!
YOU WERE GREAT ON THE TONIGHT SHOW!
ARE YOU STILL MAD AT ANONYMOOSE?
MOM...I'M SCARED...
SHHH, HONEY!
DO YOU SIGN AUTO-GRAPHS?
I'M NOT MUCH AT AUTOGRAPHS, BUT I'LL BEND SOME PENNIES FOR YOU.
HUH?
SURE. GIVE ME SOME PENNIES.
STRETCH YOUR LEGS, TRIPOD.
AND TAKE A LEAK, TOO, MAYBE...
WHOA, COOL!
DO ONE FOR ME! FOR ME!
NO, ME!
HANG ON... I'LL GET TO EVERY-BODY.
HEY, LOOK! THE DOG ONLY HAS THREE LEGS! HERE, BOY... SHAKE! C'MON, SHAKE!
OH, STOP IT, NICK!
UH, MR. CONCRETE--? WOULD YOU MIND POSING BY OUR SON?
JOHNNY CASH DID IT FOR US BACK IN '74...
Roy
Roy
LARRY? MAUREEN? I'VE DECIDED. FROM NOW ON I TRAVEL INCOGNITO.
GAS
SO LONG!

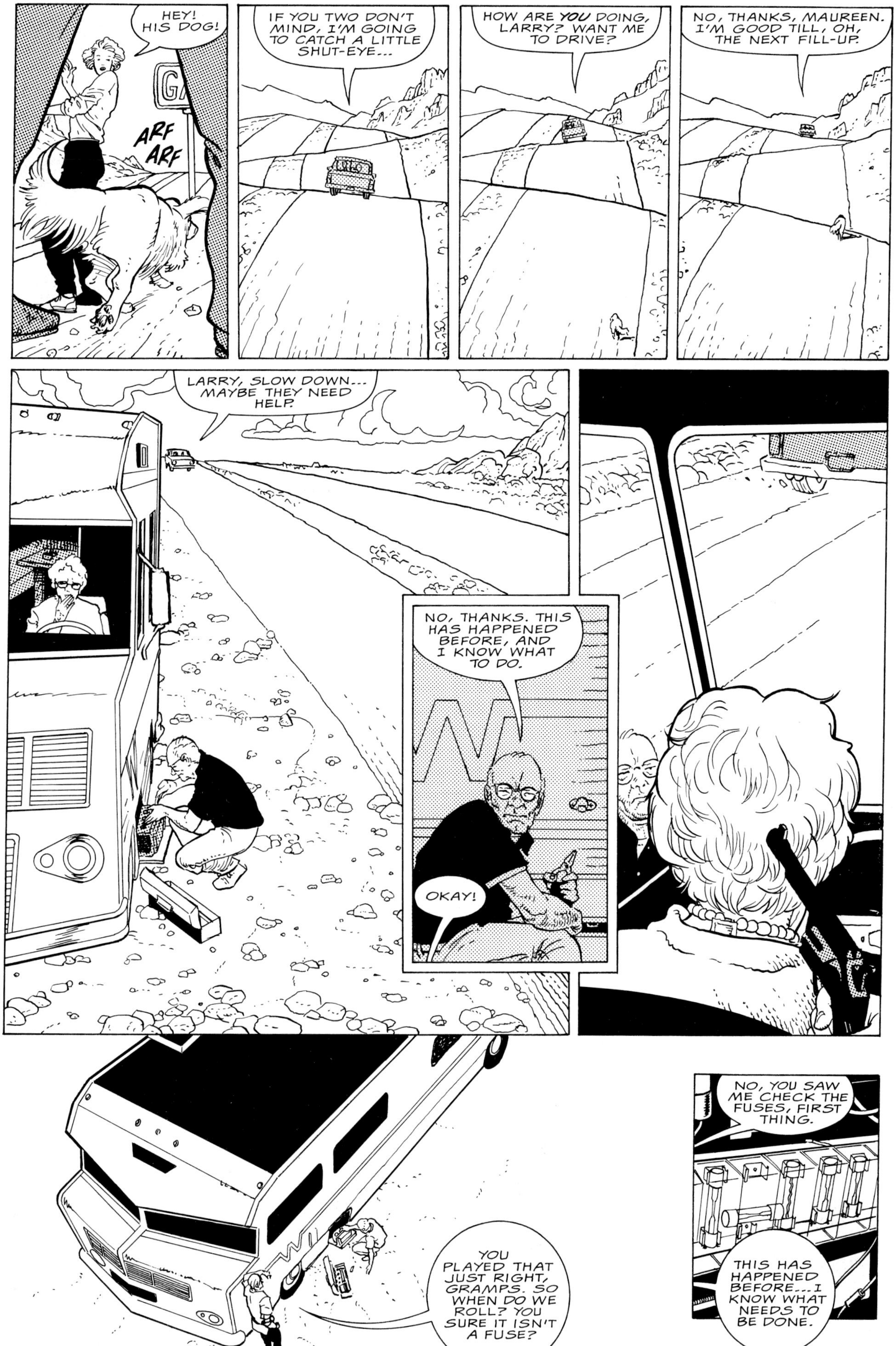
HEY! HIS DOG!
GA
ARF ARF
IF YOU TWO DON'T MIND, I'M GOING TO CATCH A LITTLE SHUT-EYE...
HOW ARE YOU DOING, LARRY? WANT ME TO DRIVE?
NO, THANKS, MAUREEN. I'M GOOD TILL, OH, THE NEXT FILL-UP.
LARRY, SLOW DOWN... MAYBE THEY NEED HELP.
NO, THANKS. THIS HAS HAPPENED BEFORE, AND I KNOW WHAT TO DO.
OKAY!
YOU PLAYED THAT JUST RIGHT, GRAMPS. SO WHEN DO WE ROLL? YOU SURE IT ISN'T A FUSE?
NO, YOU SAW ME CHECK THE FUSES, FIRST THING.
THIS HAS HAPPENED BEFORE... I KNOW WHAT NEEDS TO BE DONE.

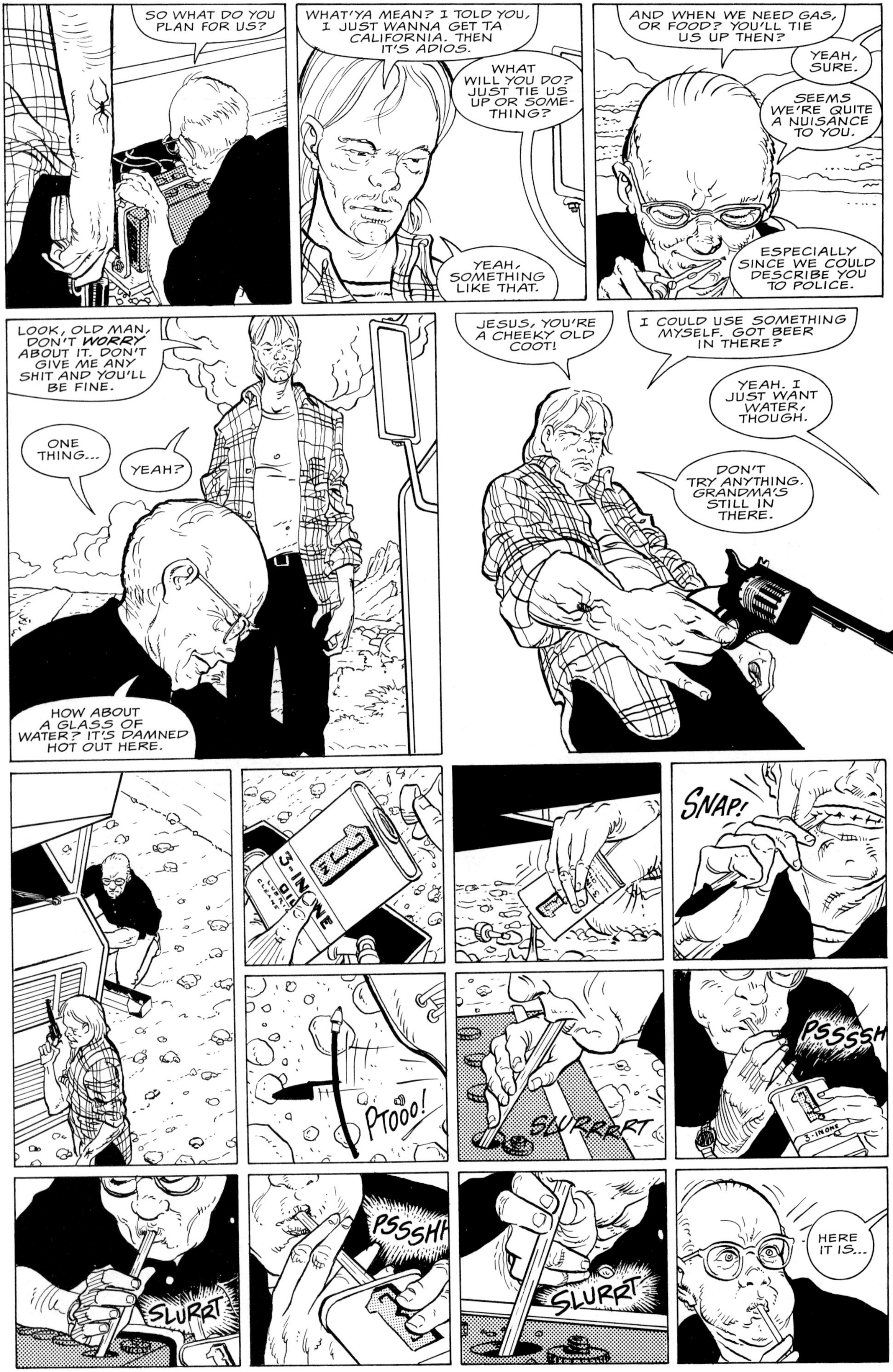
SO WHAT DO YOU PLAN FOR US?
WHAT'YA MEAN? I TOLD YOU, I JUST WANNA GET TA CALIFORNIA. THEN IT'S ADIOS.
WHAT WILL YOU DO? JUST TIE US UP OR SOME-THING?
YEAH, SOMETHING LIKE THAT.
AND WHEN WE NEED GAS, OR FOOD? YOU'LL TIE US UP THEN?
YEAH, SURE.
SEEMS WE'RE QUITE A NUISANCE TO YOU.
ESPECIALLY SINCE WE COULD DESCRIBE YOU TO POLICE.
LOOK, OLD MAN, DON'T WORRY ABOUT IT. DON'T GIVE ME ANY SHIT AND YOU'LL BE FINE.
ONE THING...
YEAH?
HOW ABOUT A GLASS OF WATER? IT'S DAMNED HOT OUT HERE.
JESUS, YOU'RE A CHEEKY OLD COOT!
I COULD USE SOMETHING MYSELF. GOT BEER IN THERE?
YEAH. I JUST WANT WATER, THOUGH.
DON'T TRY ANYTHING. GRANDMA'S STILL IN THERE.
3-IN-ONE OIL
SNAP!
PTOOO!
SLURRRRT
PSSSSH
SLURRT
PSSSHH
SLURRT
HERE IT IS...

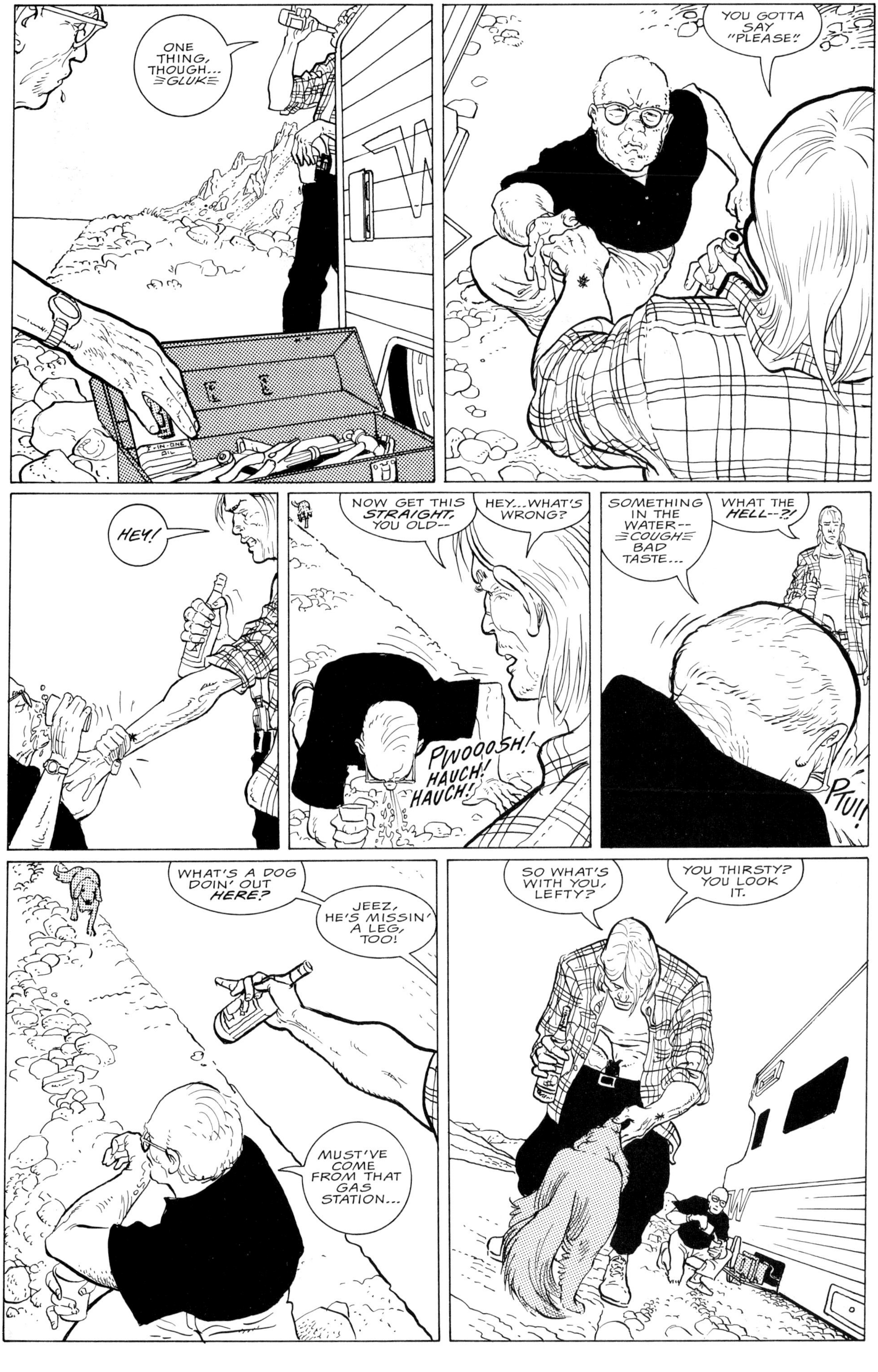
ONE THING, THOUGH... GLUK
YOU GOTTA SAY "PLEASE."
HEY!
NOW GET THIS STRAIGHT, YOU OLD--
HEY...WHAT'S WRONG?
PWOOOSH! HAUCH! HAUCH!
SOMETHING IN THE WATER-- COUGH BAD TASTE...
WHAT THE HELL--?!
PTUI!
WHAT'S A DOG DOIN' OUT HERE?
JEEZ, HE'S MISSIN' A LEG, TOO!
MUST'VE COME FROM THAT GAS STATION...
SO WHAT'S WITH YOU, LEFTY?
YOU THIRSTY? YOU LOOK IT.

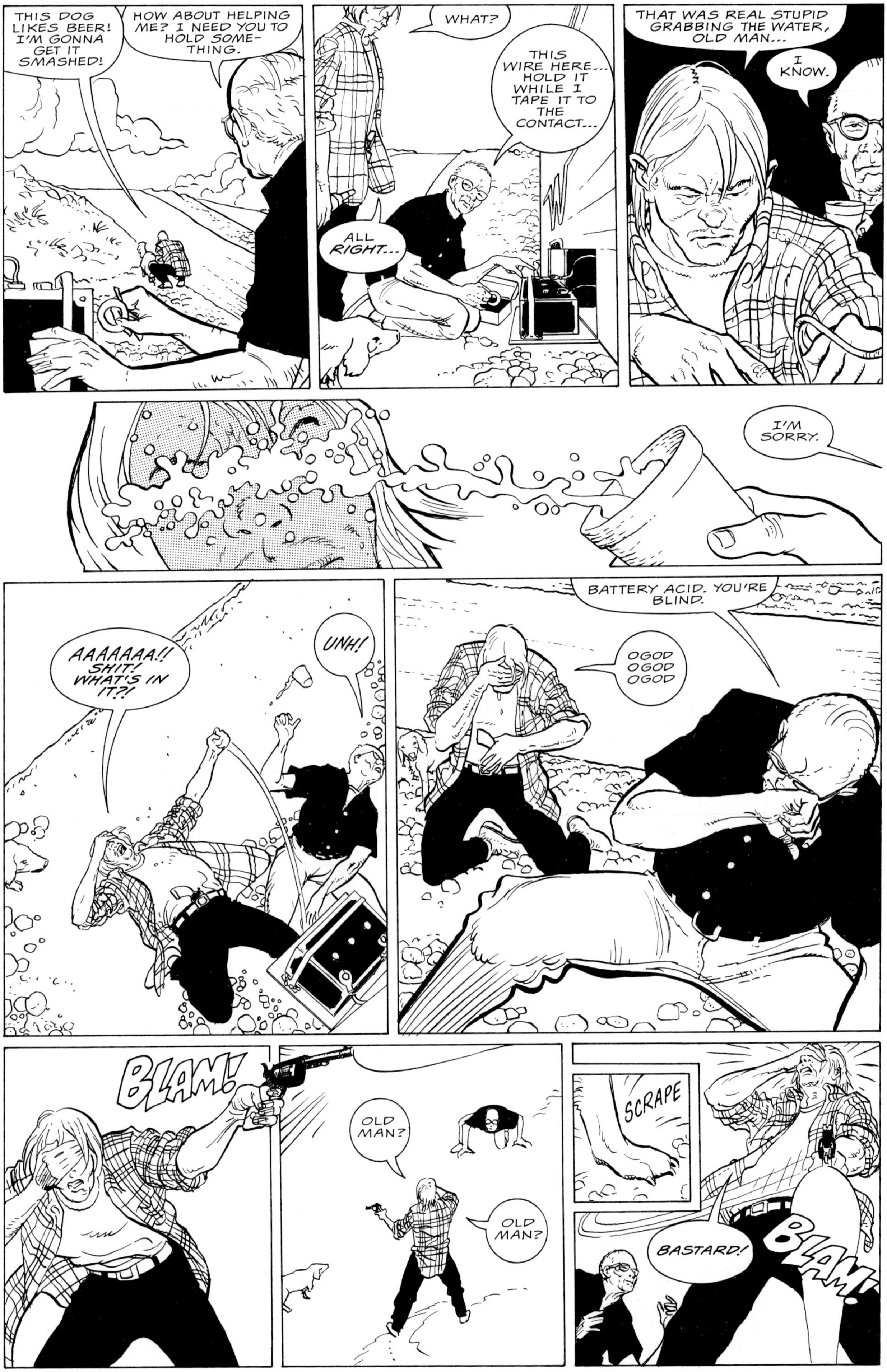
THIS DOG LIKES BEER! I'M GONNA GET IT SMASHED!
HOW ABOUT HELPING ME? I NEED YOU TO HOLD SOMETHING.
WHAT?
THIS WIRE HERE... HOLD IT WHILE I TAPE IT TO THE CONTACT...
ALL RIGHT...
THAT WAS REAL STUPID GRABBING THE WATER, OLD MAN...
I KNOW.
I'M SORRY.
AAAAAAA!! SHIT! WHAT'S IN IT?!
UNH!
BATTERY ACID. YOU'RE BLIND.
OGOD OGOD OGOD
BLAM!
OLD MAN?
OLD MAN?
SCRAPE
BASTARD!
BLAM!

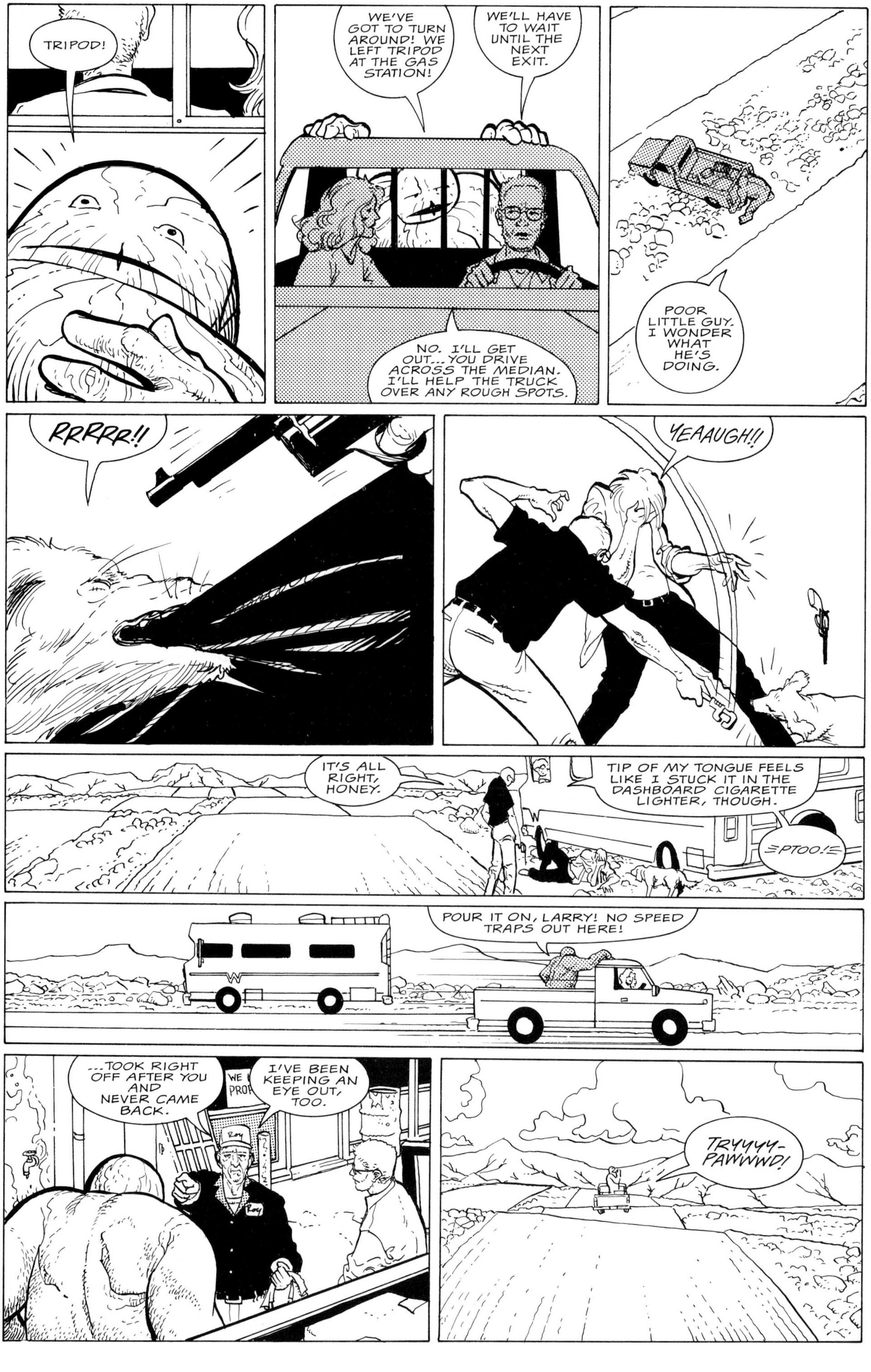
TRIPOD!
WE'VE GOT TO TURN AROUND! WE LEFT TRIPOD AT THE GAS STATION!
WE'LL HAVE TO WAIT UNTIL THE NEXT EXIT.
NO. I'LL GET OUT... YOU DRIVE ACROSS THE MEDIAN. I'LL HELP THE TRUCK OVER ANY ROUGH SPOTS.
POOR LITTLE GUY. I WONDER WHAT HE'S DOING.
RRRRR!!
YEAAUGH!!
IT'S ALL RIGHT, HONEY.
TIP OF MY TONGUE FEELS LIKE I STUCK IT IN THE DASHBOARD CIGARETTE LIGHTER, THOUGH.
PTOO!
POUR IT ON, LARRY! NO SPEED TRAPS OUT HERE!
...TOOK RIGHT OFF AFTER YOU AND NEVER CAME BACK.
I'VE BEEN KEEPING AN EYE OUT, TOO.
TRYYYY-PAWWWD!

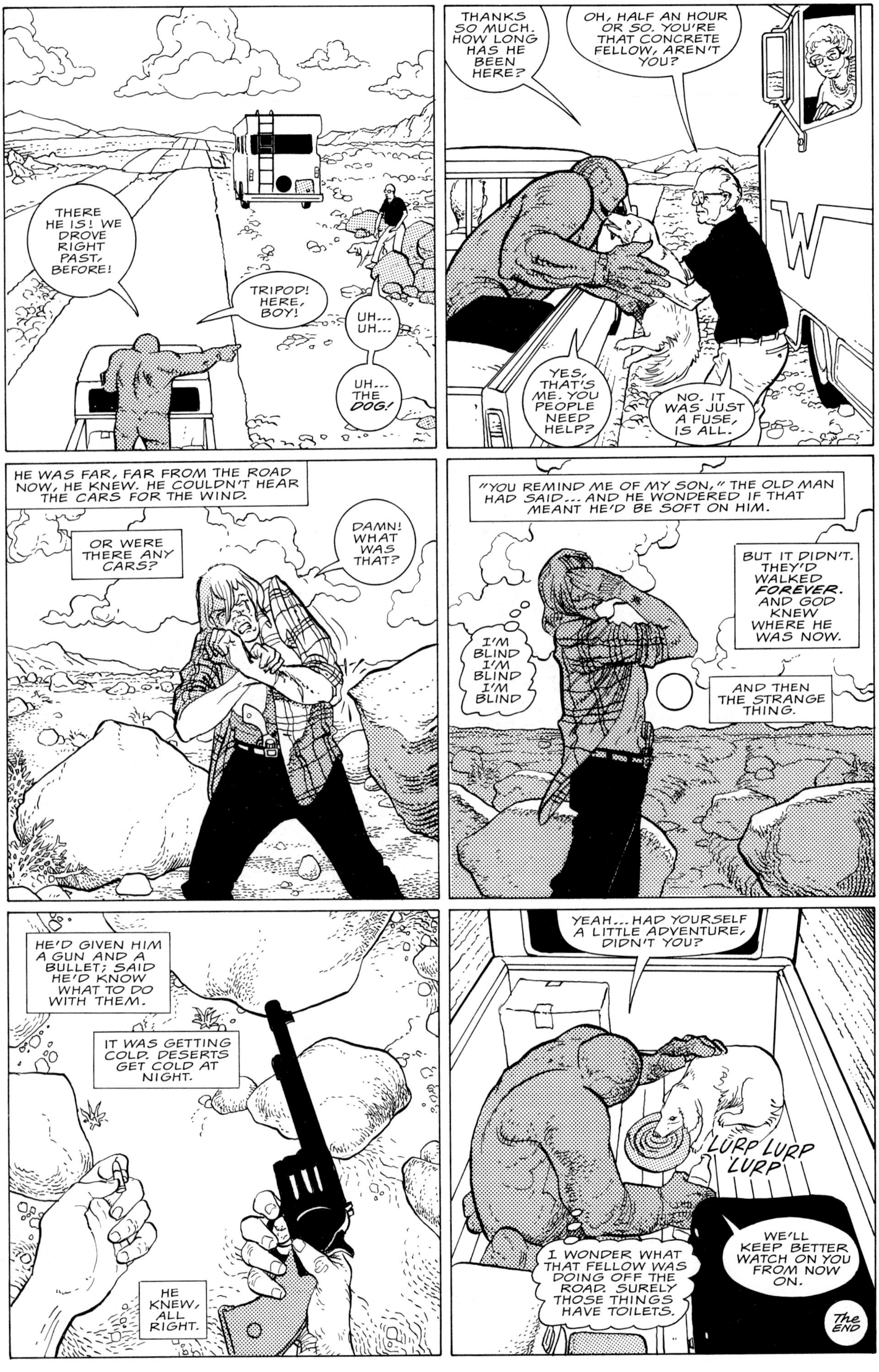
THERE HE IS! WE DROVE RIGHT PAST, BEFORE!
TRIPOD! HERE, BOY!
UH... UH...
UH... THE DOG!
THANKS SO MUCH. HOW LONG HAS HE BEEN HERE?
OH, HALF AN HOUR OR SO. YOU'RE THAT CONCRETE FELLOW, AREN'T YOU?
YES, THAT'S ME. YOU PEOPLE NEED HELP?
NO. IT WAS JUST A FUSE, IS ALL.
HE WAS FAR, FAR FROM THE ROAD NOW, HE KNEW. HE COULDN'T HEAR THE CARS FOR THE WIND.
OR WERE THERE ANY CARS?
DAMN! WHAT WAS THAT?
"YOU REMIND ME OF MY SON," THE OLD MAN HAD SAID... AND HE WONDERED IF THAT MEANT HE'D BE SOFT ON HIM.
BUT IT DIDN'T. THEY'D WALKED FOREVER. AND GOD KNEW WHERE HE WAS NOW.
I'M BLIND I'M BLIND I'M BLIND I'M BLIND
AND THEN THE STRANGE THING.
HE'D GIVEN HIM A GUN AND A BULLET; SAID HE'D KNOW WHAT TO DO WITH THEM.
IT WAS GETTING COLD. DESERTS GET COLD AT NIGHT.
HE KNEW, ALL RIGHT.
YEAH... HAD YOURSELF A LITTLE ADVENTURE, DIDN'T YOU?
LURP LURP LURP
I WONDER WHAT THAT FELLOW WAS DOING OFF THE ROAD. SURELY THOSE THINGS HAVE TOILETS.
WE'LL KEEP BETTER WATCH ON YOU FROM NOW ON.
The END

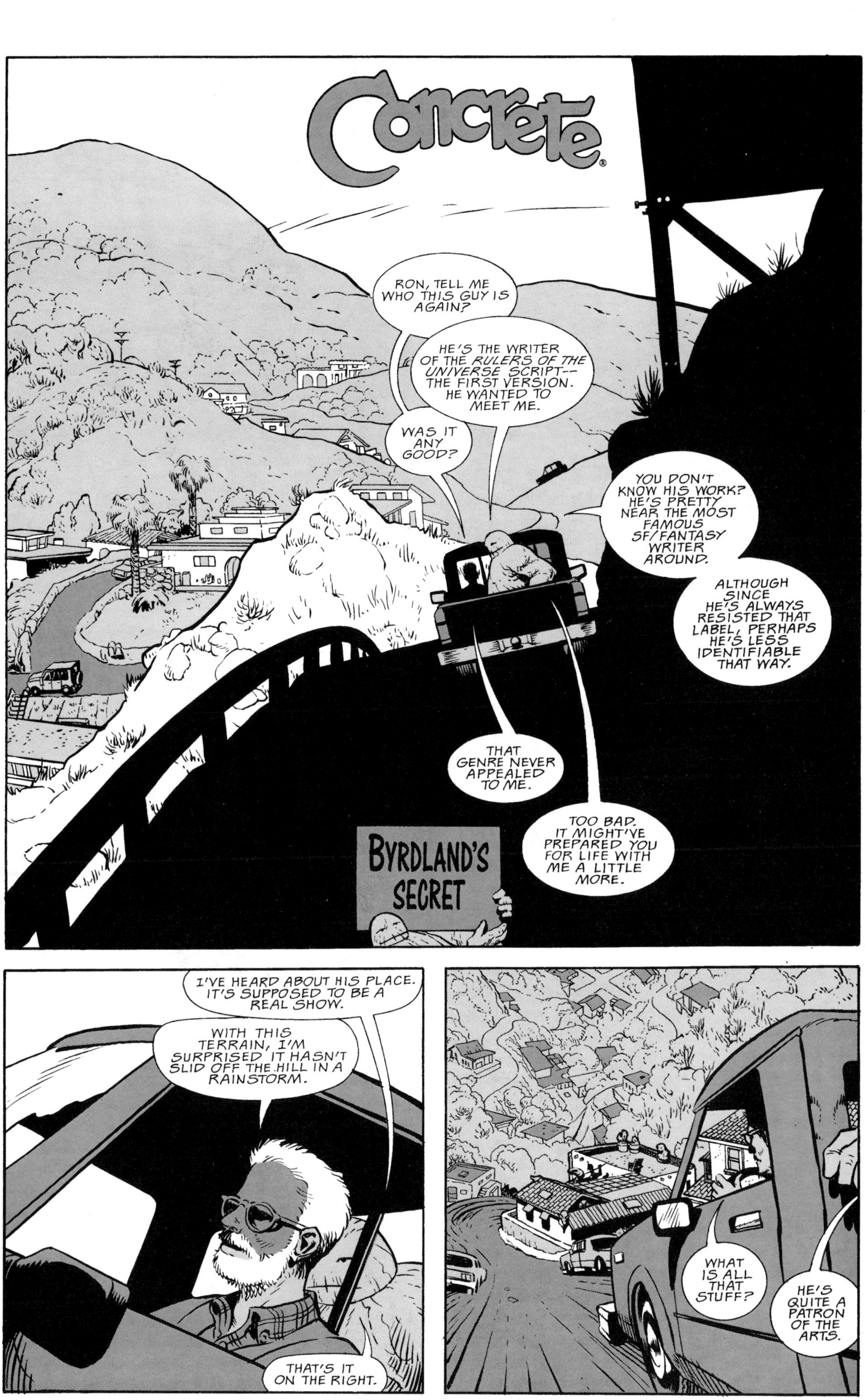
Concrete®
RON, TELL ME WHO THIS GUY IS AGAIN?
HE'S THE WRITER OF THE *RULERS OF THE UNIVERSE* SCRIPT-- THE FIRST VERSION. HE WANTED TO MEET ME.
WAS IT ANY GOOD?
YOU DON'T KNOW HIS WORK? HE'S PRETTY NEAR THE MOST FAMOUS SF/FANTASY WRITER AROUND.
ALTHOUGH SINCE HE'S ALWAYS RESISTED THAT LABEL, PERHAPS HE'S LESS IDENTIFIABLE THAT WAY.
THAT GENRE NEVER APPEALED TO ME.
TOO BAD. IT MIGHT'VE PREPARED YOU FOR LIFE WITH ME A LITTLE MORE.
BYRDLAND'S SECRET
I'VE HEARD ABOUT HIS PLACE. IT'S SUPPOSED TO BE A REAL SHOW.
WITH THIS TERRAIN, I'M SURPRISED IT HASN'T SLID OFF THE HILL IN A RAINSTORM.
THAT'S IT ON THE RIGHT.
WHAT IS ALL THAT STUFF?
HE'S QUITE A PATRON OF THE ARTS.

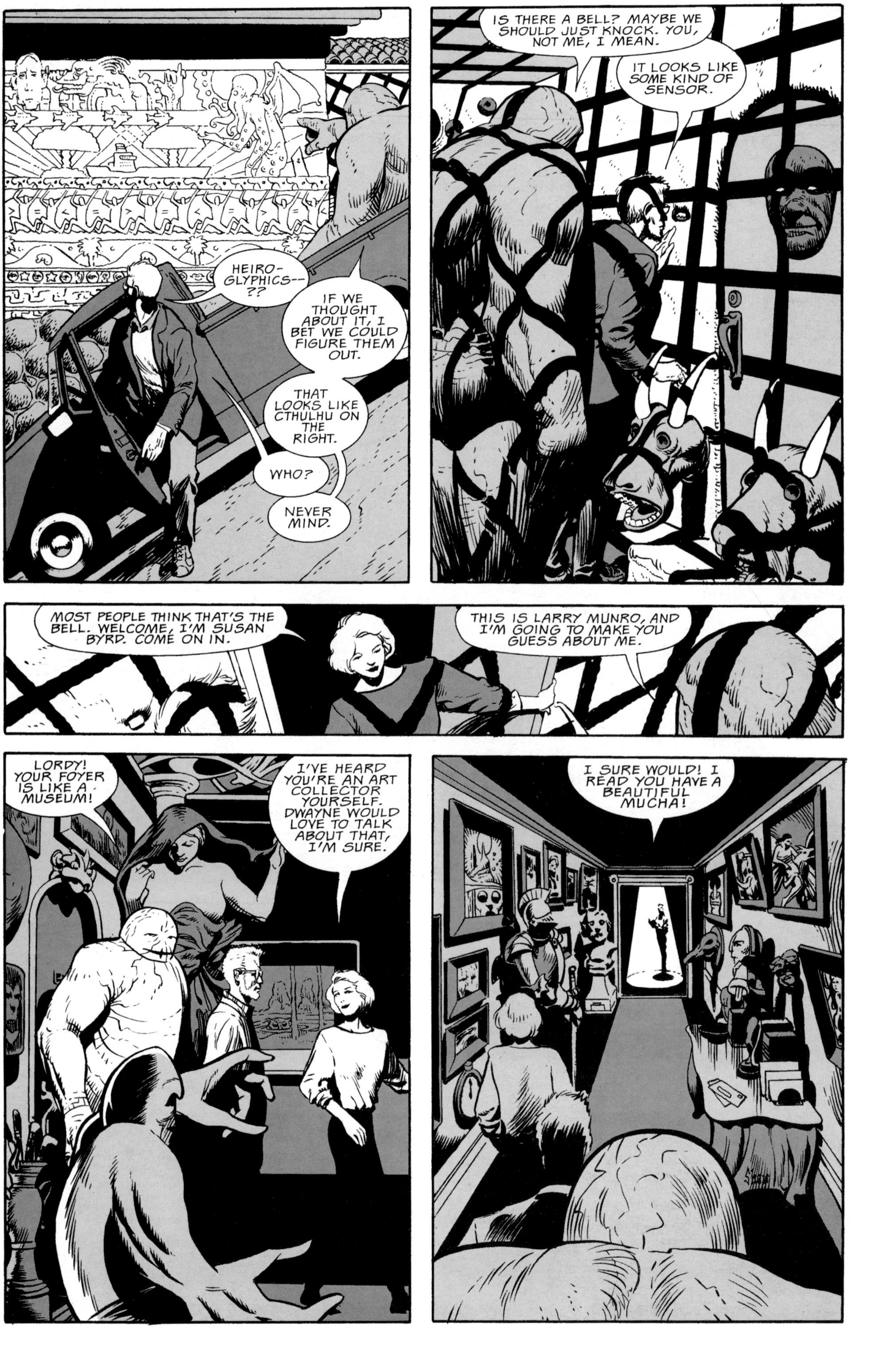
HEIRO-GLYPHICS--??
IF WE THOUGHT ABOUT IT, I BET WE COULD FIGURE THEM OUT.
THAT LOOKS LIKE CTHULHU ON THE RIGHT.
WHO?
NEVER MIND.
IS THERE A BELL? MAYBE WE SHOULD JUST KNOCK. YOU, NOT ME, I MEAN.
IT LOOKS LIKE SOME KIND OF SENSOR.
MOST PEOPLE THINK THAT'S THE BELL. WELCOME, I'M SUSAN BYRD. COME ON IN.
THIS IS LARRY MUNRO, AND I'M GOING TO MAKE YOU GUESS ABOUT ME.
LORDY! YOUR FOYER IS LIKE A MUSEUM!
I'VE HEARD YOU'RE AN ART COLLECTOR YOURSELF. DWAYNE WOULD LOVE TO TALK ABOUT THAT, I'M SURE.
I SURE WOULD! I READ YOU HAVE A BEAUTIFUL MUCHA!

INTRODUCTIONS ARE MADE IN A ROOM CRAMMED WITH IMAGES, CHEERFULLY CRASS PULP ART HARD BY SIXTIES ABSTRACTS AND UNCLASSIFIABLE PERSONAL VISIONS.

CONCRETE HAS TROUBLE MEETING BYRD'S EYE, SO MANY FRAMED INVITATIONS TO OTHER WORLDS PULLING AT HIS ATTENTION.

THE MUCHA'S JUST A PRINT. BUT A NICE ONE, A MODERN REPRODUCTION OF ONE OF HIS FEW OIL PAINTINGS. LIMITED EDITION THING.

I HAVE A COUPLE OF PAGES FROM HIS ILSEE-- CAN YOU IMAGINE SOMEBODY TEARING THAT UP? I'LL SHOW YOU IN A BIT.

CAN I GET YOU TWO ANYTHING?

NOTHING, THANKS.

AM I CORRECT IN ASSUMING YOU HAD THIS MADE JUST FOR MY VISIT?

DON'T BE IMPRESSED. I'VE EMPLOYED SO MANY CRAFTSMEN ON THIS PLACE I CAN GET ANYTHING I NEED. A GUY THREW THIS TOGETHER IN HALF A DAY.

CONCRETE

I'M GOING TO DENT IT, I'M AFRAID.

THAT'S THE POINT. I'LL HAVE A MEMENTO OF YOUR VISIT.

MY SEAT-PRINT? ALL RIGHT...

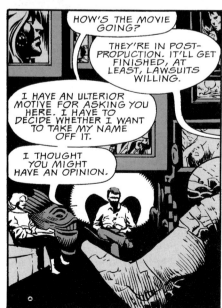

HOW'S THE MOVIE GOING?

THEY'RE IN POST-PRODUCTION. IT'LL GET FINISHED, AT LEAST, LAWSUITS WILLING.

I HAVE AN ULTERIOR MOTIVE FOR ASKING YOU HERE. I HAVE TO DECIDE WHETHER I WANT TO TAKE MY NAME OFF IT.

I THOUGHT YOU MIGHT HAVE AN OPINION.

I NEVER SAW YOUR SCRIPT, BUT I THOUGHT THE ONE DATASNOUTE DID WAS PRETTY INTERESTING.

I WAS GONE BEFORE THAT, OF COURSE. GIVEN THE LIMITATIONS OF THOSE MORONIC TOYS, I WAS TRYING TO SAY SOMETHING ABOUT LOYALTY, AND ACCEPTING CHANGE, AND WHEN TO RESIST IT.

I CAN SEE SOME OF THAT. WHEN KO'S SEVERED ARM KEEPS FIGHTING AFTER HE'S KILLED, IT'S TOUCHING IN A BIZARRE SORT OF WAY.

THAT WAS MINE.

51

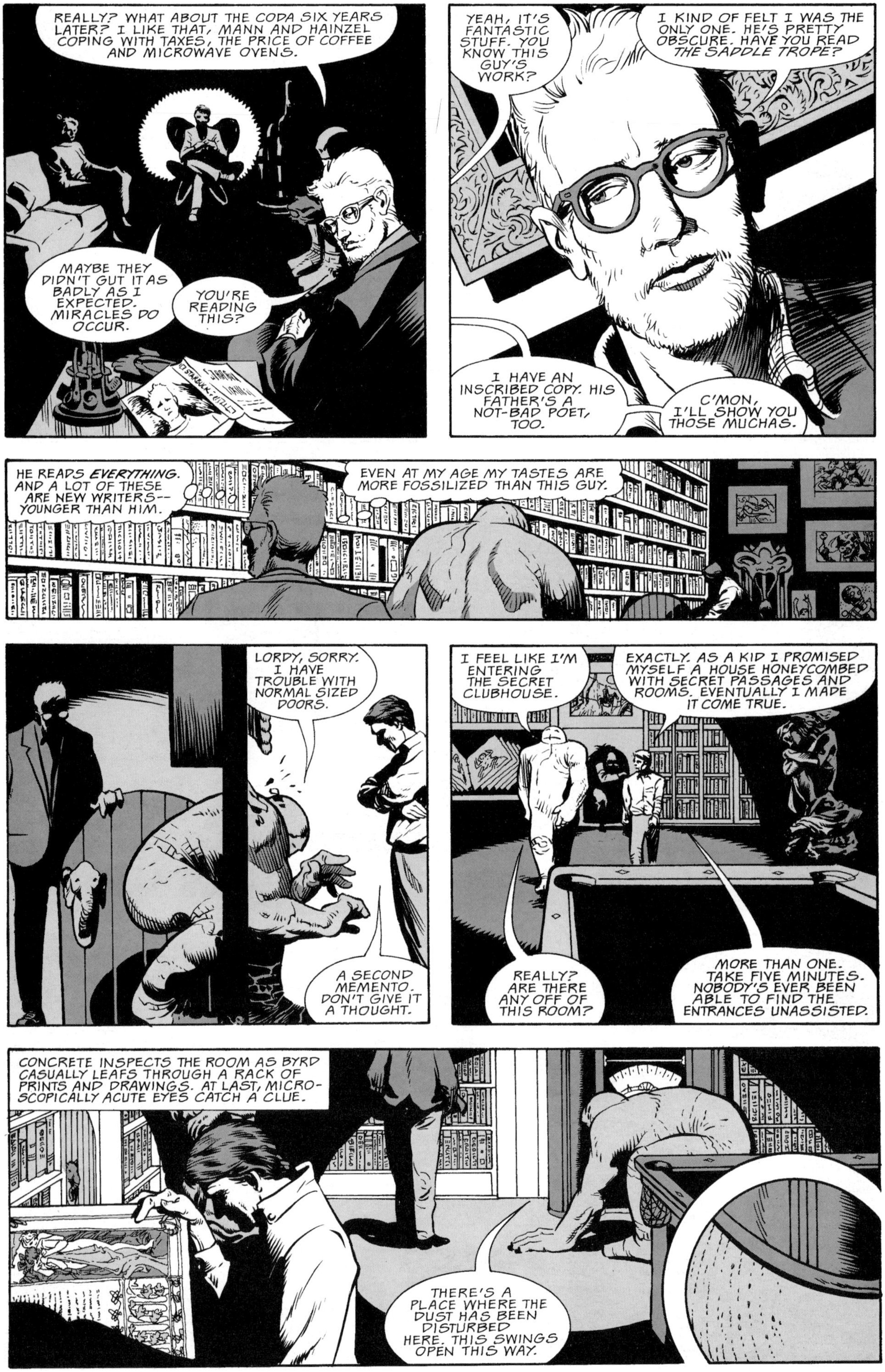
REALLY? WHAT ABOUT THE CODA SIX YEARS LATER? I LIKE THAT, MANN AND HAINZEL COPING WITH TAXES, THE PRICE OF COFFEE AND MICROWAVE OVENS.
MAYBE THEY DIDN'T GUT IT AS BADLY AS I EXPECTED. MIRACLES DO OCCUR.
YOU'RE READING THIS?
YEAH, IT'S FANTASTIC STUFF. YOU KNOW THIS GUY'S WORK?
I KIND OF FELT I WAS THE ONLY ONE. HE'S PRETTY OBSCURE. HAVE YOU READ THE SADDLE TROPE?
I HAVE AN INSCRIBED COPY. HIS FATHER'S A NOT-BAD POET, TOO.
C'MON, I'LL SHOW YOU THOSE MUCHAS.
HE READS EVERYTHING. AND A LOT OF THESE ARE NEW WRITERS-- YOUNGER THAN HIM.
EVEN AT MY AGE MY TASTES ARE MORE FOSSILIZED THAN THIS GUY.
LORDY, SORRY. I HAVE TROUBLE WITH NORMAL SIZED DOORS.
A SECOND MEMENTO. DON'T GIVE IT A THOUGHT.
I FEEL LIKE I'M ENTERING THE SECRET CLUBHOUSE.
EXACTLY. AS A KID I PROMISED MYSELF A HOUSE HONEYCOMBED WITH SECRET PASSAGES AND ROOMS. EVENTUALLY I MADE IT COME TRUE.
REALLY? ARE THERE ANY OFF OF THIS ROOM?
MORE THAN ONE. TAKE FIVE MINUTES. NOBODY'S EVER BEEN ABLE TO FIND THE ENTRANCES UNASSISTED.
CONCRETE INSPECTS THE ROOM AS BYRD CASUALLY LEAFS THROUGH A RACK OF PRINTS AND DRAWINGS. AT LAST, MICRO-SCOPICALLY ACUTE EYES CATCH A CLUE.
THERE'S A PLACE WHERE THE DUST HAS BEEN DISTURBED HERE. THIS SWINGS OPEN THIS WAY.

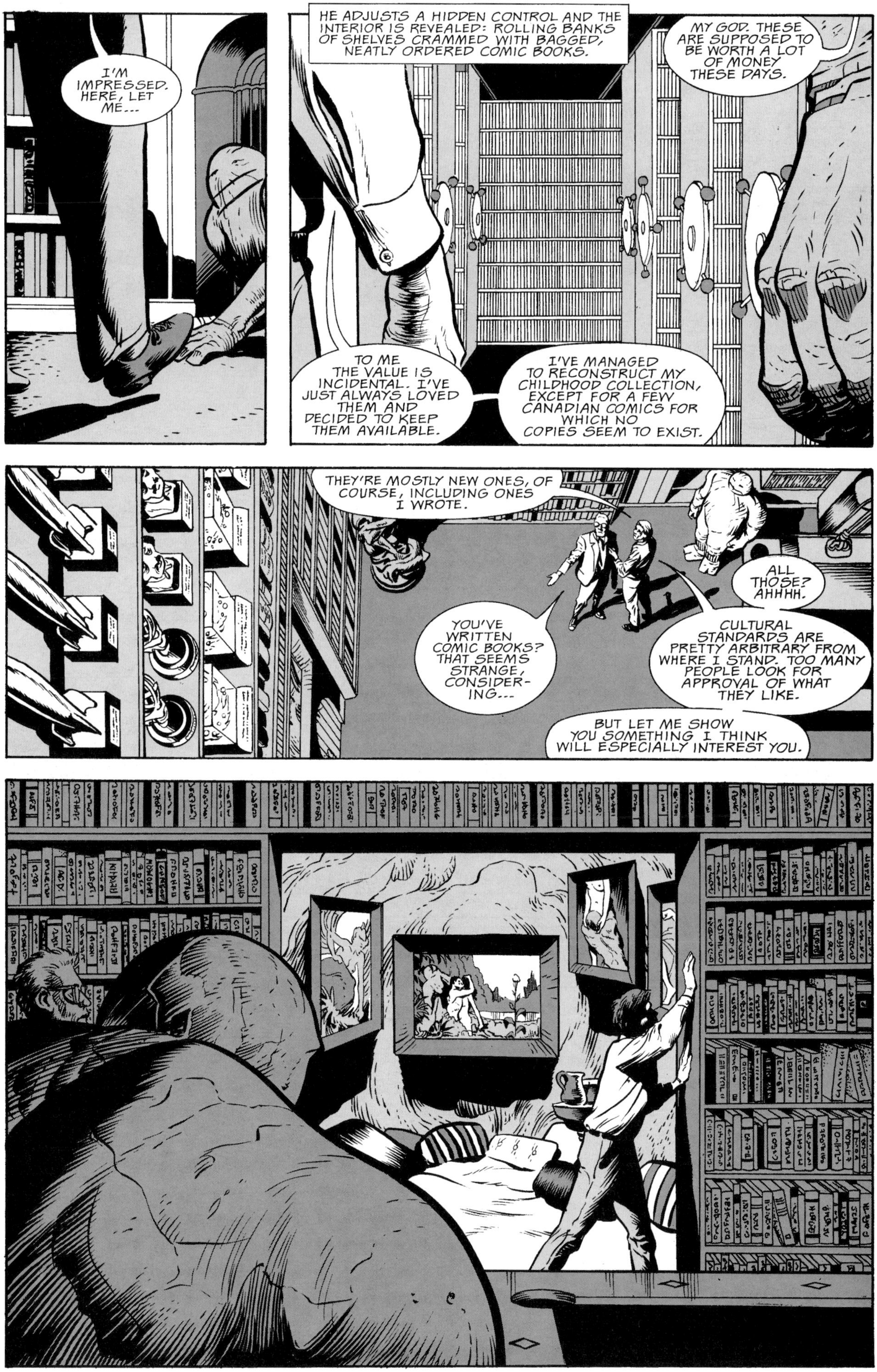
I'M IMPRESSED. HERE, LET ME...
HE ADJUSTS A HIDDEN CONTROL AND THE INTERIOR IS REVEALED: ROLLING BANKS OF SHELVES CRAMMED WITH BAGGED, NEATLY ORDERED COMIC BOOKS.
MY GOD. THESE ARE SUPPOSED TO BE WORTH A LOT OF MONEY THESE DAYS.
TO ME THE VALUE IS INCIDENTAL. I'VE JUST ALWAYS LOVED THEM AND DECIDED TO KEEP THEM AVAILABLE.
I'VE MANAGED TO RECONSTRUCT MY CHILDHOOD COLLECTION, EXCEPT FOR A FEW CANADIAN COMICS FOR WHICH NO COPIES SEEM TO EXIST.
THEY'RE MOSTLY NEW ONES, OF COURSE, INCLUDING ONES I WROTE.
ALL THOSE? AHHHH.
YOU'VE WRITTEN COMIC BOOKS? THAT SEEMS STRANGE, CONSIDER-ING...
CULTURAL STANDARDS ARE PRETTY ARBITRARY FROM WHERE I STAND. TOO MANY PEOPLE LOOK FOR APPROVAL OF WHAT THEY LIKE.
BUT LET ME SHOW YOU SOMETHING I THINK WILL ESPECIALLY INTEREST YOU.

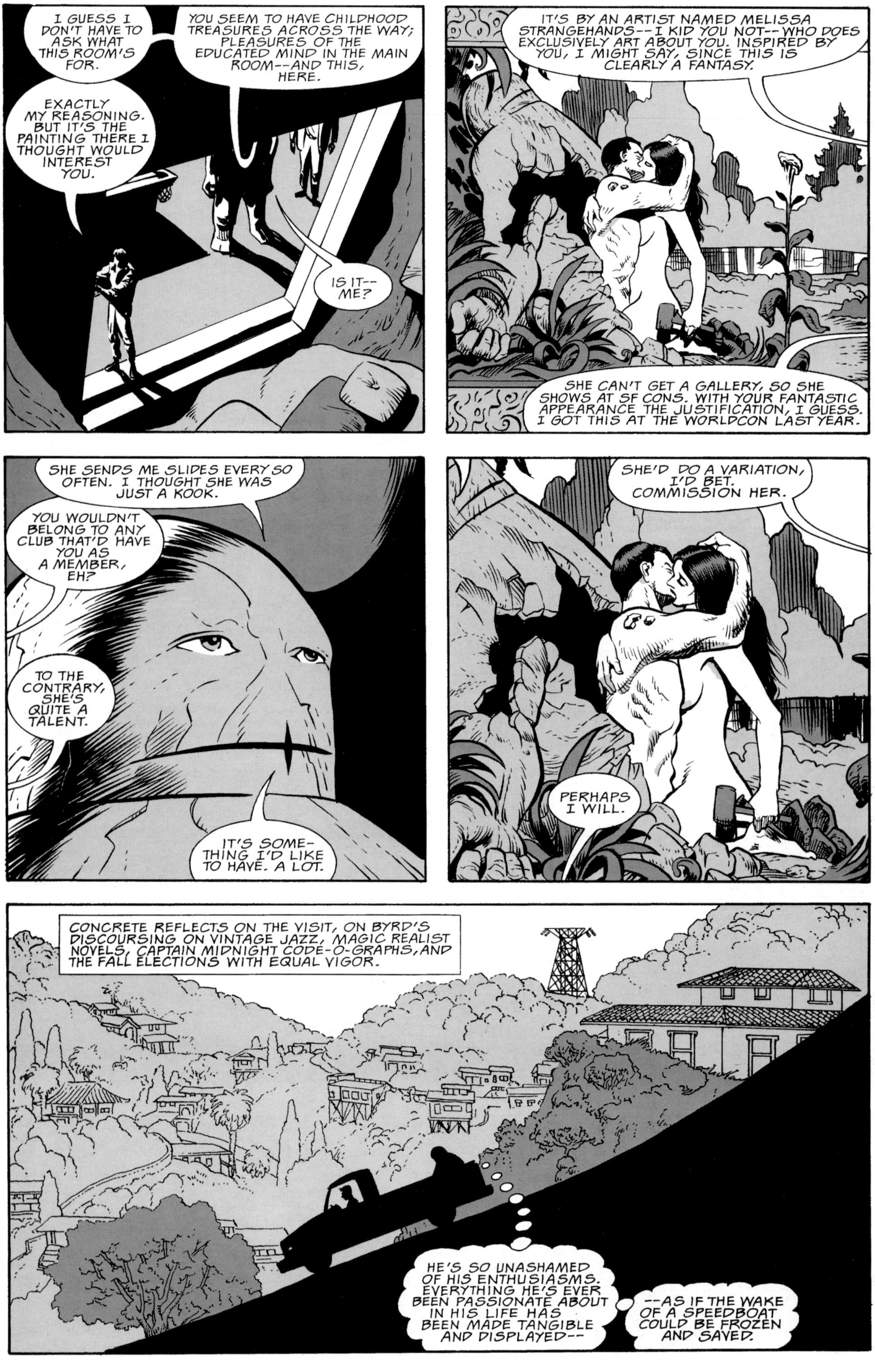
I GUESS I DON'T HAVE TO ASK WHAT THIS ROOM'S FOR.
YOU SEEM TO HAVE CHILDHOOD TREASURES ACROSS THE WAY; PLEASURES OF THE EDUCATED MIND IN THE MAIN ROOM--AND THIS, HERE.
EXACTLY MY REASONING. BUT IT'S THE PAINTING THERE I THOUGHT WOULD INTEREST YOU.
IS IT-- ME?
IT'S BY AN ARTIST NAMED MELISSA STRANGEHANDS--I KID YOU NOT--WHO DOES EXCLUSIVELY ART ABOUT YOU. INSPIRED BY YOU, I MIGHT SAY, SINCE THIS IS CLEARLY A FANTASY.
SHE CAN'T GET A GALLERY, SO SHE SHOWS AT SF CONS. WITH YOUR FANTASTIC APPEARANCE THE JUSTIFICATION, I GUESS. I GOT THIS AT THE WORLDCON LAST YEAR.
SHE SENDS ME SLIDES EVERY SO OFTEN. I THOUGHT SHE WAS JUST A KOOK.
YOU WOULDN'T BELONG TO ANY CLUB THAT'D HAVE YOU AS A MEMBER, EH?
TO THE CONTRARY, SHE'S QUITE A TALENT.
IT'S SOMETHING I'D LIKE TO HAVE. A LOT.
SHE'D DO A VARIATION, I'D BET. COMMISSION HER.
PERHAPS I WILL.
CONCRETE REFLECTS ON THE VISIT, ON BYRD'S DISCOURSING ON VINTAGE JAZZ, MAGIC REALIST NOVELS, CAPTAIN MIDNIGHT CODE-O-GRAPHS, AND THE FALL ELECTIONS WITH EQUAL VIGOR.
HE'S SO UNASHAMED OF HIS ENTHUSIASMS. EVERYTHING HE'S EVER BEEN PASSIONATE ABOUT IN HIS LIFE HAS BEEN MADE TANGIBLE AND DISPLAYED--
--AS IF THE WAKE OF A SPEEDBOAT COULD BE FROZEN AND SAVED.

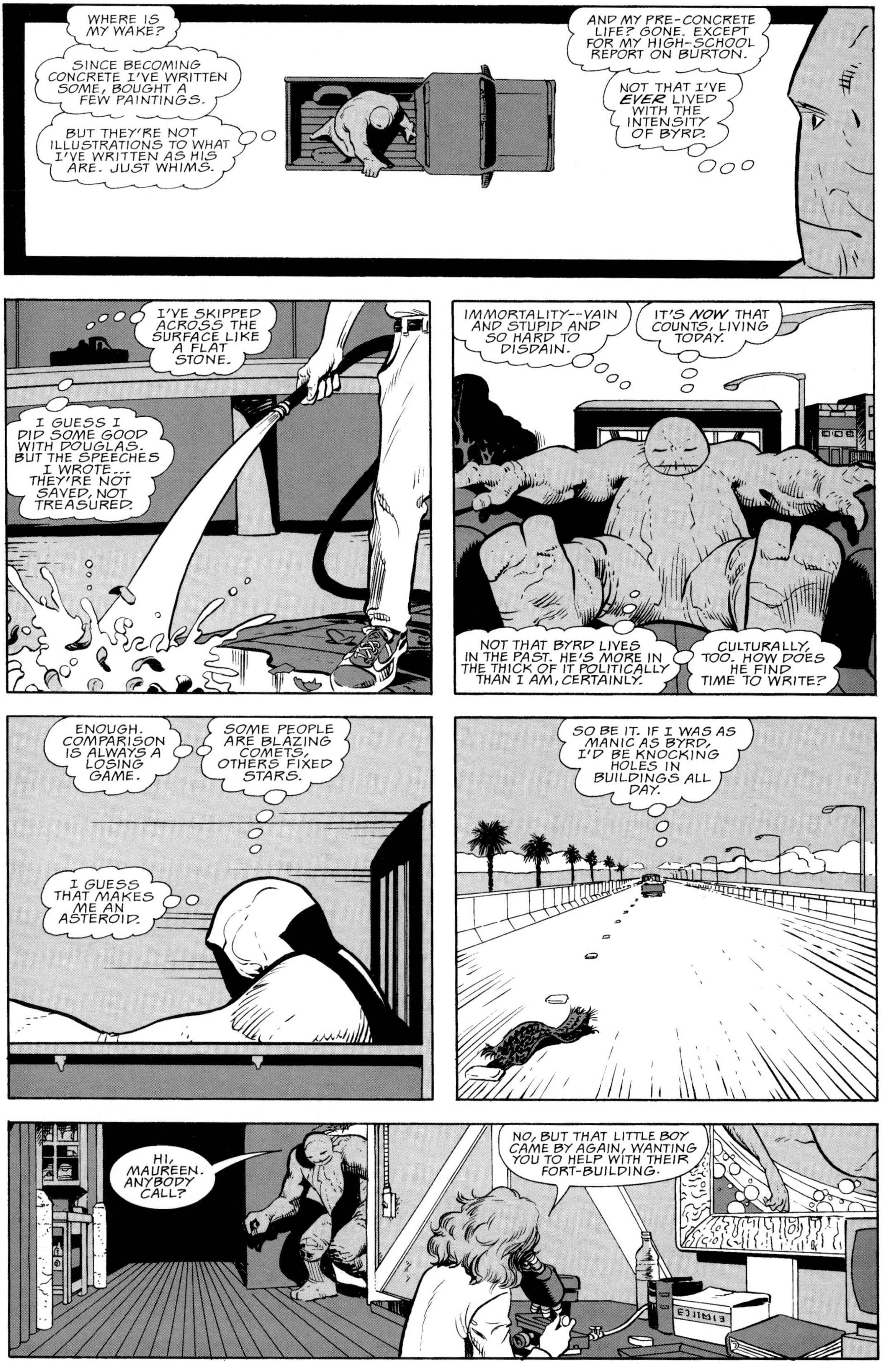
WHERE IS MY WAKE?
SINCE BECOMING CONCRETE I'VE WRITTEN SOME, BOUGHT A FEW PAINTINGS.
BUT THEY'RE NOT ILLUSTRATIONS TO WHAT I'VE WRITTEN AS HIS ARE. JUST WHIMS.
AND MY PRE-CONCRETE LIFE? GONE. EXCEPT FOR MY HIGH-SCHOOL REPORT ON BURTON.
NOT THAT I'VE EVER LIVED WITH THE INTENSITY OF BYRD.
I'VE SKIPPED ACROSS THE SURFACE LIKE A FLAT STONE.
I GUESS I DID SOME GOOD WITH DOUGLAS. BUT THE SPEECHES I WROTE... THEY'RE NOT SAVED, NOT TREASURED.
IMMORTALITY--VAIN AND STUPID AND SO HARD TO DISDAIN.
IT'S NOW THAT COUNTS, LIVING TODAY.
NOT THAT BYRD LIVES IN THE PAST. HE'S MORE IN THE THICK OF IT POLITICALLY THAN I AM, CERTAINLY.
CULTURALLY, TOO. HOW DOES HE FIND TIME TO WRITE?
ENOUGH. COMPARISON IS ALWAYS A LOSING GAME.
SOME PEOPLE ARE BLAZING COMETS, OTHERS FIXED STARS.
I GUESS THAT MAKES ME AN ASTEROID.
SO BE IT. IF I WAS AS MANIC AS BYRD, I'D BE KNOCKING HOLES IN BUILDINGS ALL DAY.
HI, MAUREEN. ANYBODY CALL?
NO, BUT THAT LITTLE BOY CAME BY AGAIN, WANTING YOU TO HELP WITH THEIR FORT-BUILDING.

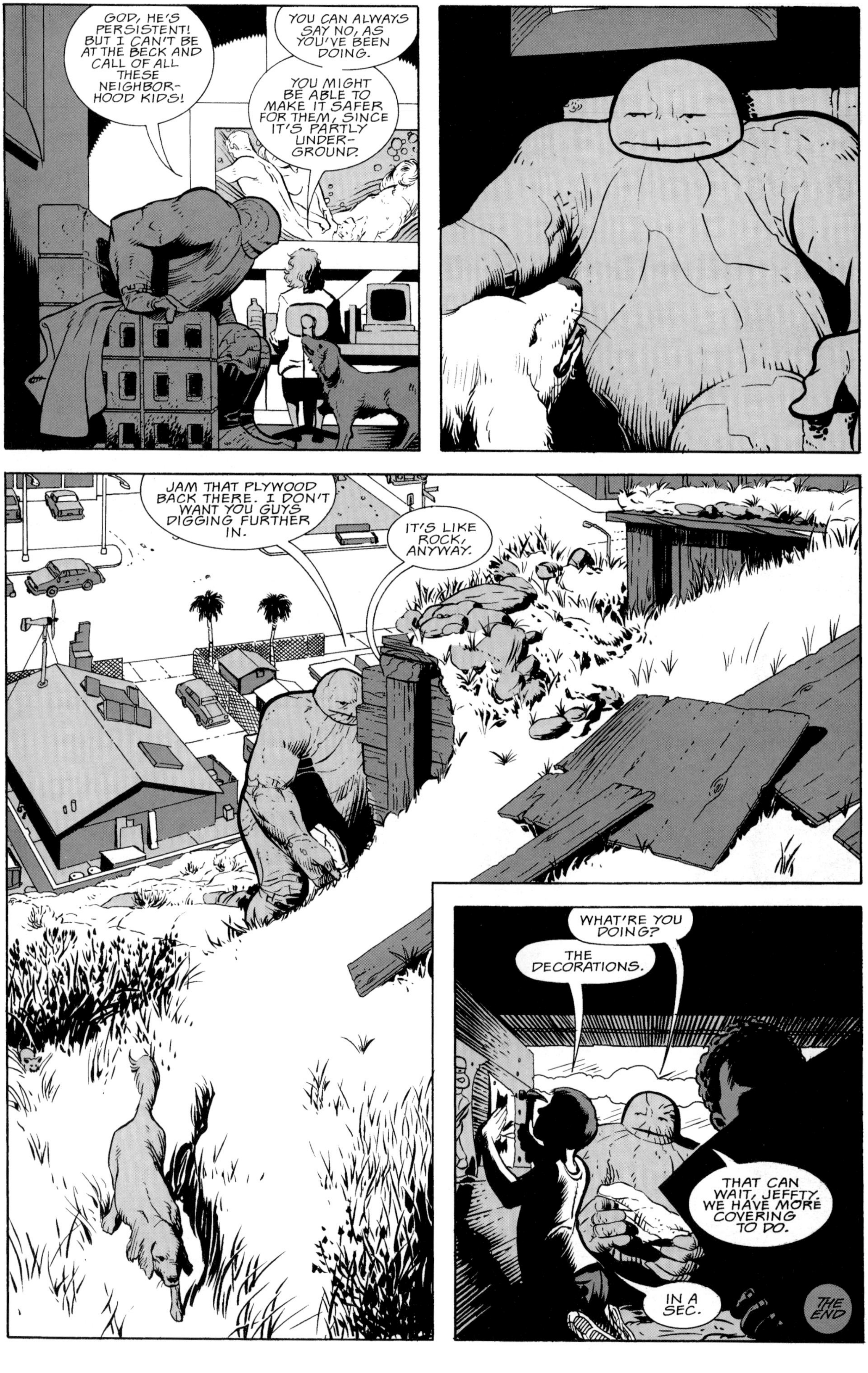
GOD, HE'S PERSISTENT! BUT I CAN'T BE AT THE BECK AND CALL OF ALL THESE NEIGHBOR-HOOD KIDS!
YOU CAN ALWAYS SAY NO, AS YOU'VE BEEN DOING.
YOU MIGHT BE ABLE TO MAKE IT SAFER FOR THEM, SINCE IT'S PARTLY UNDER-GROUND.
JAM THAT PLYWOOD BACK THERE. I DON'T WANT YOU GUYS DIGGING FURTHER IN.
IT'S LIKE ROCK, ANYWAY.
WHAT'RE YOU DOING?
THE DECORATIONS.
THAT CAN WAIT, JEFFTY. WE HAVE MORE COVERING TO DO.
IN A SEC.
THE END

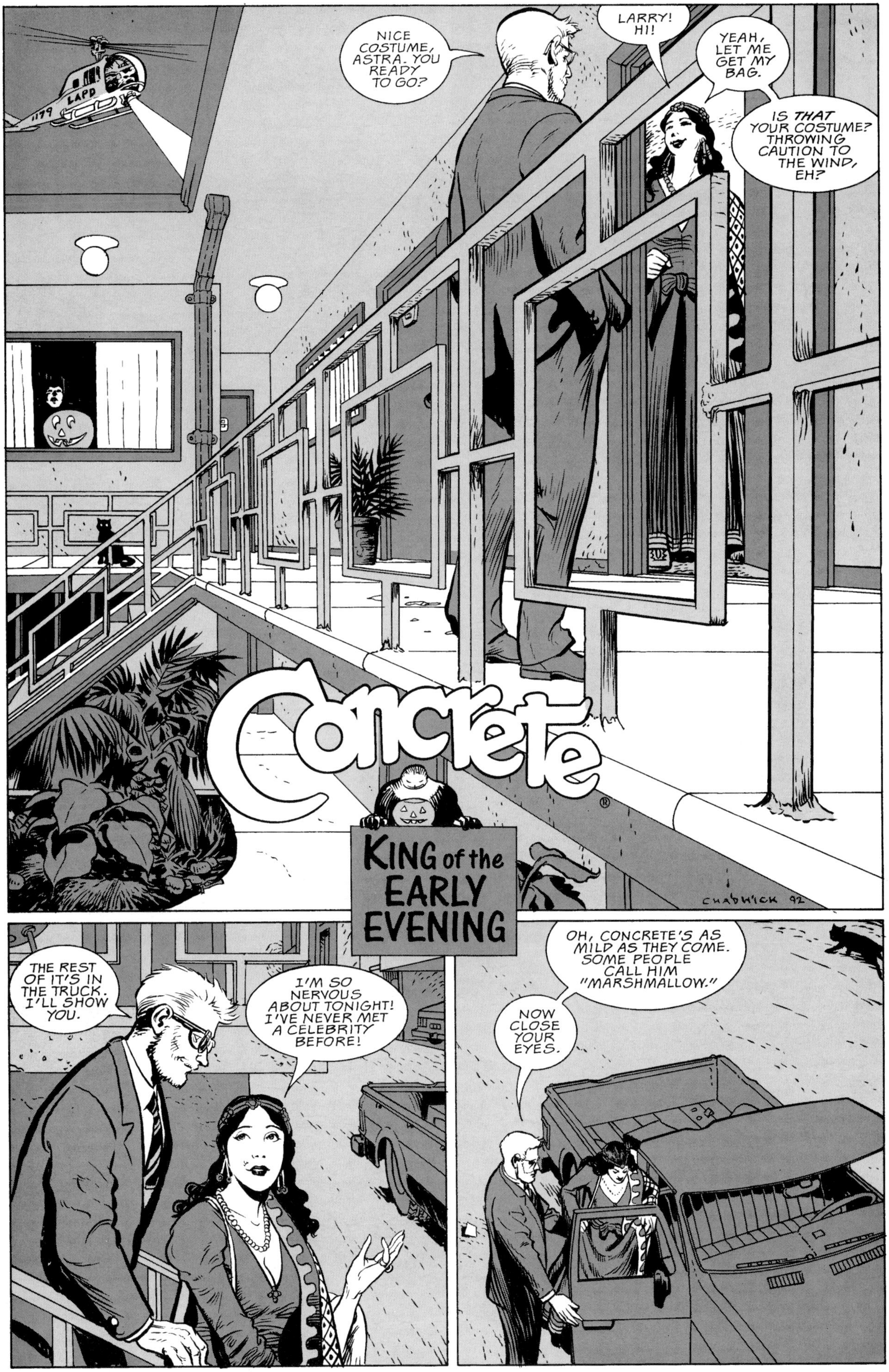
1179 LAPD
NICE COSTUME, ASTRA. YOU READY TO GO?
LARRY! HI!
YEAH, LET ME GET MY BAG.
IS THAT YOUR COSTUME? THROWING CAUTION TO THE WIND, EH?
Concrete®
KING of the EARLY EVENING
CHADWICK 92
THE REST OF IT'S IN THE TRUCK. I'LL SHOW YOU.
I'M SO NERVOUS ABOUT TONIGHT! I'VE NEVER MET A CELEBRITY BEFORE!
OH, CONCRETE'S AS MILD AS THEY COME. SOME PEOPLE CALL HIM "MARSHMALLOW."
NOW CLOSE YOUR EYES.

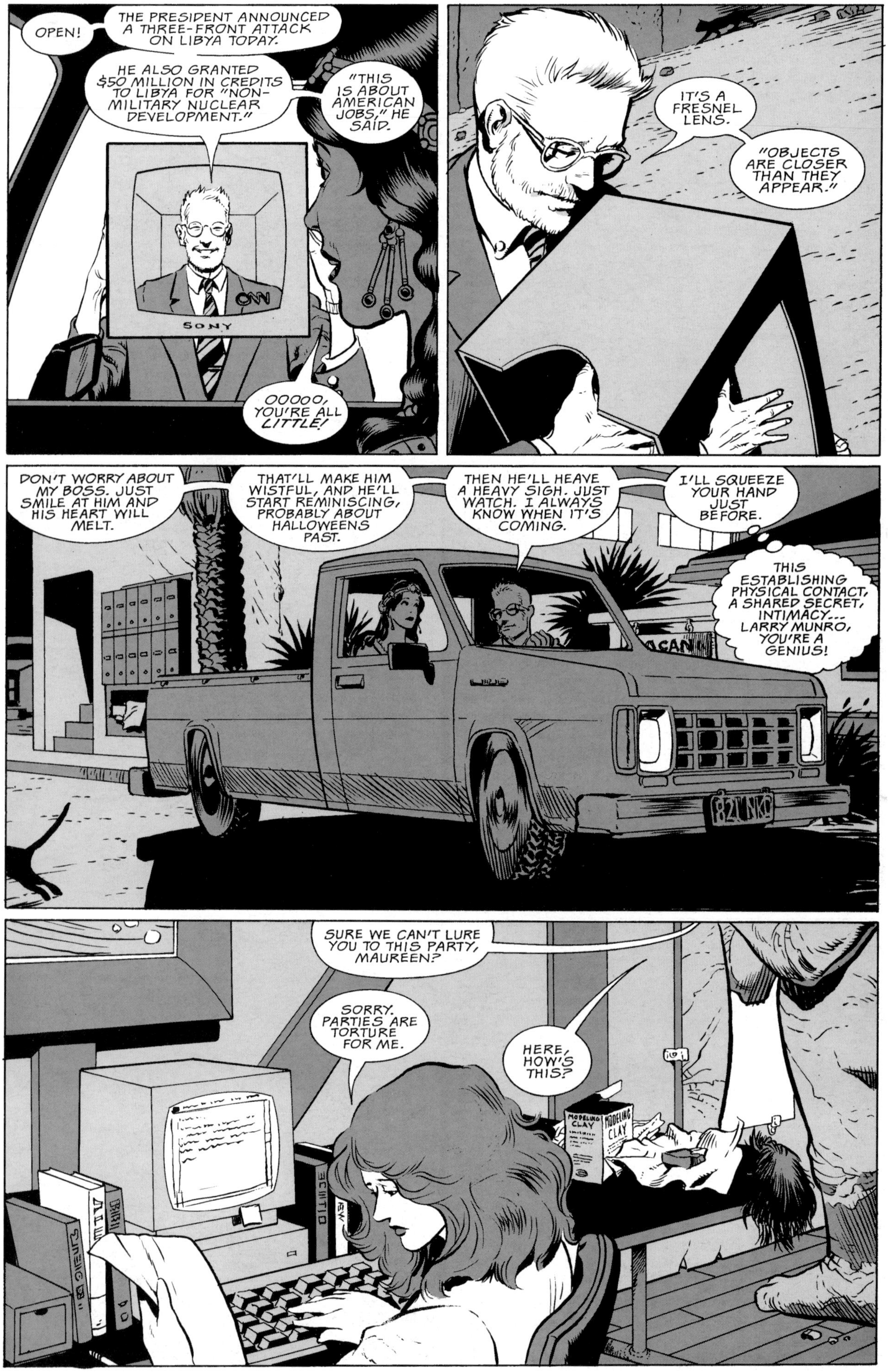
OPEN!
THE PRESIDENT ANNOUNCED A THREE-FRONT ATTACK ON LIBYA TODAY.
HE ALSO GRANTED $50 MILLION IN CREDITS TO LIBYA FOR "NON-MILITARY NUCLEAR DEVELOPMENT."
"THIS IS ABOUT AMERICAN JOBS," HE SAID.
CNN
SONY
OOOOO, YOU'RE ALL LITTLE!
IT'S A FRESNEL LENS.
"OBJECTS ARE CLOSER THAN THEY APPEAR."
DON'T WORRY ABOUT MY BOSS. JUST SMILE AT HIM AND HIS HEART WILL MELT.
THAT'LL MAKE HIM WISTFUL, AND HE'LL START REMINISCING, PROBABLY ABOUT HALLOWEENS PAST.
THEN HE'LL HEAVE A HEAVY SIGH. JUST WATCH. I ALWAYS KNOW WHEN IT'S COMING.
I'LL SQUEEZE YOUR HAND JUST BEFORE.
THIS ESTABLISHING PHYSICAL CONTACT, A SHARED SECRET, INTIMACY... LARRY MUNRO, YOU'RE A GENIUS!
SURE WE CAN'T LURE YOU TO THIS PARTY, MAUREEN?
SORRY. PARTIES ARE TORTURE FOR ME.
HERE, HOW'S THIS?
MODELING CLAY
MODELING CLAY

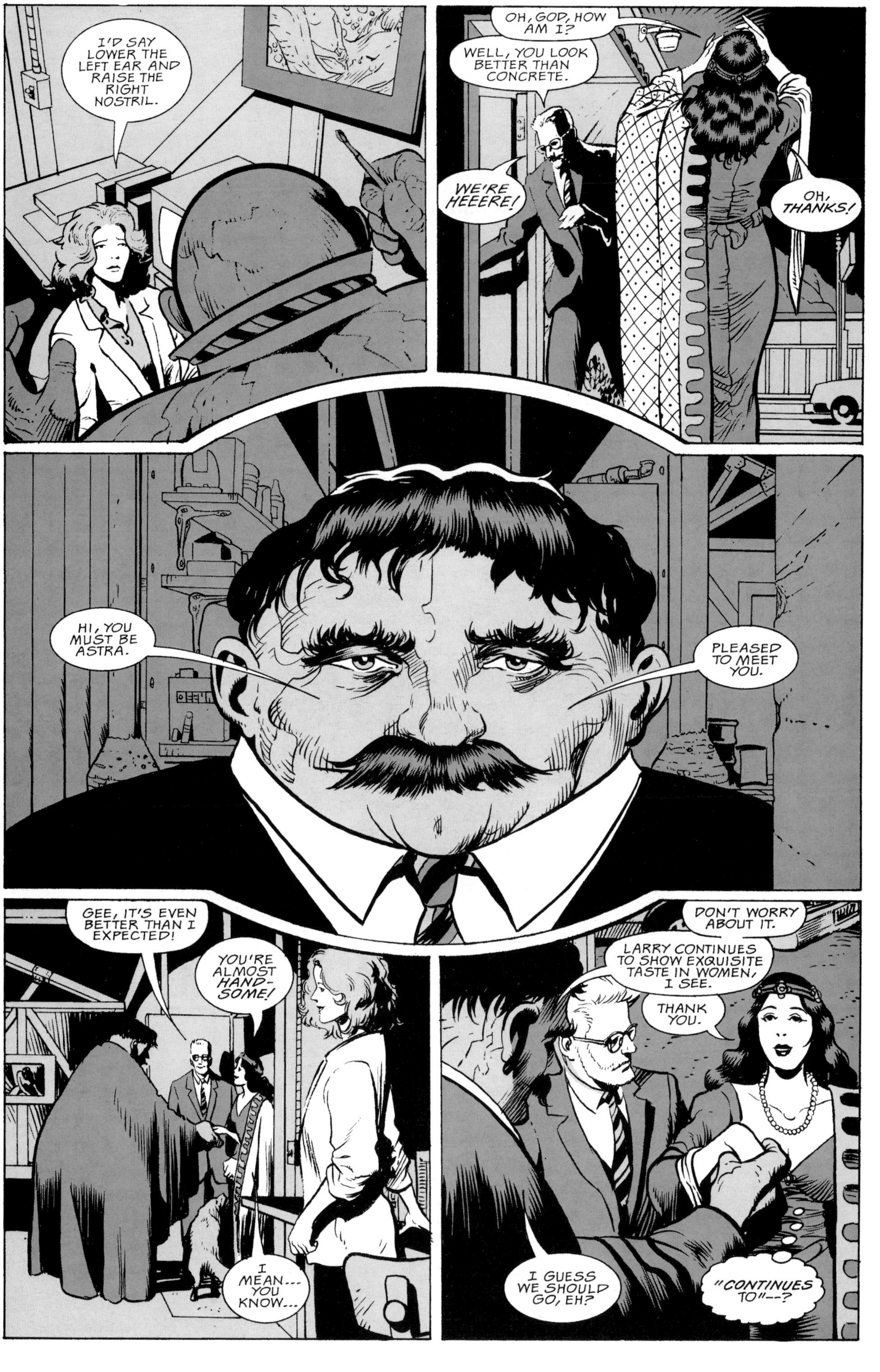
I'D SAY LOWER THE LEFT EAR AND RAISE THE RIGHT NOSTRIL.
OH, GOD, HOW AM I?
WELL, YOU LOOK BETTER THAN CONCRETE.
WE'RE HEEERE!
OH, THANKS!
HI, YOU MUST BE ASTRA.
PLEASED TO MEET YOU.
GEE, IT'S EVEN BETTER THAN I EXPECTED!
YOU'RE ALMOST HAND-SOME!
I MEAN--- YOU KNOW...
DON'T WORRY ABOUT IT.
LARRY CONTINUES TO SHOW EXQUISITE TASTE IN WOMEN, I SEE.
THANK YOU.
I GUESS WE SHOULD GO, EH?
"CONTINUES TO"--?

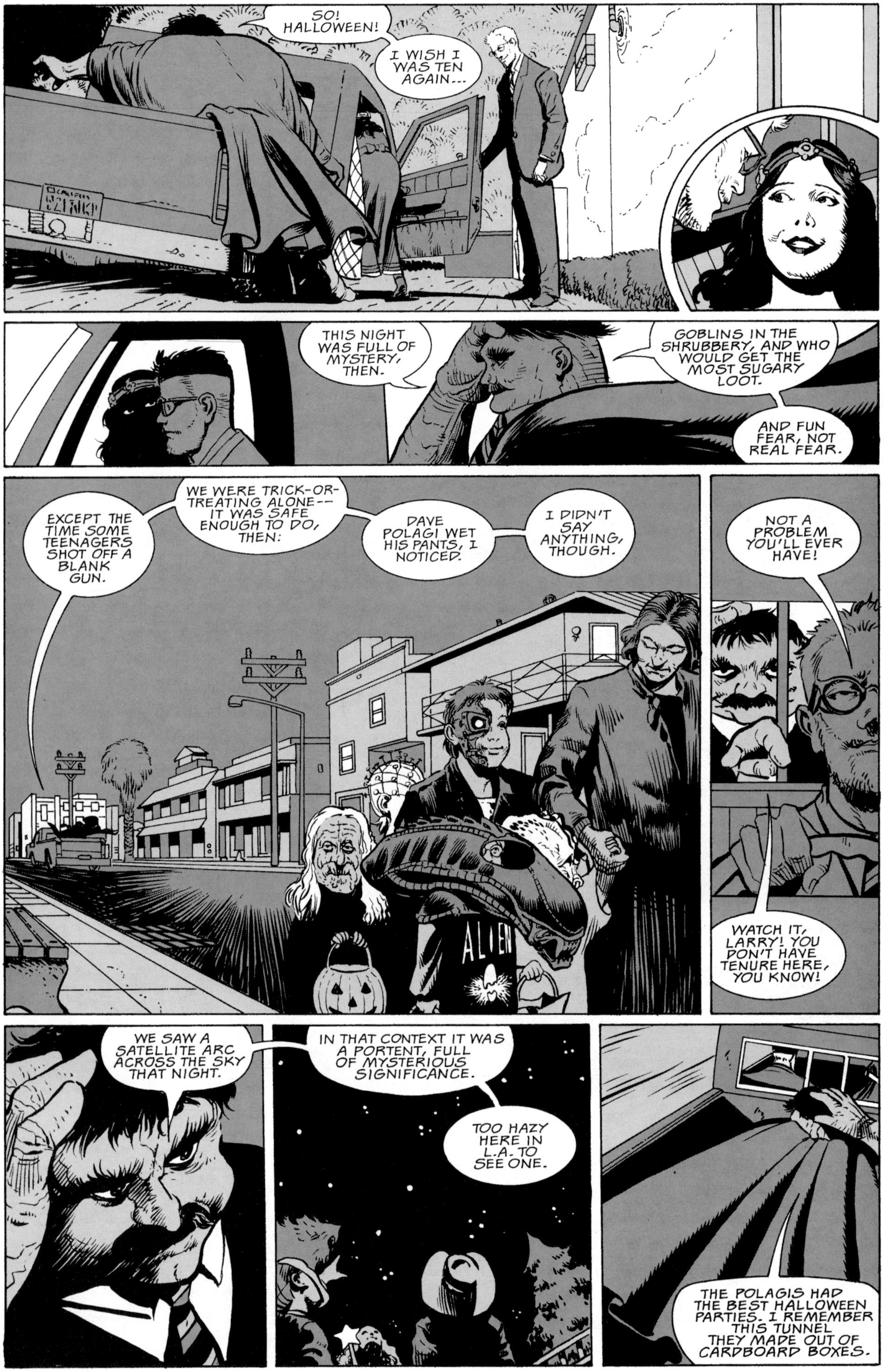
SO! HALLOWEEN!
I WISH I WAS TEN AGAIN...
THIS NIGHT WAS FULL OF MYSTERY, THEN.
GOBLINS IN THE SHRUBBERY, AND WHO WOULD GET THE MOST SUGARY LOOT.
AND FUN FEAR, NOT REAL FEAR.
EXCEPT THE TIME SOME TEENAGERS SHOT OFF A BLANK GUN.
WE WERE TRICK-OR-TREATING ALONE-- IT WAS SAFE ENOUGH TO DO, THEN.
DAVE POLAGI WET HIS PANTS, I NOTICED.
I DIDN'T SAY ANYTHING, THOUGH.
NOT A PROBLEM YOU'LL EVER HAVE!
WATCH IT, LARRY! YOU DON'T HAVE TENURE HERE, YOU KNOW!
ALIEN
WE SAW A SATELLITE ARC ACROSS THE SKY THAT NIGHT.
IN THAT CONTEXT IT WAS A PORTENT, FULL OF MYSTERIOUS SIGNIFICANCE.
TOO HAZY HERE IN L.A. TO SEE ONE.
THE POLAGIS HAD THE BEST HALLOWEEN PARTIES. I REMEMBER THIS TUNNEL THEY MADE OUT OF CARDBOARD BOXES.

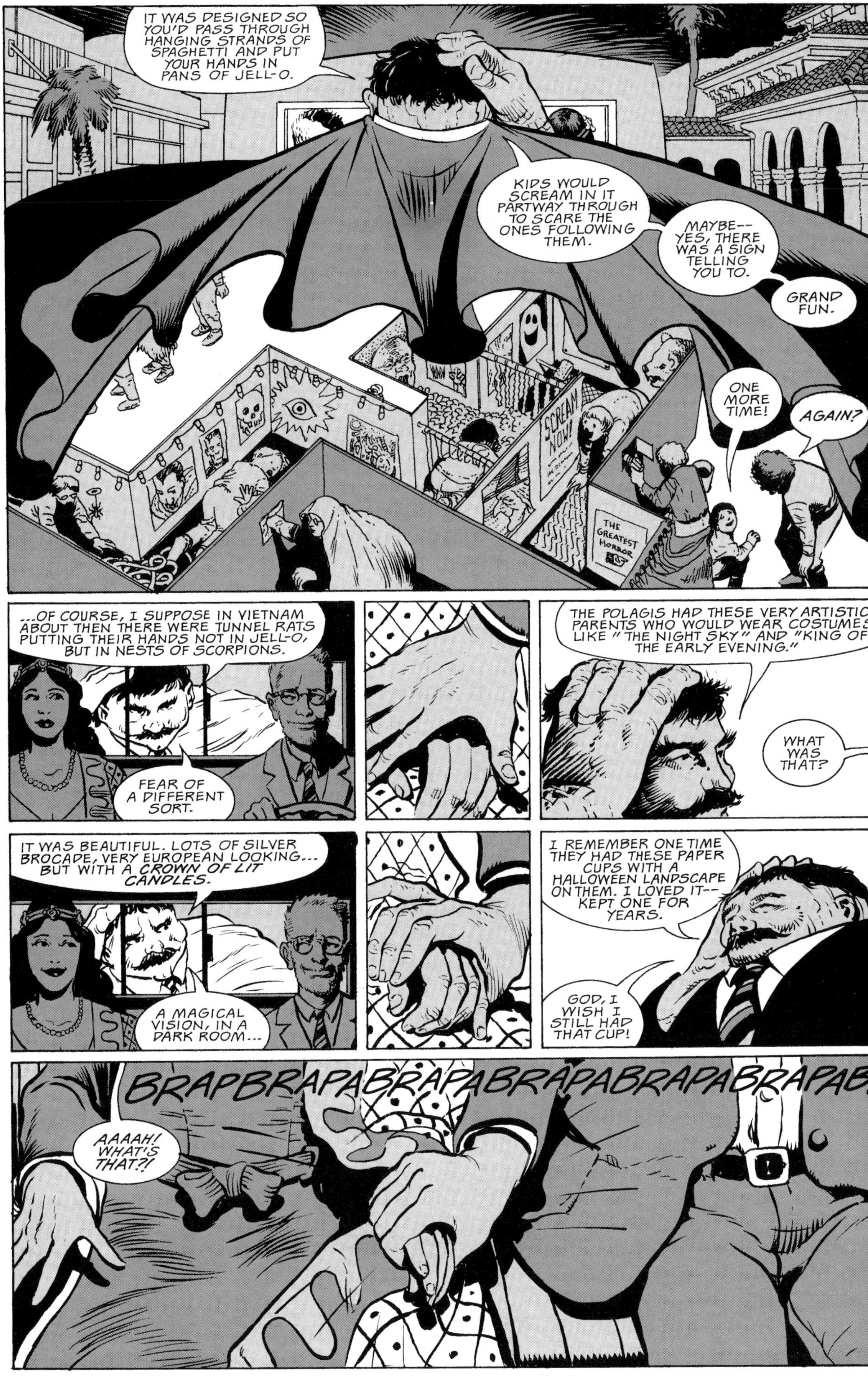

IT WAS DESIGNED SO YOU'D PASS THROUGH HANGING STRANDS OF SPAGHETTI AND PUT YOUR HANDS IN PANS OF JELL-O.
KIDS WOULD SCREAM IN IT PARTWAY THROUGH TO SCARE THE ONES FOLLOWING THEM.
MAYBE-- YES, THERE WAS A SIGN TELLING YOU TO.
GRAND FUN.
SCREAM NOW!
THE GREATEST HORROR
ONE MORE TIME!
AGAIN?
...OF COURSE, I SUPPOSE IN VIETNAM ABOUT THEN THERE WERE TUNNEL RATS PUTTING THEIR HANDS NOT IN JELL-O, BUT IN NESTS OF SCORPIONS.
FEAR OF A DIFFERENT SORT.
THE POLAGIS HAD THESE VERY ARTISTIC PARENTS WHO WOULD WEAR COSTUMES LIKE "THE NIGHT SKY" AND "KING OF THE EARLY EVENING."
WHAT WAS THAT?
IT WAS BEAUTIFUL. LOTS OF SILVER BROCADE, VERY EUROPEAN LOOKING... BUT WITH A CROWN OF LIT CANDLES.
A MAGICAL VISION, IN A DARK ROOM...
I REMEMBER ONE TIME THEY HAD THESE PAPER CUPS WITH A HALLOWEEN LANDSCAPE ON THEM. I LOVED IT-- KEPT ONE FOR YEARS.
GOD, I WISH I STILL HAD THAT CUP!
BRAPBRAPABRAPABRAPABRAPABRAPABRAPABR
AAAAH! WHAT'S THAT?!

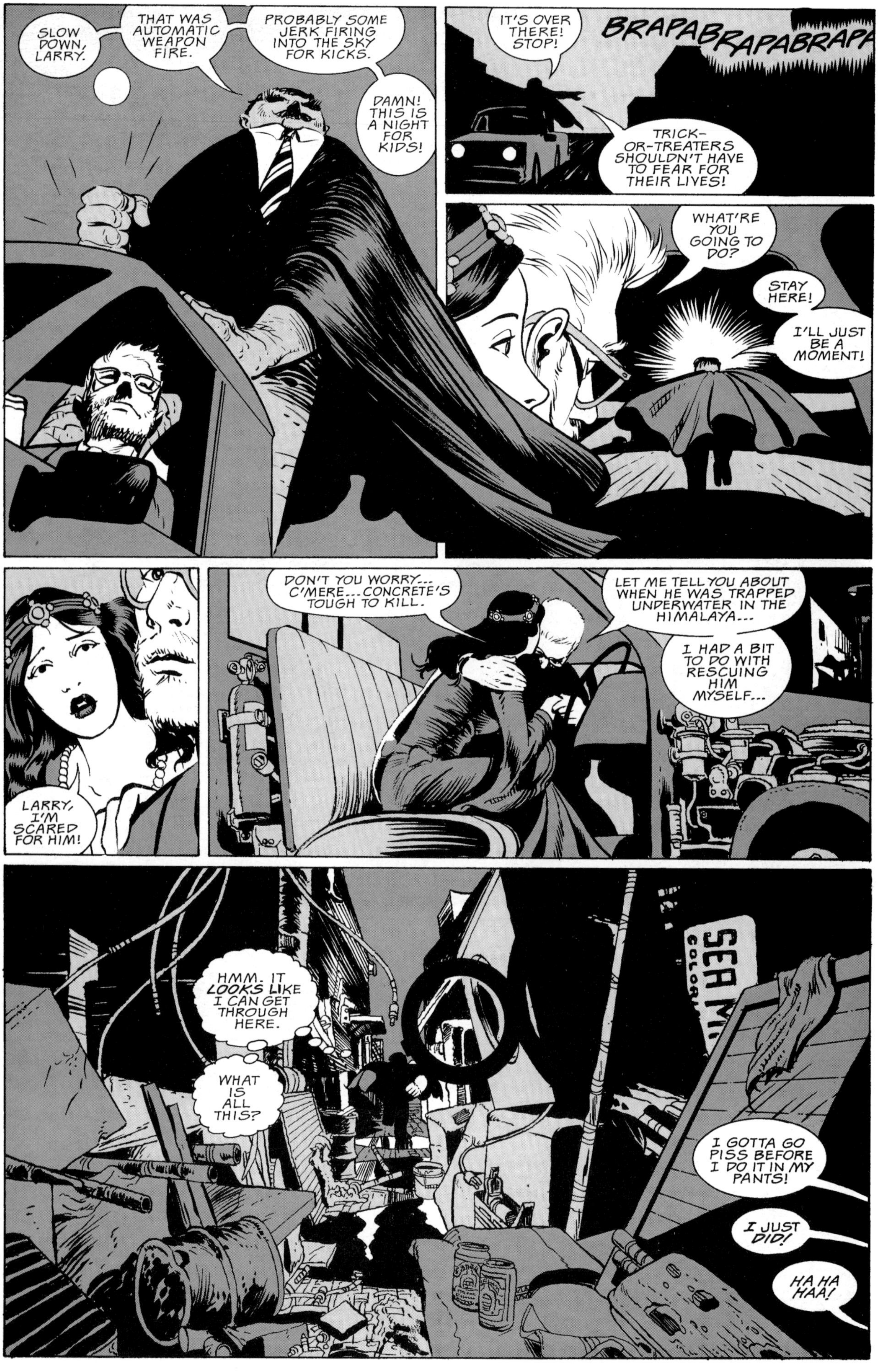

SLOW DOWN, LARRY.
THAT WAS AUTOMATIC WEAPON FIRE.
PROBABLY SOME JERK FIRING INTO THE SKY FOR KICKS.
DAMN! THIS IS A NIGHT FOR KIDS!
IT'S OVER THERE! STOP!
BRAPABRAPABRAPABRAPA
TRICK-OR-TREATERS SHOULDN'T HAVE TO FEAR FOR THEIR LIVES!
WHAT'RE YOU GOING TO DO?
STAY HERE!
I'LL JUST BE A MOMENT!
LARRY, I'M SCARED FOR HIM!
DON'T YOU WORRY... C'MERE... CONCRETE'S TOUGH TO KILL.
LET ME TELL YOU ABOUT WHEN HE WAS TRAPPED UNDERWATER IN THE HIMALAYA...
I HAD A BIT TO DO WITH RESCUING HIM MYSELF...
HMM. IT LOOKS LIKE I CAN GET THROUGH HERE.
WHAT IS ALL THIS?
I GOTTA GO PISS BEFORE I DO IT IN MY PANTS!
I JUST DID!
HA HA HAA!

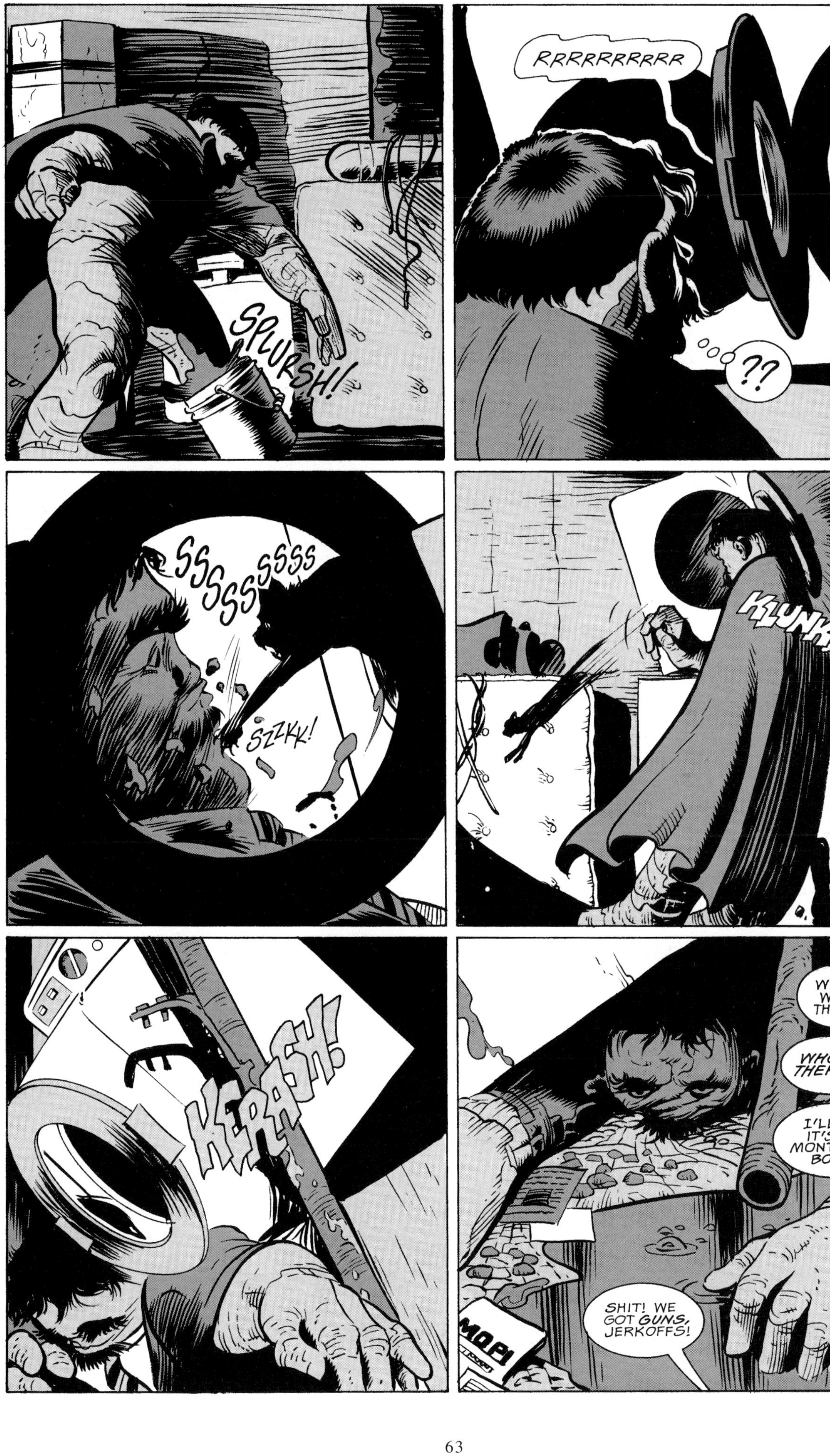
SPLURSH!
RRRRRRRRRR
??
SSSSSSSSSS
SZZKK!
KLUNK!
KERASH!
WHAT WAS THAT?
WHO'S THERE?!
I'LL BET IT'S THE MONTERREY BOYS!
SHIT! WE GOT GUNS, JERKOFFS!

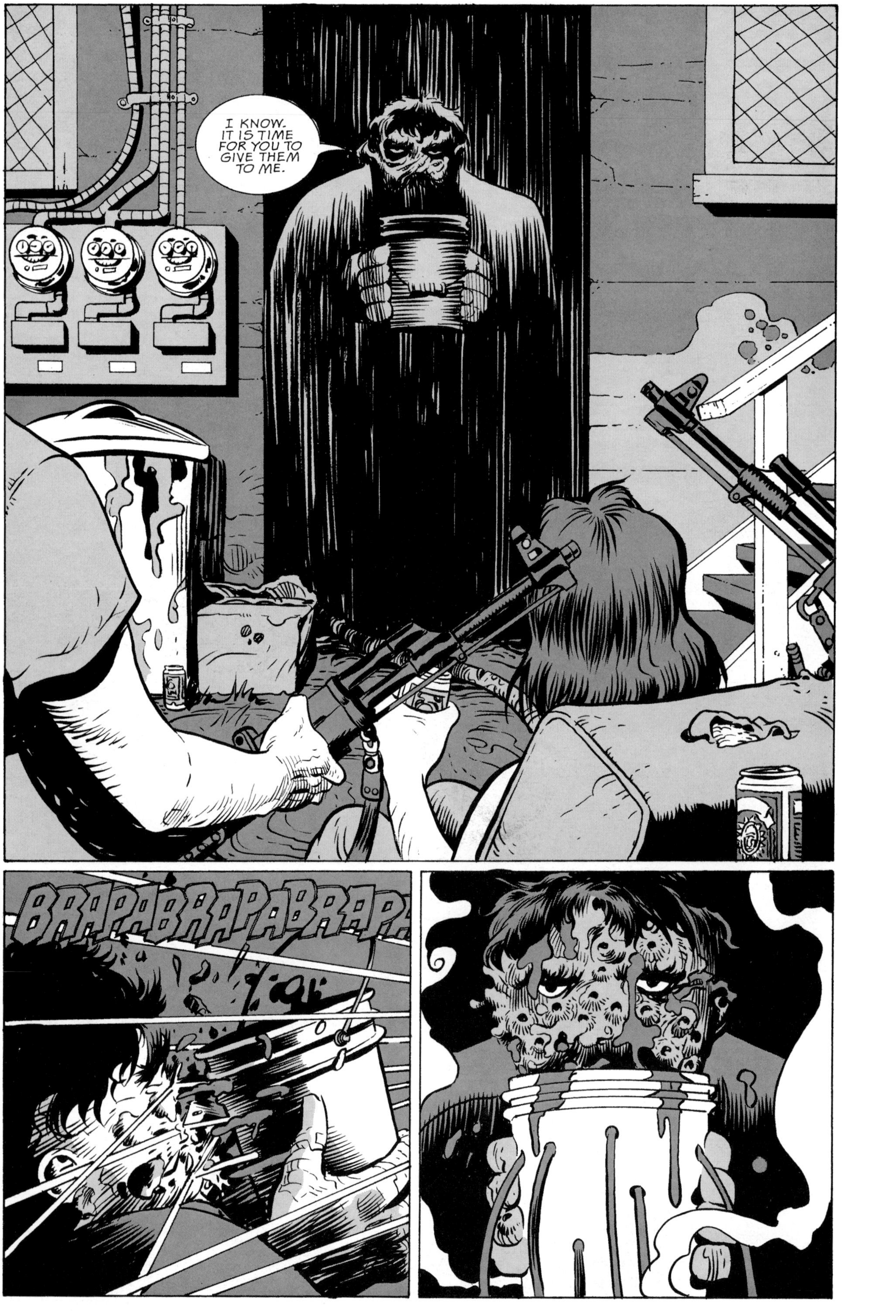
I KNOW. IT IS TIME FOR YOU TO GIVE THEM TO ME.
BRAPABRAPABRAPA

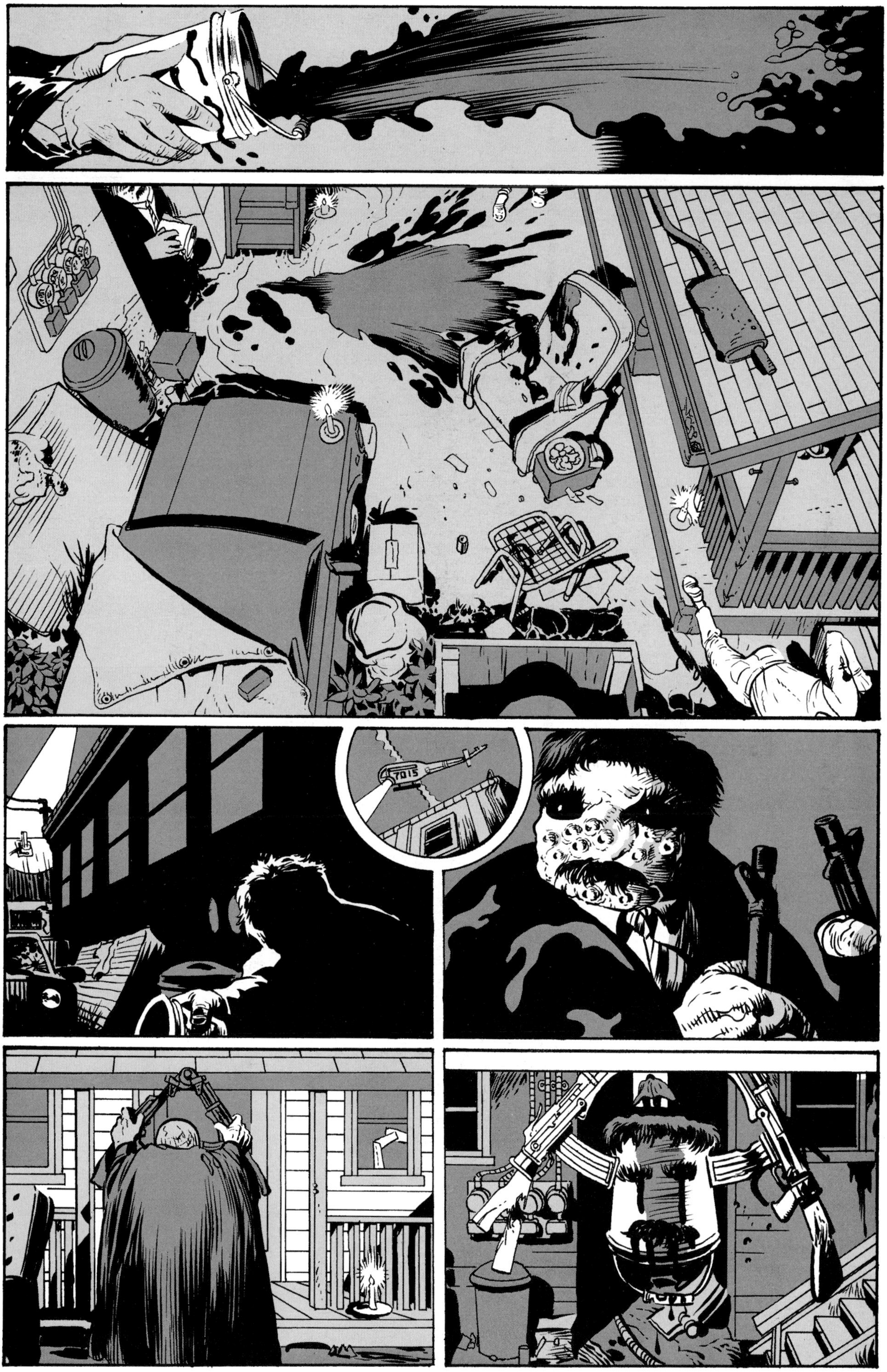
7D15

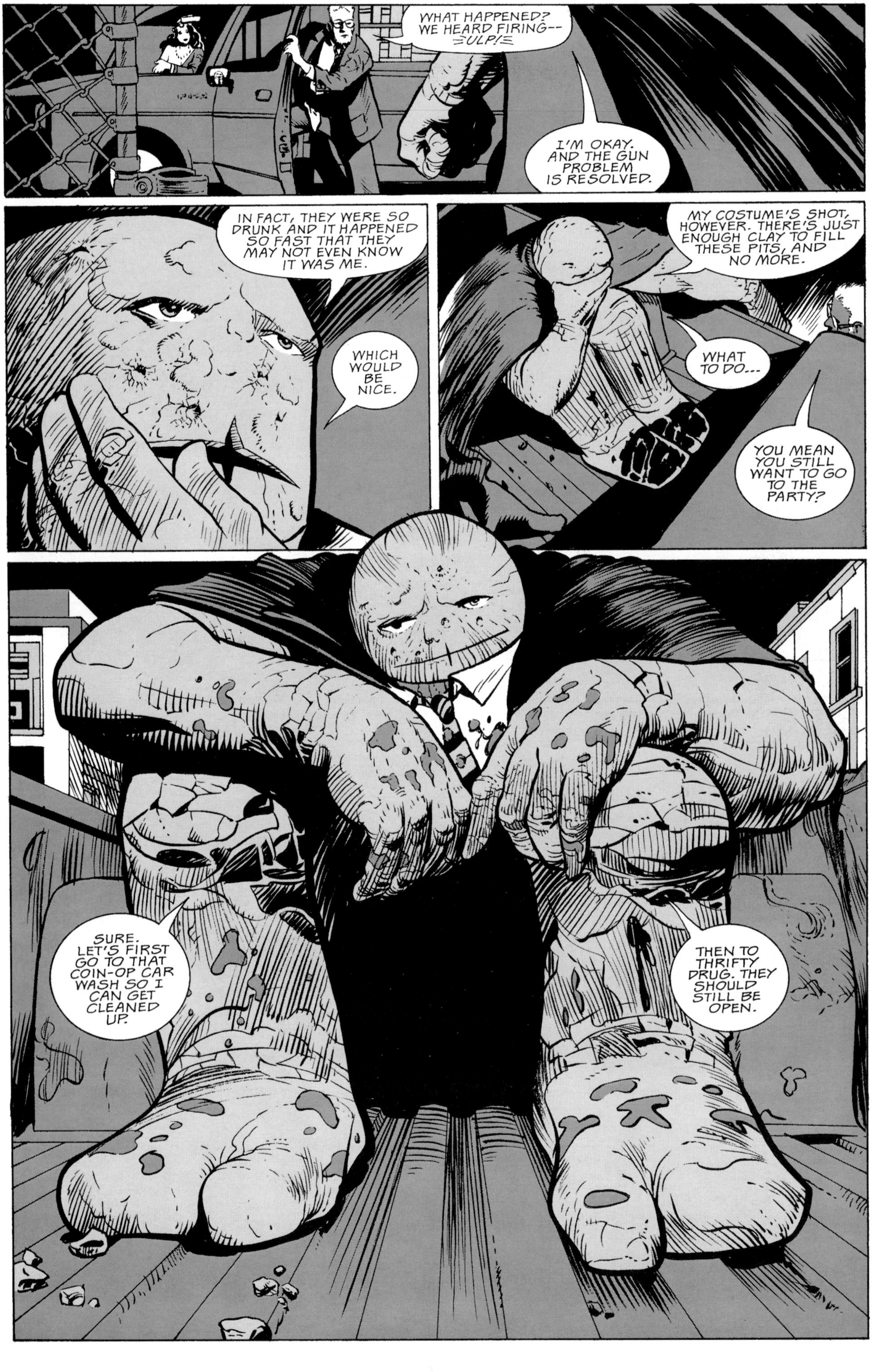
WHAT HAPPENED? WE HEARD FIRING-- GULP!
I'M OKAY. AND THE GUN PROBLEM IS RESOLVED.
IN FACT, THEY WERE SO DRUNK AND IT HAPPENED SO FAST THAT THEY MAY NOT EVEN KNOW IT WAS ME.
WHICH WOULD BE NICE.
MY COSTUME'S SHOT, HOWEVER. THERE'S JUST ENOUGH CLAY TO FILL THESE PITS, AND NO MORE.
WHAT TO DO...
YOU MEAN YOU STILL WANT TO GO TO THE PARTY?
SURE. LET'S FIRST GO TO THAT COIN-OP CAR WASH SO I CAN GET CLEANED UP.
THEN TO THRIFTY DRUG. THEY SHOULD STILL BE OPEN.

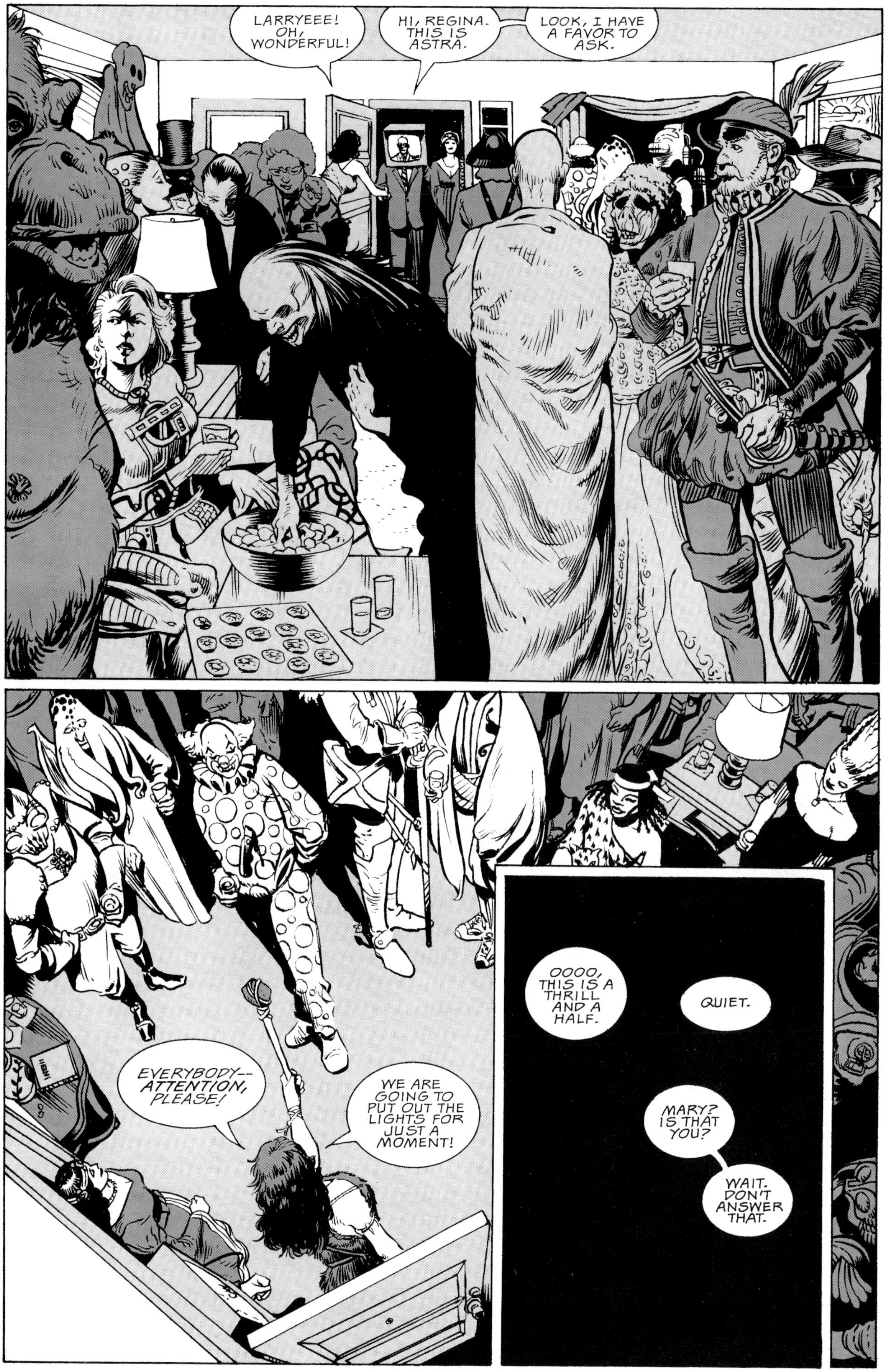

LARRYEEE! OH, WONDERFUL!
HI, REGINA. THIS IS ASTRA.
LOOK, I HAVE A FAVOR TO ASK.
EVERYBODY-- ATTENTION, PLEASE!
WE ARE GOING TO PUT OUT THE LIGHTS FOR JUST A MOMENT!
OOOO, THIS IS A THRILL AND A HALF.
QUIET.
MARY? IS THAT YOU?
WAIT. DON'T ANSWER THAT.

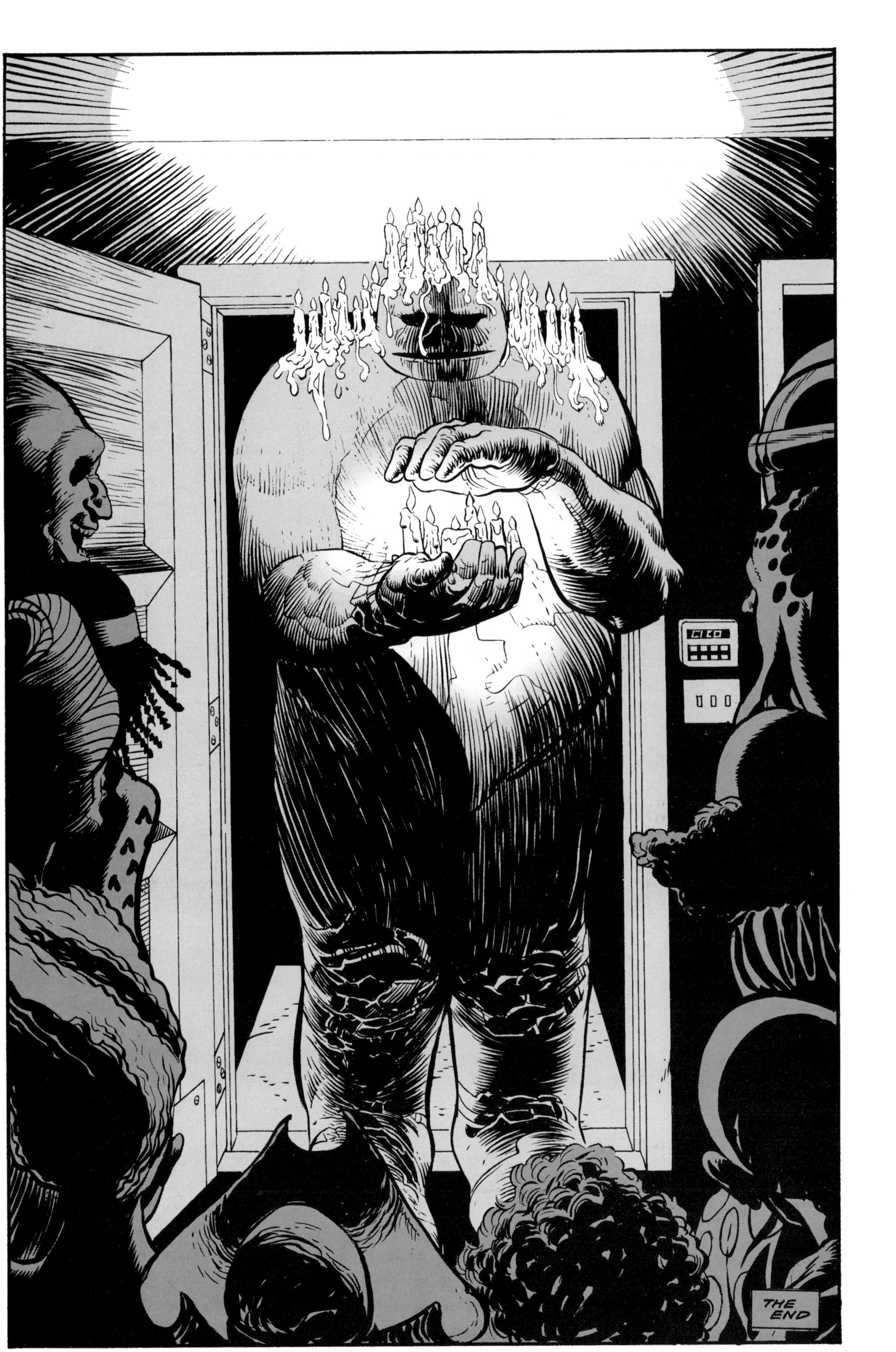
THE END

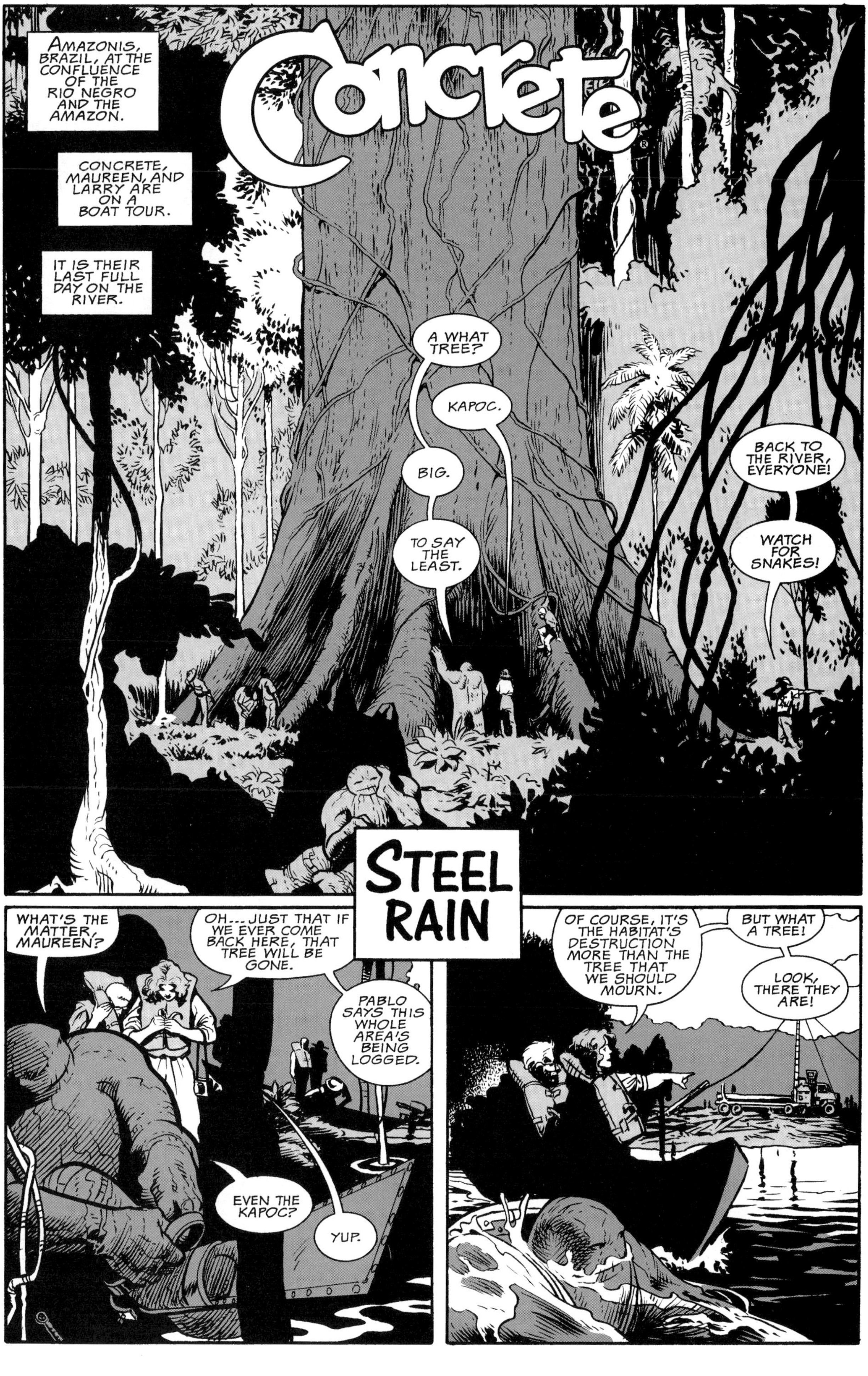

AMAZONIS, BRAZIL, AT THE CONFLUENCE OF THE RIO NEGRO AND THE AMAZON.
Concrete
CONCRETE, MAUREEN, AND LARRY ARE ON A BOAT TOUR.
IT IS THEIR LAST FULL DAY ON THE RIVER.
A WHAT TREE?
KAPOC.
BIG.
TO SAY THE LEAST.
BACK TO THE RIVER, EVERYONE!
WATCH FOR SNAKES!
STEEL RAIN
WHAT'S THE MATTER, MAUREEN?
OH... JUST THAT IF WE EVER COME BACK HERE, THAT TREE WILL BE GONE.
PABLO SAYS THIS WHOLE AREA'S BEING LOGGED.
EVEN THE KAPOC?
YUP.
OF COURSE, IT'S THE HABITAT'S DESTRUCTION MORE THAN THE TREE THAT WE SHOULD MOURN.
BUT WHAT A TREE!
LOOK, THERE THEY ARE!

HOW FAR?

HOW FAR DO YOU HAVE TO GO ON THIS PLANET TO FIND A PLACE THAT ISN'T BEING LEVELED FOR MARGINAL PROFIT?

UH, CONCRETE-- NOT SO NEAR THE RAILING, OKAY? BOAT'S TIPPING.

OKAY, PABLO.

LOOK OUT, PIRANHA!

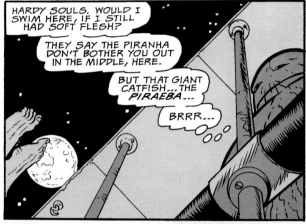

HARDY SOULS. WOULD I SWIM HERE, IF I STILL HAD SOFT FLESH?

THEY SAY THE PIRANHA DON'T BOTHER YOU OUT IN THE MIDDLE, HERE.

BUT THAT GIANT CATFISH...THE PIRAEBA...

BRRR...

WERE THEY KIDDING WHEN THEY SAID A DEAD PIRAEBA HAD WASHED UP WITH A HUMAN LIMB IN ITS MOUTH?

IT DRAGS YOU DOWN UNTIL YOU DROWN, AND EATS YOU AT ITS LEISURE, SUPPOSEDLY.

I SHOULD HAVE MY FINS ON IN CASE...

NO... THEY'RE GETTING OUT.

OF COURSE, IF A PIRAEBA DID GRAB SOMEONE, IT'D BE WITHIN ITS RIGHTS... WE'RE THE INVADERS.

FISH RIGHTS. I HAVE BEEN TALKING A LOT WITH THE BIOCENTRISM CROWD, HAVEN'T I?

THEY'D BE CHAINED TO THAT KAPOC TREE RIGHT NOW IF THEY WERE HERE.

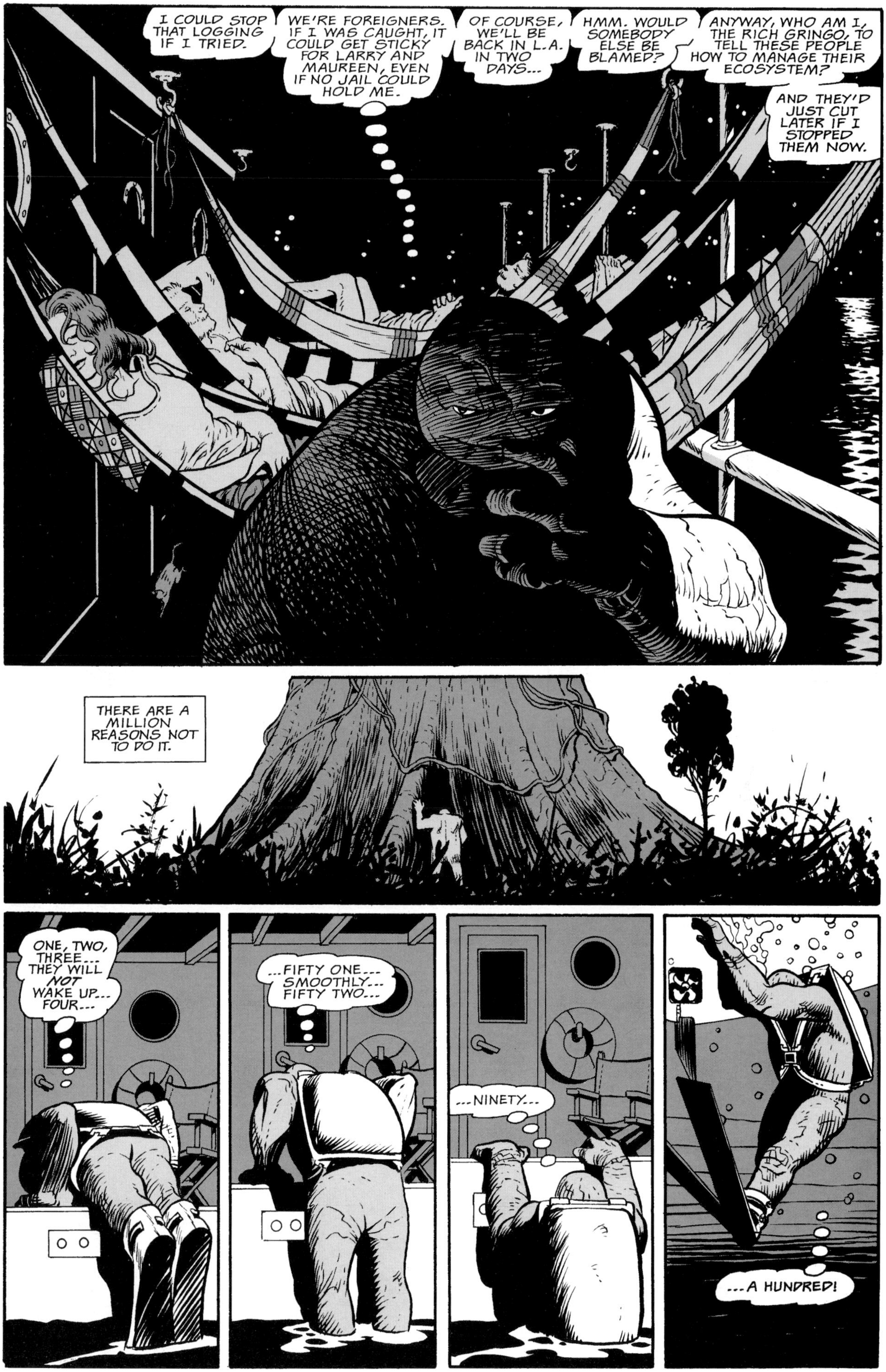

I COULD STOP THAT LOGGING IF I TRIED.
WE'RE FOREIGNERS. IF I WAS CAUGHT, IT COULD GET STICKY FOR LARRY AND MAUREEN, EVEN IF NO JAIL COULD HOLD ME.
OF COURSE, WE'LL BE BACK IN L.A. IN TWO DAYS...
HMM. WOULD SOMEBODY ELSE BE BLAMED?
ANYWAY, WHO AM I, THE RICH GRINGO, TO TELL THESE PEOPLE HOW TO MANAGE THEIR ECOSYSTEM?
AND THEY'D JUST CUT LATER IF I STOPPED THEM NOW.
THERE ARE A MILLION REASONS NOT TO DO IT.
ONE, TWO, THREE... THEY WILL NOT WAKE UP... FOUR...
...FIFTY ONE... SMOOTHLY... FIFTY TWO...
...NINETY...
...A HUNDRED!

BREAKFAST IS SERVED!

YOU'RE OUT HERE! I WONDERED WHERE YOU WERE WALKING ABOUT LAST NIGHT!

AND I THOUGHT I WAS BEING SNEAKY! COULD YOU SENSE MY LEAVING THE BOAT?

NO... WHERE'D YOU GO?

THE LOGGING TRUCK?!

QUIET.

TOOK A WHILE. THING HAD TEN WHEELS.

NINE ARE FLOATING DOWNRIVER NOW... TO BE SNAGGED BY CABOCLOS, NO DOUBT, WHO WILL SURELY FIND SOME USE FOR THEM.

AND THE TENTH?

IT'S... SENDING A MESSAGE ABOUT A TREE.

YOU SAVED THE KAPOC!

POSSIBLY.

NOT WITHOUT MISGIVINGS, PRACTICAL AND ETHICAL.

WELL, THAT'S YOU, ISN'T IT?

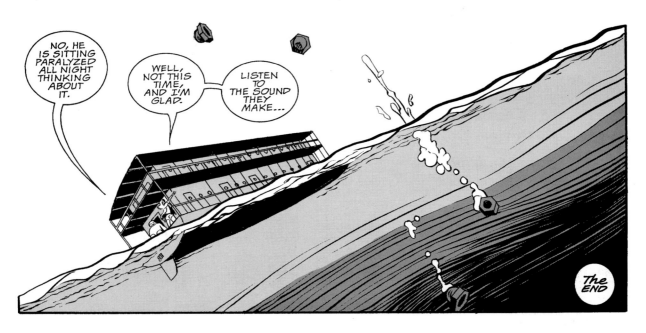

NO, HE IS SITTING PARALYZED ALL NIGHT THINKING ABOUT IT.

WELL, NOT THIS TIME, AND I'M GLAD.

LISTEN TO THE SOUND THEY MAKE...

The END

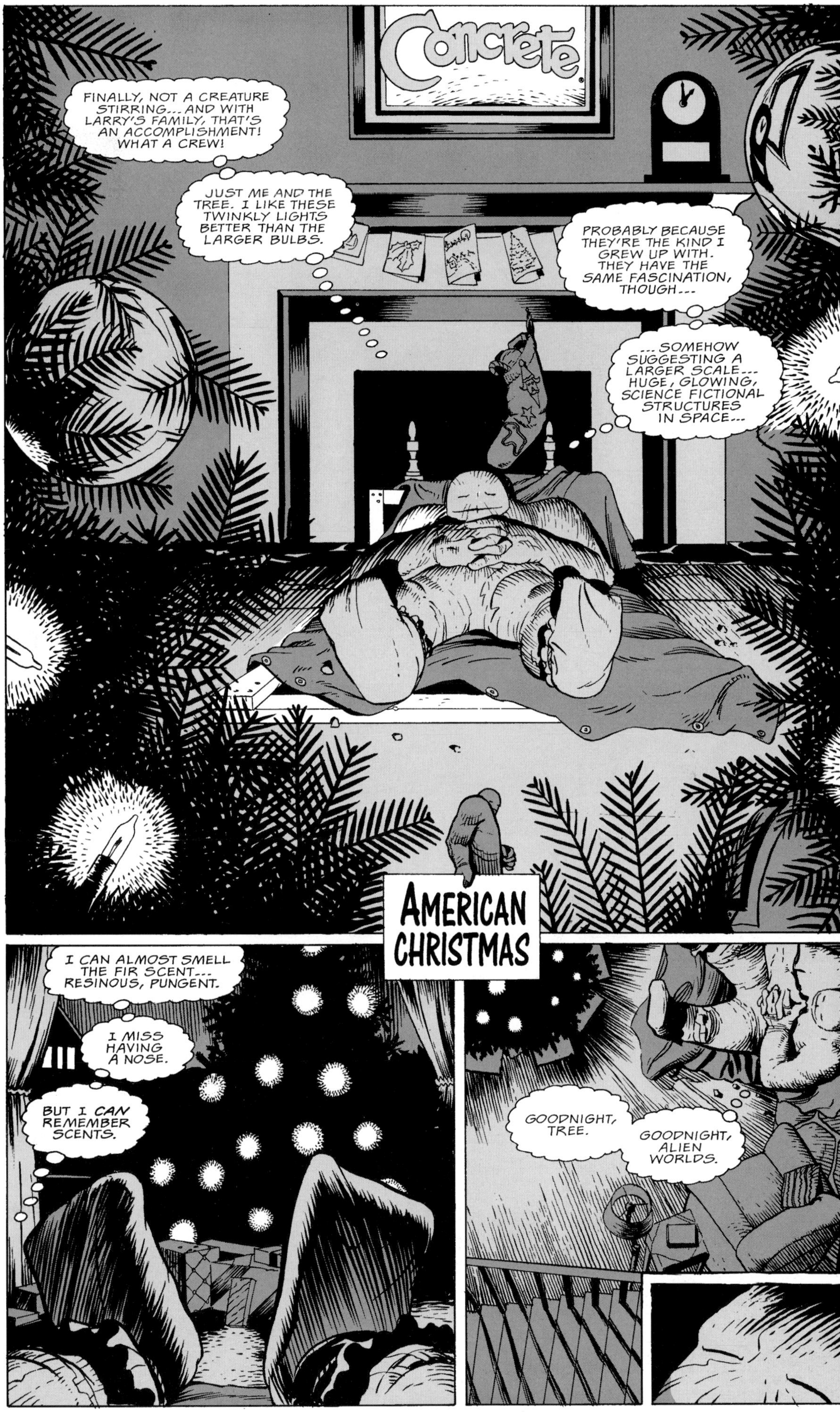
Concrete
FINALLY, NOT A CREATURE STIRRING... AND WITH LARRY'S FAMILY, THAT'S AN ACCOMPLISHMENT! WHAT A CREW!
JUST ME AND THE TREE. I LIKE THESE TWINKLY LIGHTS BETTER THAN THE LARGER BULBS.
PROBABLY BECAUSE THEY'RE THE KIND I GREW UP WITH. THEY HAVE THE SAME FASCINATION, THOUGH---
---SOMEHOW SUGGESTING A LARGER SCALE--- HUGE, GLOWING, SCIENCE FICTIONAL STRUCTURES IN SPACE---
AMERICAN CHRISTMAS
I CAN ALMOST SMELL THE FIR SCENT--- RESINOUS, PUNGENT.
I MISS HAVING A NOSE.
BUT I CAN REMEMBER SCENTS.
GOODNIGHT, TREE.
GOODNIGHT, ALIEN WORLDS.

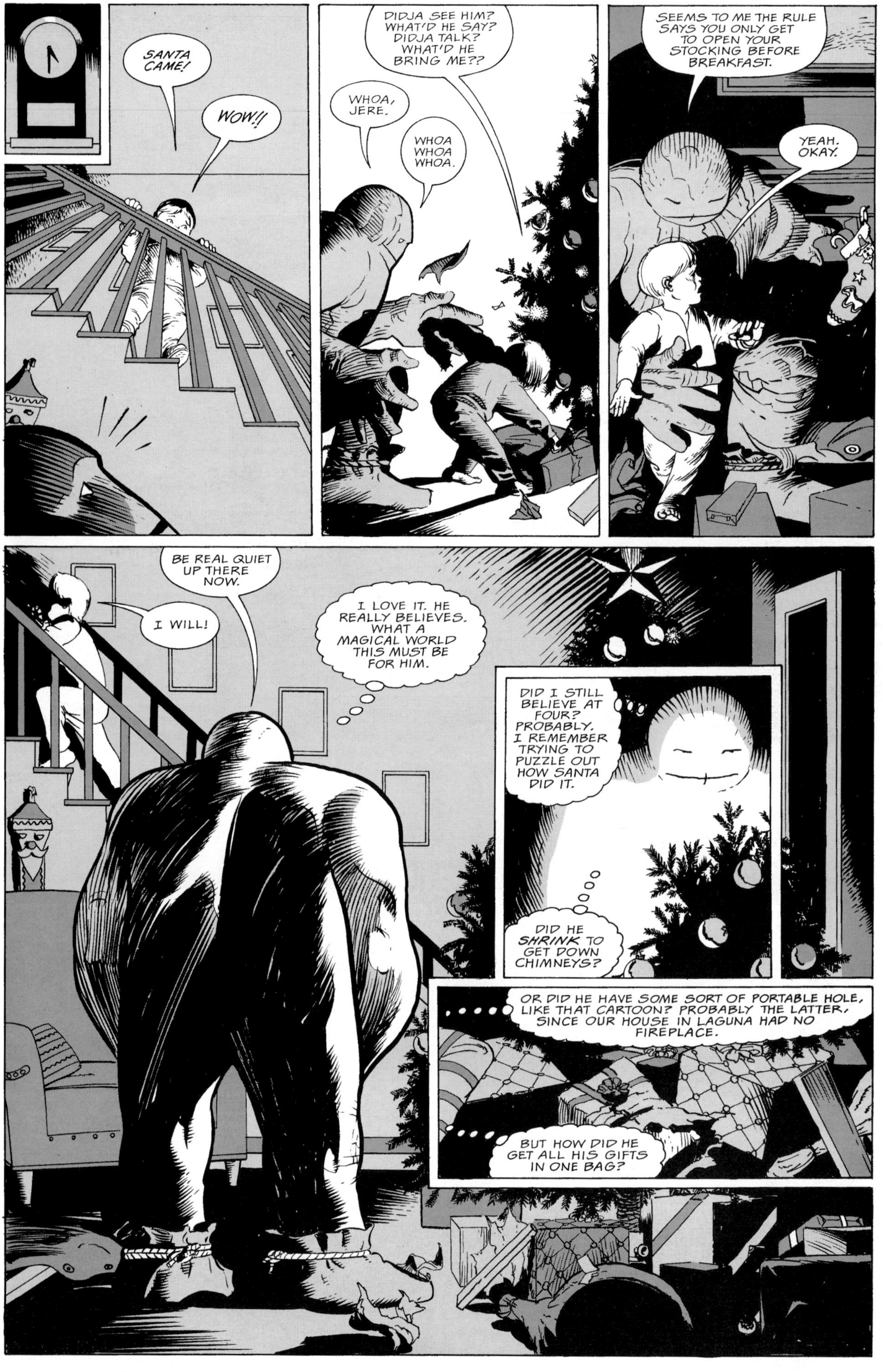
SANTA CAME!
WOW!!
DIDJA SEE HIM? WHAT'D HE SAY? DIDJA TALK? WHAT'D HE BRING ME??
WHOA, JERE.
WHOA WHOA WHOA.
SEEMS TO ME THE RULE SAYS YOU ONLY GET TO OPEN YOUR STOCKING BEFORE BREAKFAST.
YEAH. OKAY.
BE REAL QUIET UP THERE NOW.
I WILL!
I LOVE IT. HE REALLY BELIEVES. WHAT A MAGICAL WORLD THIS MUST BE FOR HIM.
DID I STILL BELIEVE AT FOUR? PROBABLY. I REMEMBER TRYING TO PUZZLE OUT HOW SANTA DID IT.
DID HE SHRINK TO GET DOWN CHIMNEYS?
OR DID HE HAVE SOME SORT OF PORTABLE HOLE, LIKE THAT CARTOON? PROBABLY THE LATTER, SINCE OUR HOUSE IN LAGUNA HAD NO FIREPLACE.
BUT HOW DID HE GET ALL HIS GIFTS IN ONE BAG?

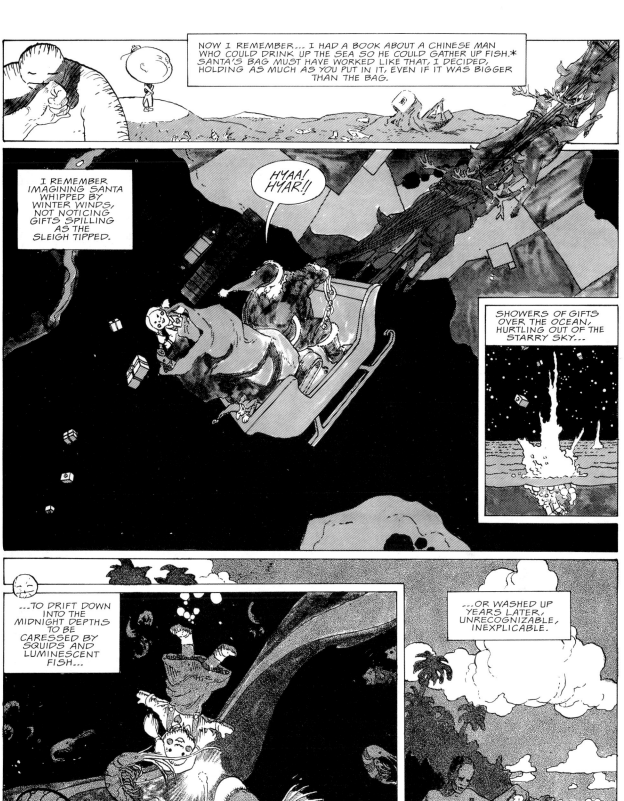

NOW I REMEMBER... I HAD A BOOK ABOUT A CHINESE MAN WHO COULD DRINK UP THE SEA SO HE COULD GATHER UP FISH.* SANTA'S BAG MUST HAVE WORKED LIKE THAT, I DECIDED, HOLDING AS MUCH AS YOU PUT IN IT, EVEN IF IT WAS BIGGER THAN THE BAG.

I REMEMBER IMAGINING SANTA WHIPPED BY WINTER WINDS, NOT NOTICING GIFTS SPILLING AS THE SLEIGH TIPPED.

HYAA! HYAR!!

SHOWERS OF GIFTS OVER THE OCEAN, HURTLING OUT OF THE STARRY SKY...

...TO DRIFT DOWN INTO THE MIDNIGHT DEPTHS TO BE CARESSED BY SQUIDS AND LUMINESCENT FISH...

...OR WASHED UP YEARS LATER, UNRECOGNIZABLE, INEXPLICABLE.

GOOD MORNING, CONCRETE!

THE BEST PART OF CHILDHOOD CHRISTMAS ISN'T INDULGED ACQUISITIVENESS, BUT SPURRED IMAGINATION.

* THE FIVE CHINESE BROTHERS, BY CLAIRE H. BISHOP AND KURT WIESE.

ADAM! YOU'RE UP EARLY.

THOUGHT I'D GET IN A RUN BEFORE BREAKFAST.

THIS WAY I'LL BE WARMED UP FOR THE TRADITIONAL GAME AT MUNRO FAMILY GATHERINGS.

WHAT'S THAT?

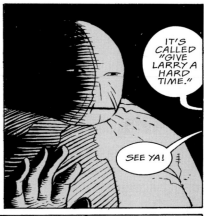

IT'S CALLED "GIVE LARRY A HARD TIME."

SEE YA!

...LIKE A BABY. HOW'D YOU SLEEP, LARRY?

I...

LARRY'S THE UNDEFEATED CHAMPION SLEEPER IN THE FAMILY!

KNOWN TO SLEEP PAST NOON, ALL RIGHT.

FIRST BATCH!

THANKS, HONEY.

C'MON, EAT, EVERY- ONE!

ONLY AFTER I'D BEEN UP ALL NIGHT WRITING.

SO GOES THE STORY...

NOW YOU LAY OFF POOR LARRY...

STILL DEFENDING YOUR BIG BROTHER, JANE?

I DON'T WORRY ABOUT LARRY SINCE HE HOOKED UP WITH YOU, CONCRETE.

I DON'T KNOW WHAT HE WOULD'VE DONE IF HE HADN'T...

HE MIGHT'VE BEEN FORCED TO JOIN HIS DAD'S REPAIR BUSINESS... HORRIBLE THOUGHT!

DAD...

THREE SONS...THREE! AND NOT ONE SEES FIT TO THROW IN WITH THE OLD MAN. NO...WE HAVE AN EASEL PAINTER, A STUNTMAN, AND A...A...

WRITER.

NOT A REAL WRITER.

WHAT--?!

YOU'RE NOT A REAL WRITER 'TIL YOU'RE PUBLISHED.

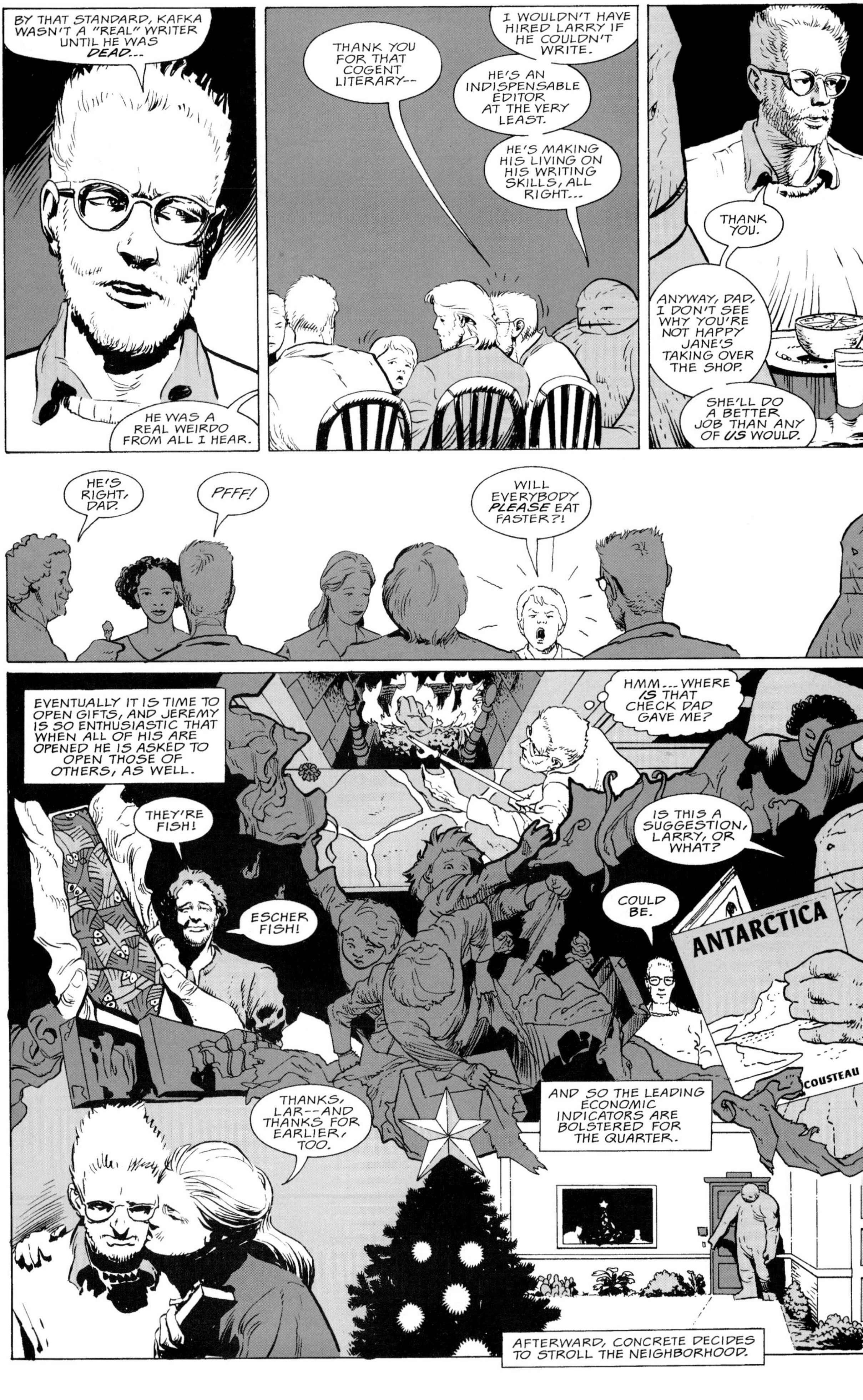
BY THAT STANDARD, KAFKA WASN'T A "REAL" WRITER UNTIL HE WAS DEAD--
HE WAS A REAL WEIRDO FROM ALL I HEAR.
THANK YOU FOR THAT COGENT LITERARY--
I WOULDN'T HAVE HIRED LARRY IF HE COULDN'T WRITE.
HE'S AN INDISPENSABLE EDITOR AT THE VERY LEAST.
HE'S MAKING HIS LIVING ON HIS WRITING SKILLS, ALL RIGHT...
THANK YOU.
ANYWAY, DAD, I DON'T SEE WHY YOU'RE NOT HAPPY JANE'S TAKING OVER THE SHOP.
SHE'LL DO A BETTER JOB THAN ANY OF US WOULD.
HE'S RIGHT, DAD.
PFFF!
WILL EVERYBODY PLEASE EAT FASTER?!
EVENTUALLY IT IS TIME TO OPEN GIFTS, AND JEREMY IS SO ENTHUSIASTIC THAT WHEN ALL OF HIS ARE OPENED HE IS ASKED TO OPEN THOSE OF OTHERS, AS WELL.
HMM... WHERE IS THAT CHECK DAD GAVE ME?
THEY'RE FISH!
ESCHER FISH!
IS THIS A SUGGESTION, LARRY, OR WHAT?
COULD BE.
ANTARCTICA
COUSTEAU
THANKS, LAR--AND THANKS FOR EARLIER, TOO.
AND SO THE LEADING ECONOMIC INDICATORS ARE BOLSTERED FOR THE QUARTER.
AFTERWARD, CONCRETE DECIDES TO STROLL THE NEIGHBORHOOD.

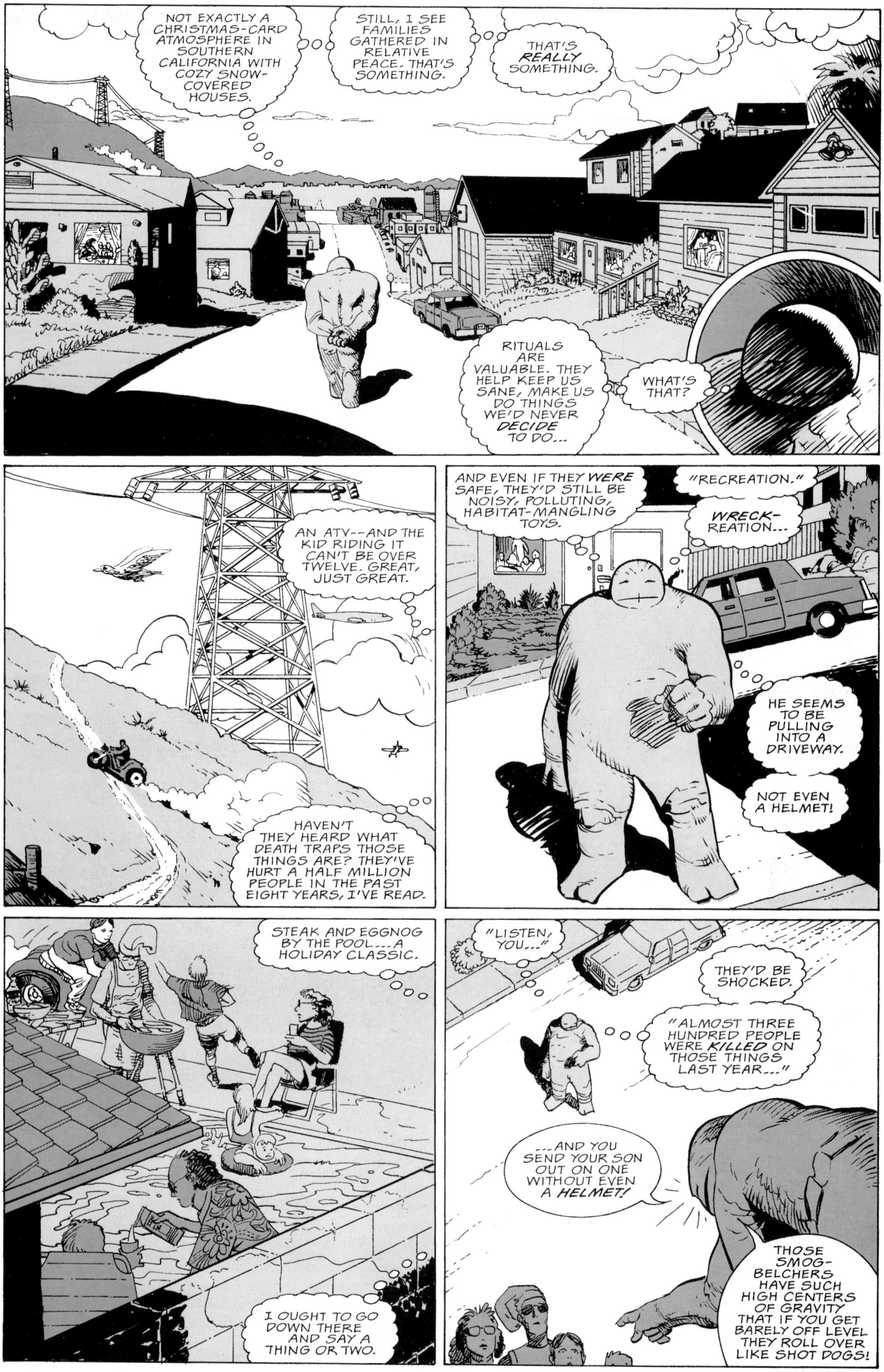
NOT EXACTLY A CHRISTMAS-CARD ATMOSPHERE IN SOUTHERN CALIFORNIA WITH COZY SNOW-COVERED HOUSES.
STILL, I SEE FAMILIES GATHERED IN RELATIVE PEACE. THAT'S SOMETHING.
THAT'S REALLY SOMETHING.
RITUALS ARE VALUABLE. THEY HELP KEEP US SANE, MAKE US DO THINGS WE'D NEVER DECIDE TO DO...
WHAT'S THAT?
AN ATV--AND THE KID RIDING IT CAN'T BE OVER TWELVE. GREAT, JUST GREAT.
HAVEN'T THEY HEARD WHAT DEATH TRAPS THOSE THINGS ARE? THEY'VE HURT A HALF MILLION PEOPLE IN THE PAST EIGHT YEARS, I'VE READ.
AND EVEN IF THEY WERE SAFE, THEY'D STILL BE NOISY, POLLUTING, HABITAT-MANGLING TOYS.
"RECREATION."
WRECK-REATION...
HE SEEMS TO BE PULLING INTO A DRIVEWAY.
NOT EVEN A HELMET!
STEAK AND EGGNOG BY THE POOL... A HOLIDAY CLASSIC.
I OUGHT TO GO DOWN THERE AND SAY A THING OR TWO.
"LISTEN, YOU..."
THEY'D BE SHOCKED.
"ALMOST THREE HUNDRED PEOPLE WERE KILLED ON THOSE THINGS LAST YEAR..."
...AND YOU SEND YOUR SON OUT ON ONE WITHOUT EVEN A HELMET!
THOSE SMOG-BELCHERS HAVE SUCH HIGH CENTERS OF GRAVITY THAT IF YOU GET BARELY OFF LEVEL THEY ROLL OVER LIKE SHOT DOGS!

IMAGINE THIS HUNDREDS OF POUNDS OF NOISY METAL ROLLING OVER ON YOUR SON...

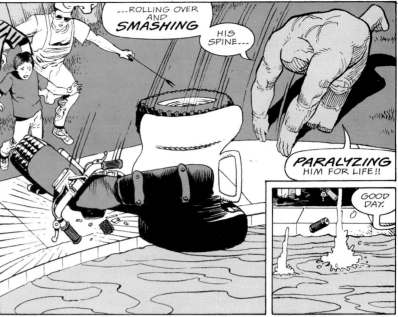

...ROLLING OVER AND **SMASHING** HIS SPINE...

PARALYZING HIM FOR LIFE!!

GOOD DAY.

YEAH, THAT'D MAKE AN IMPRESSION.

WHAT RIGHT DO *YOU* HAVE TO DESTROY *MY SON'S* PROPERTY?!

YOU'LL BE HEARING FROM MY LAWYER, PAL!

WAAAAUGH!!

≡SIGH≡

WE FIND IN FAVOR OF THE PLAINTIFF, YOUR HONOR.

BAD IDEA.

Some People Just Can't Handle Fame

John Ronson

Los Angeles–Concrete found out yesterday that even if you're a celebrity that even if you're still don't have the right to be a bully. And high time, too. A county court judge slapped the rock-wristed one with a $100,000 judgement that would leave even a crusty cyborg smarting. The satisfied winners in the civil suit are the Hansen family of Woodland Hills, California, who in utter horror as their son's "noise bother" — as good as Sadd use the "noise bother as good as Sadd act as Kuwait.

I WONDER WHAT'S DOING BACK AT THE HOUSE.

HOW WAS YOUR WALK?

FINE.

YOU'RE DEAD. I ATOMIZED YOU.

DIDN'T HURT.

WHAT ARE YOU STARING AT, CONCRETE?

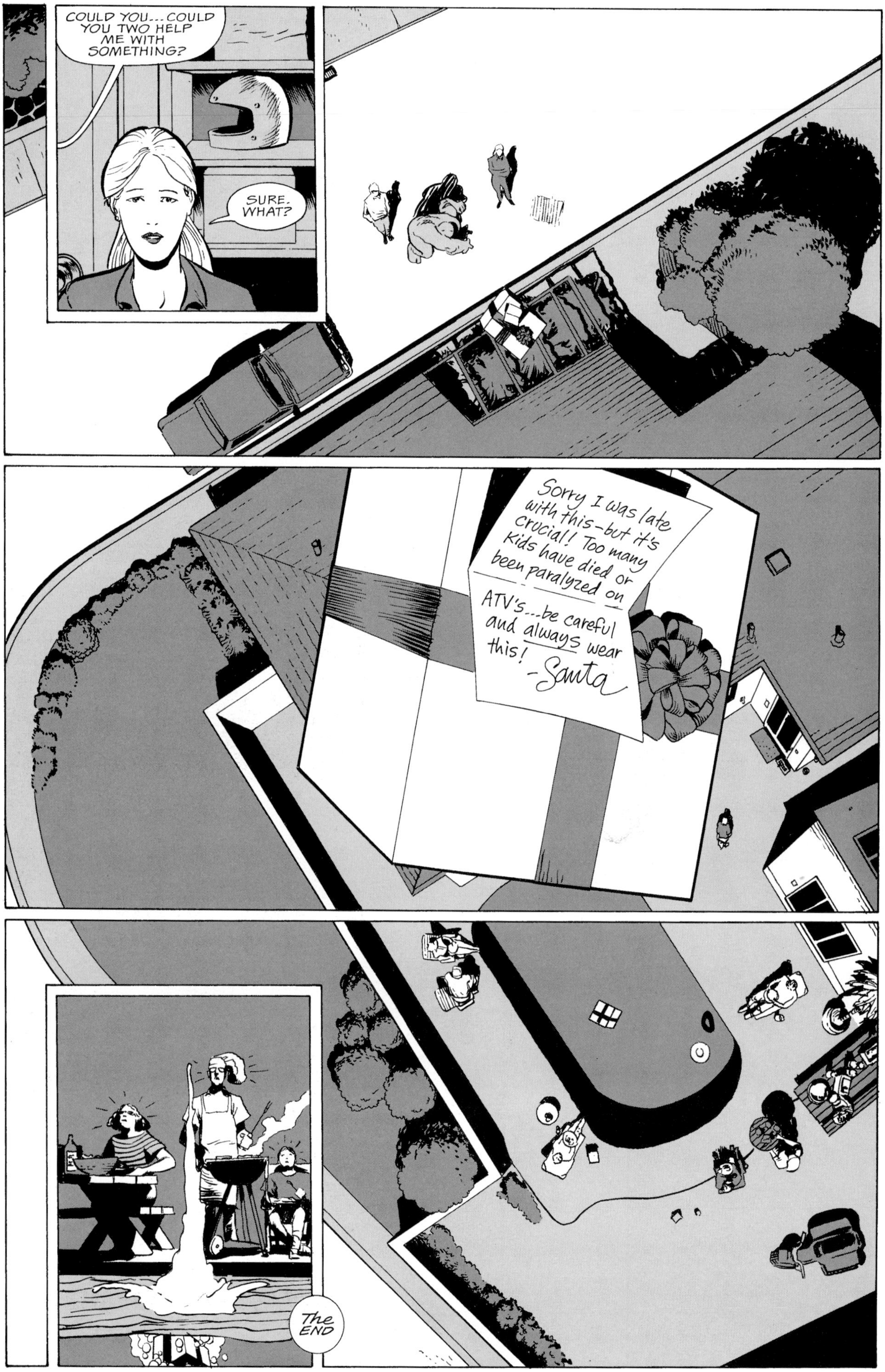
COULD YOU... COULD YOU TWO HELP ME WITH SOMETHING?
SURE. WHAT?
Sorry I was late with this—but it's crucial!! Too many kids have died or been paralyzed on ATV's...be careful and always wear this! -Santa
The END

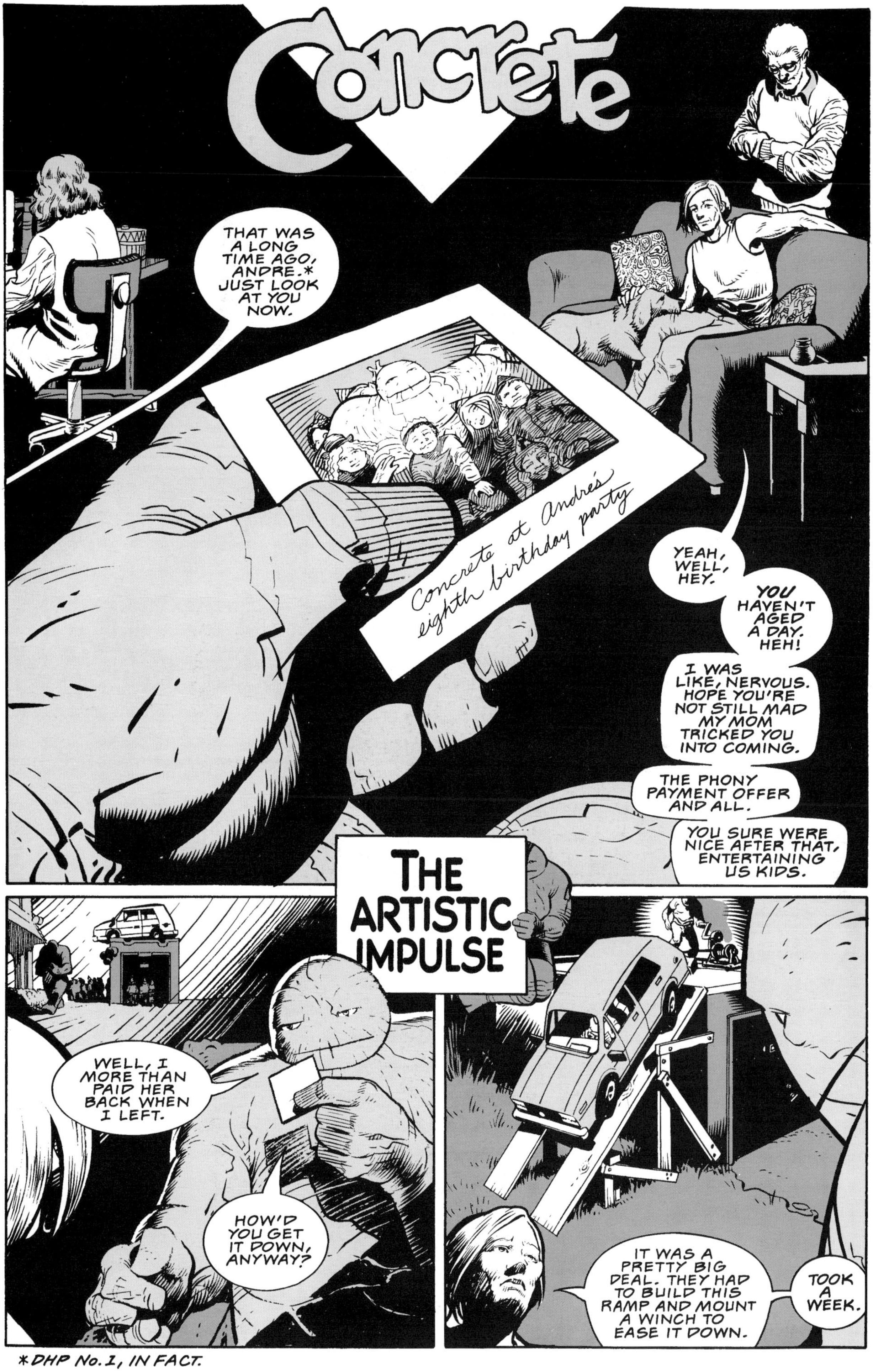
Concrete
THAT WAS A LONG TIME AGO, ANDRE.* JUST LOOK AT YOU NOW.
Concrete at Andre's eighth birthday party
YEAH, WELL, HEY.
YOU HAVEN'T AGED A DAY. HEH!
I WAS LIKE, NERVOUS. HOPE YOU'RE NOT STILL MAD MY MOM TRICKED YOU INTO COMING.
THE PHONY PAYMENT OFFER AND ALL.
YOU SURE WERE NICE AFTER THAT, ENTERTAINING US KIDS.
THE ARTISTIC IMPULSE
WELL, I MORE THAN PAID HER BACK WHEN I LEFT.
HOW'D YOU GET IT DOWN, ANYWAY?
IT WAS A PRETTY BIG DEAL. THEY HAD TO BUILD THIS RAMP AND MOUNT A WINCH TO EASE IT DOWN.
TOOK A WEEK.

*DHP No. 1, IN FACT.

I FEEL AWFUL. A PETTY, MEAN TRICK. WHAT A BULLY.

HEY, SHE TRICKED YOU FIRST!

BUT I LEAPT AT THE BAIT-- THINKING I DESERVED A THOUSAND BUCKS FOR MINGLING AT A PARTY!

FIFTEEN HUNDRED, ACTUALLY.

ANYWAY, WE'RE NOT MAD ANYMORE. IT WAS FUNNY.

AND YOU COULD MORE THAN MAKE UP FOR IT IF YOU WANTED.

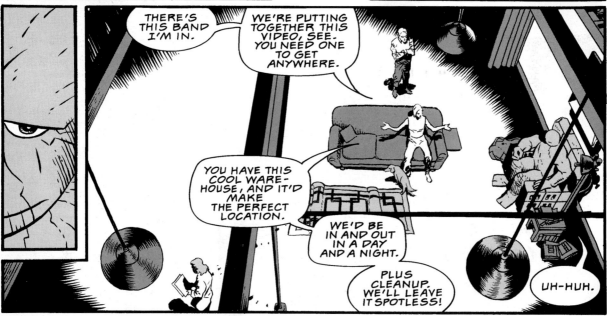

THERE'S THIS BAND I'M IN.

WE'RE PUTTING TOGETHER THIS VIDEO, SEE. YOU NEED ONE TO GET ANYWHERE.

YOU HAVE THIS COOL WAREHOUSE, AND IT'D MAKE THE PERFECT LOCATION.

WE'D BE IN AND OUT IN A DAY AND A NIGHT.

PLUS CLEANUP. WE'LL LEAVE IT SPOTLESS!

UH-HUH.

LOOK, IT'D MEAN A WHOLE LOT.

WE REALLY, REALLY COULD USE IT.

IT'S LIKE, THIS COULD MAKE US!

IT'LL BE GREAT!

FUN FOR YOU, TOO!

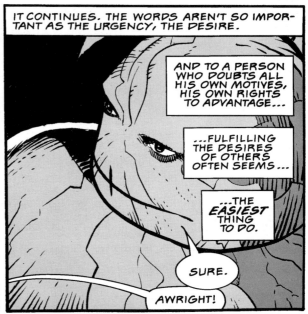

IT CONTINUES. THE WORDS AREN'T SO IMPORTANT AS THE URGENCY, THE DESIRE.

AND TO A PERSON WHO DOUBTS ALL HIS OWN MOTIVES, HIS OWN RIGHTS TO ADVANTAGE...

...FULFILLING THE DESIRES OF OTHERS OFTEN SEEMS...

...THE EASIEST THING TO DO.

SURE.

AWRIGHT!

SOON THE DAY OF PREPARATION IS AT HAND, AND CONCRETE RECALLS ANOTHER "SHOOT" WITH WARMTH.*

IT'S THAT SAME ENERGY I FELT AS PART OF THE "RULERS" CREW--

THOUGH I'M NOT REALLY *ON* THIS TEAM...

MRS. GRACE-- WHAT'S THAT YOU'RE DOING?

JUST PROTECTING YOUR ARTWORK!

THIS IS SHRINK-WRAP FOR STORM WINDOWS!

MY COLLECTION IS GOING TO BE IN THIS? I FIGURED IT'D BE PUT SAFELY AWAY.

OH, NO! IT'S CRUCIAL FOR WHAT WE HAVE PLANNED!

I DON'T QUITE SEE HOW IT FITS YOUR THEME.

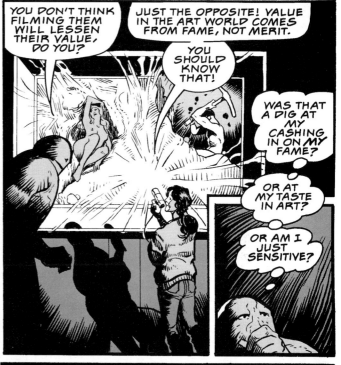

YOU DON'T THINK FILMING THEM WILL LESSEN THEIR VALUE, DO YOU?

JUST THE OPPOSITE! VALUE IN THE ART WORLD COMES FROM FAME, NOT MERIT.

YOU SHOULD KNOW THAT!

WAS THAT A DIG AT *MY* CASHING IN ON *MY* FAME?

OR AT *MY* TASTE IN ART?

OR AM I JUST SENSITIVE?

I GUESS I DID SIGN A RELEASE SAYING YOU COULD USE ANY-THING YOU FILMED IN HERE--INCLUDING ME.

OH, I'D NEVER HOLD YOU TO THAT!

THAT NIGHT, THE BAND, LEUKEMIA CLUSTER, TUNES UP...

WE'RE CREATING FAME, THE WAY A FARMER GROWS A CROP, OR A BAKER MAKES BREAD.

I GUESS I'M THE SOURDOUGH STARTER.

YA KNOW HOW IT WORKS. WE JUST REPEAT THE ONE TUNE. LATER WE CUT THE NIGHT'S FILMING TOGETHER... WELL, *YOU* KNOW.

SO OKAY. A-ONE... TWO...

*CONCRETE: FRAGILE CREATURE 1-4.

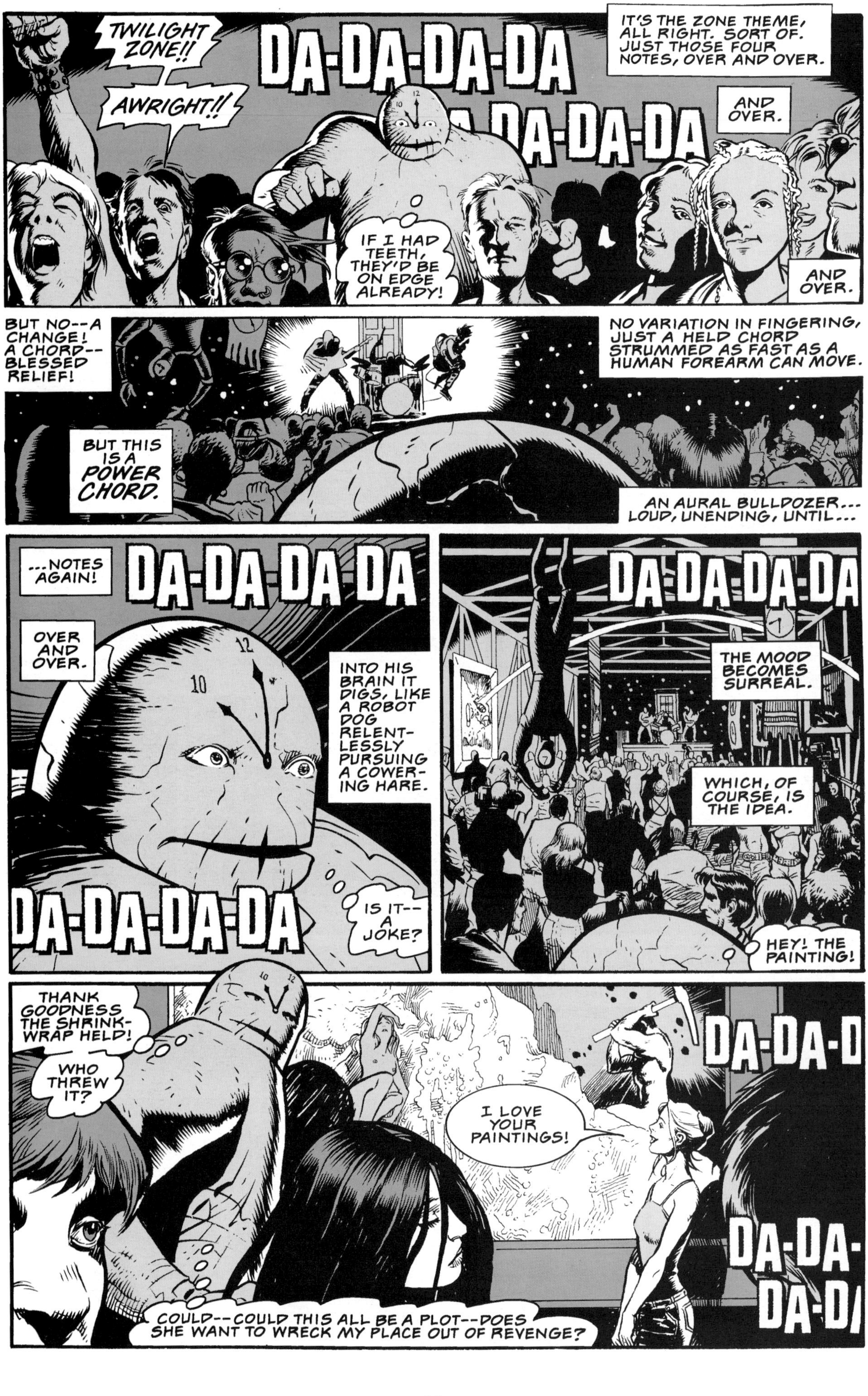
TWILIGHT ZONE!!
DA-DA-DA-DA
IT'S THE ZONE THEME, ALL RIGHT. SORT OF. JUST THOSE FOUR NOTES, OVER AND OVER.
AWRIGHT!!
DA-DA-DA
AND OVER.
IF I HAD TEETH, THEY'D BE ON EDGE ALREADY!
AND OVER.
BUT NO--A CHANGE! A CHORD--BLESSED RELIEF!
NO VARIATION IN FINGERING, JUST A HELD CHORD STRUMMED AS FAST AS A HUMAN FOREARM CAN MOVE.
BUT THIS IS A POWER CHORD.
AN AURAL BULLDOZER... LOUD, UNENDING, UNTIL...
...NOTES AGAIN!
DA-DA-DA-DA
OVER AND OVER.
INTO HIS BRAIN IT DIGS, LIKE A ROBOT DOG RELENT-LESSLY PURSUING A COWER-ING HARE.
DA-DA-DA-DA
IS IT--A JOKE?
DA-DA-DA-DA
THE MOOD BECOMES SURREAL.
WHICH, OF COURSE, IS THE IDEA.
HEY! THE PAINTING!
THANK GOODNESS THE SHRINK-WRAP HELD!
WHO THREW IT?
DA-DA-D
I LOVE YOUR PAINTINGS!
DA-DA-
DA-D
COULD--COULD THIS ALL BE A PLOT--DOES SHE WANT TO WRECK MY PLACE OUT OF REVENGE?

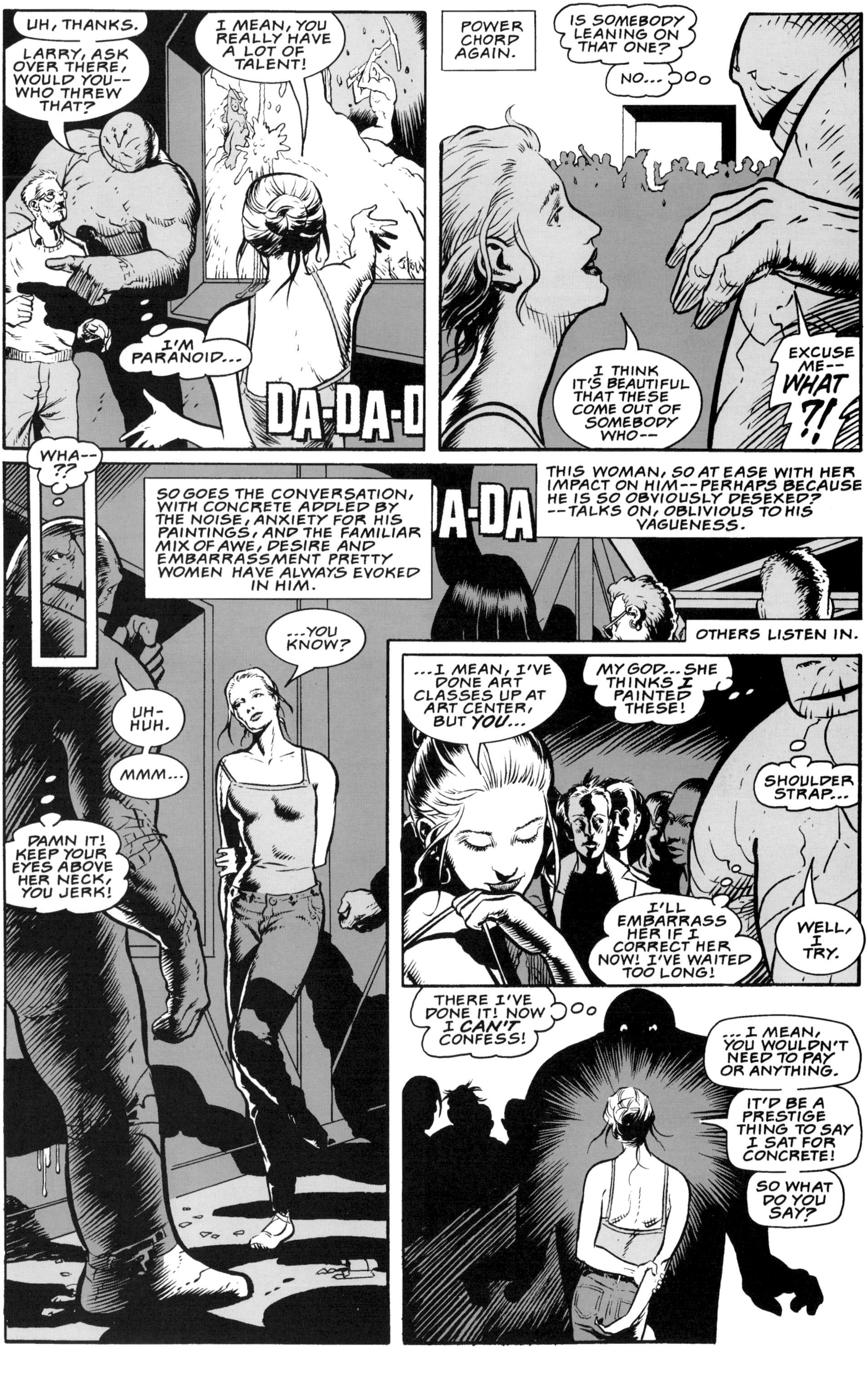
UH, THANKS.
LARRY, ASK OVER THERE, WOULD YOU-- WHO THREW THAT?
I MEAN, YOU REALLY HAVE A LOT OF TALENT!
I'M PARANOID...
DA-DA-D
POWER CHORD AGAIN.
IS SOMEBODY LEANING ON THAT ONE?
NO...
I THINK IT'S BEAUTIFUL THAT THESE COME OUT OF SOMEBODY WHO--
EXCUSE ME-- WHAT ?!
WHA-- ??
SO GOES THE CONVERSATION, WITH CONCRETE ADDLED BY THE NOISE, ANXIETY FOR HIS PAINTINGS, AND THE FAMILIAR MIX OF AWE, DESIRE AND EMBARRASSMENT PRETTY WOMEN HAVE ALWAYS EVOKED IN HIM.
DA-DA
THIS WOMAN, SO AT EASE WITH HER IMPACT ON HIM--PERHAPS BECAUSE HE IS SO OBVIOUSLY DESEXED? --TALKS ON, OBLIVIOUS TO HIS VAGUENESS.
...YOU KNOW?
UH-HUH.
MMM...
DAMN IT! KEEP YOUR EYES ABOVE HER NECK, YOU JERK!
OTHERS LISTEN IN.
...I MEAN, I'VE DONE ART CLASSES UP AT ART CENTER, BUT YOU...
MY GOD... SHE THINKS I PAINTED THESE!
SHOULDER STRAP...
I'LL EMBARRASS HER IF I CORRECT HER NOW! I'VE WAITED TOO LONG!
WELL, I TRY.
THERE I'VE DONE IT! NOW I CAN'T CONFESS!
...I MEAN, YOU WOULDN'T NEED TO PAY OR ANYTHING.
IT'D BE A PRESTIGE THING TO SAY I SAT FOR CONCRETE!
SO WHAT DO YOU SAY?

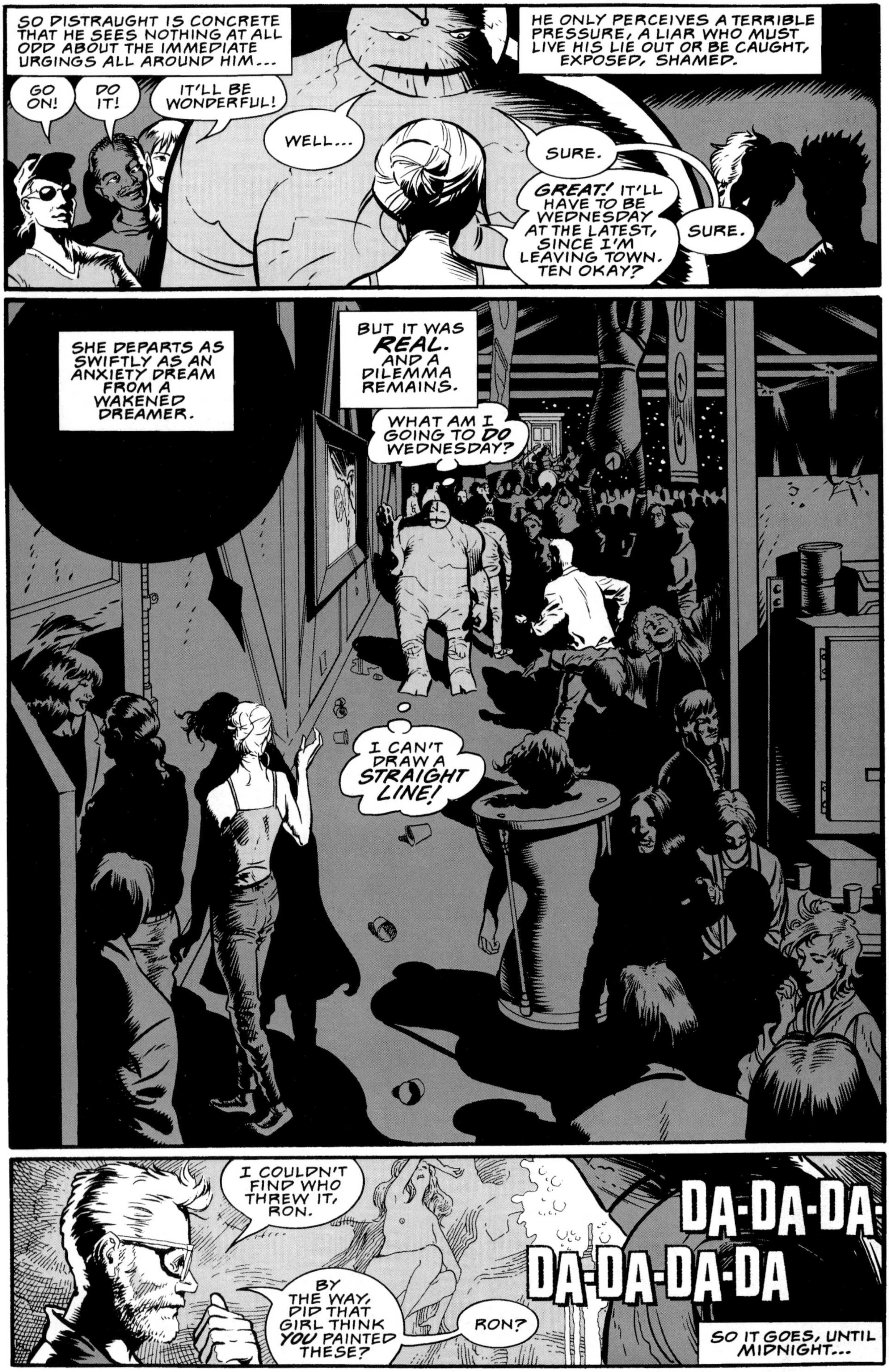
SO DISTRAUGHT IS CONCRETE THAT HE SEES NOTHING AT ALL ODD ABOUT THE IMMEDIATE URGINGS ALL AROUND HIM...
HE ONLY PERCEIVES A TERRIBLE PRESSURE, A LIAR WHO MUST LIVE HIS LIE OUT OR BE CAUGHT, EXPOSED, SHAMED.
GO ON!
DO IT!
IT'LL BE WONDERFUL!
WELL...
SURE.
GREAT! IT'LL HAVE TO BE WEDNESDAY AT THE LATEST, SINCE I'M LEAVING TOWN. TEN OKAY?
SURE.
SHE DEPARTS AS SWIFTLY AS AN ANXIETY DREAM FROM A WAKENED DREAMER.
BUT IT WAS REAL. AND A DILEMMA REMAINS.
WHAT AM I GOING TO DO WEDNESDAY?
I CAN'T DRAW A STRAIGHT LINE!
I COULDN'T FIND WHO THREW IT, RON.
BY THE WAY, DID THAT GIRL THINK YOU PAINTED THESE?
RON?
DA-DA-DA-DA-DA-DA-DA
SO IT GOES, UNTIL MIDNIGHT...

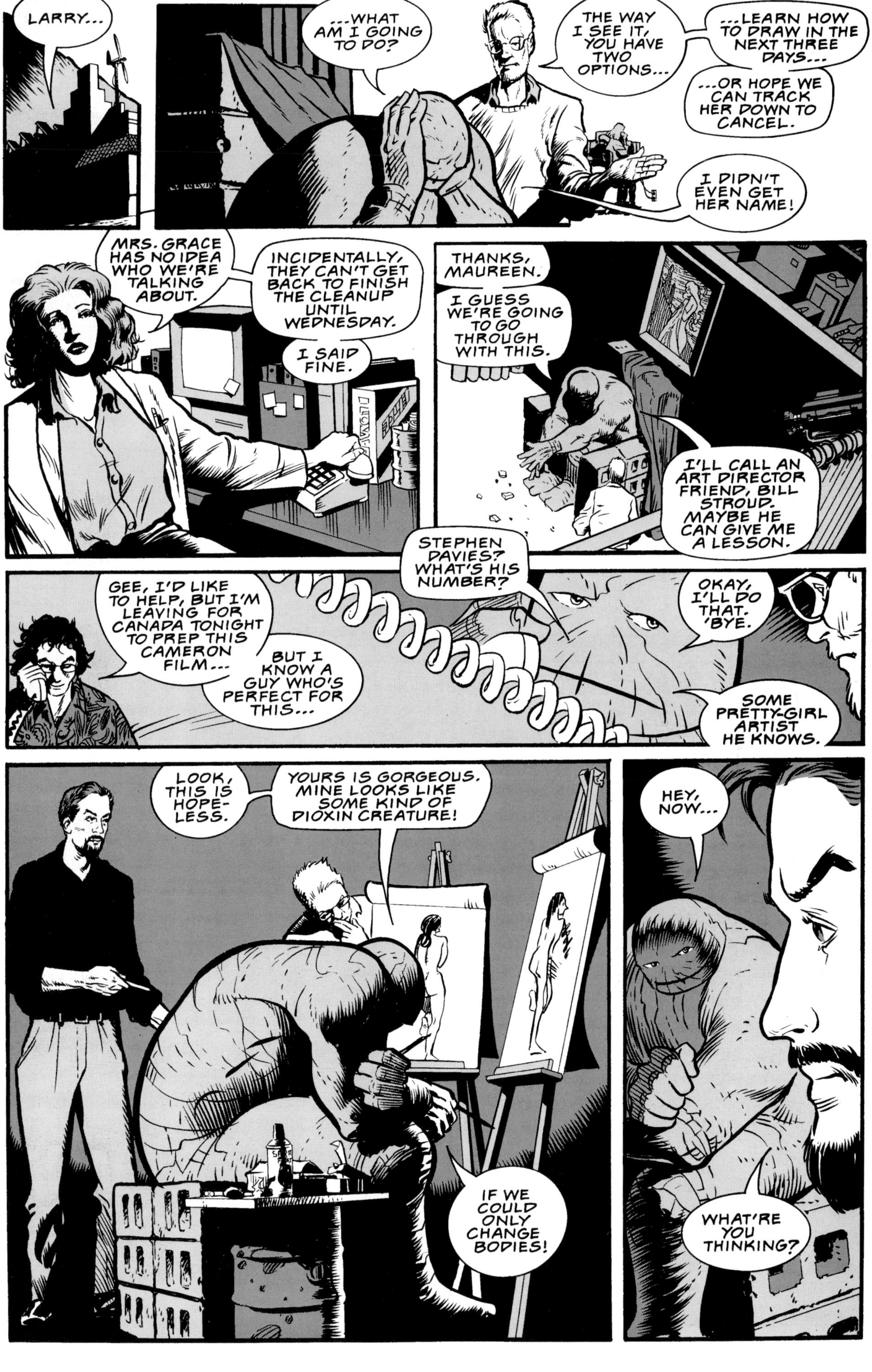
LARRY...
...WHAT AM I GOING TO DO?
THE WAY I SEE IT, YOU HAVE TWO OPTIONS...
...LEARN HOW TO DRAW IN THE NEXT THREE DAYS...
...OR HOPE WE CAN TRACK HER DOWN TO CANCEL.
I DIDN'T EVEN GET HER NAME!
MRS. GRACE HAS NO IDEA WHO WE'RE TALKING ABOUT.
INCIDENTALLY, THEY CAN'T GET BACK TO FINISH THE CLEANUP UNTIL WEDNESDAY.
I SAID FINE.
THANKS, MAUREEN.
I GUESS WE'RE GOING TO GO THROUGH WITH THIS.
I'LL CALL AN ART DIRECTOR FRIEND, BILL STROUD. MAYBE HE CAN GIVE ME A LESSON.
GEE, I'D LIKE TO HELP, BUT I'M LEAVING FOR CANADA TONIGHT TO PREP THIS CAMERON FILM...
BUT I KNOW A GUY WHO'S PERFECT FOR THIS...
STEPHEN DAVIES? WHAT'S HIS NUMBER?
OKAY, I'LL DO THAT. 'BYE.
SOME PRETTY-GIRL ARTIST HE KNOWS.
LOOK, THIS IS HOPE-LESS.
YOURS IS GORGEOUS. MINE LOOKS LIKE SOME KIND OF DIOXIN CREATURE!
IF WE COULD ONLY CHANGE BODIES!
HEY, NOW...
WHAT'RE YOU THINKING?

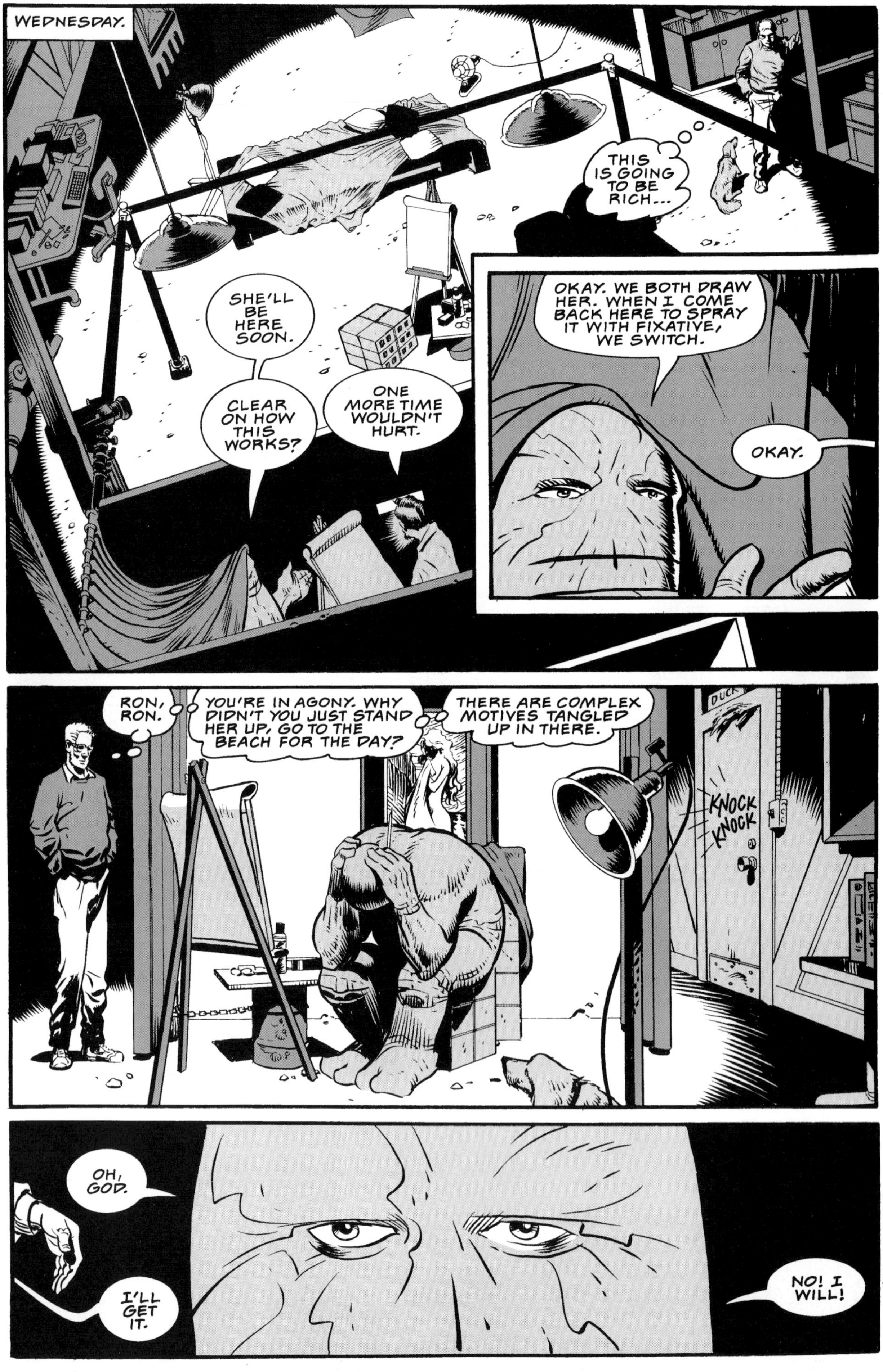
WEDNESDAY.
THIS IS GOING TO BE RICH...
SHE'LL BE HERE SOON.
CLEAR ON HOW THIS WORKS?
ONE MORE TIME WOULDN'T HURT.
OKAY. WE BOTH DRAW HER. WHEN I COME BACK HERE TO SPRAY IT WITH FIXATIVE, WE SWITCH.
OKAY.
RON, RON.
YOU'RE IN AGONY. WHY DIDN'T YOU JUST STAND HER UP, GO TO THE BEACH FOR THE DAY?
THERE ARE COMPLEX MOTIVES TANGLED UP IN THERE.
KNOCK
KNOCK
OH, GOD.
I'LL GET IT.
NO! I WILL!

HI. COME IN!

I'M SO EXCITED!

I CAN'T WAIT TO SEE WHAT YOU PRODUCE!

CAN I UNDRESS IN HERE? I'M SHY ABOUT THAT.

ULP!

UH...

NO!!

CRAZY, I KNOW.

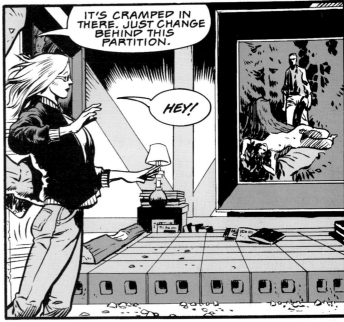

IT'S CRAMPED IN THERE. JUST CHANGE BEHIND THIS PARTITION.

HEY!

I'M TERRIBLY SORRY.

MY STRENGTH! I DON'T...

DON'T WORRY ABOUT IT.

I'VE GOTTEN LITTLE PUSHES INTO THE BEDROOM BEFORE, BUT NOT LIKE THAT!

MY GOD! IT IS MY BEDROOM!

WHAT MESSAGE DOES THAT SEND?!

LOOKS HARD!

BUT SO ARE YOU.

WHAT'S SHE MEAN?

NOTHING, GUTTER MIND!

COULD YOU-- STEP OUT A SEC?

SURE! SORRY!

89

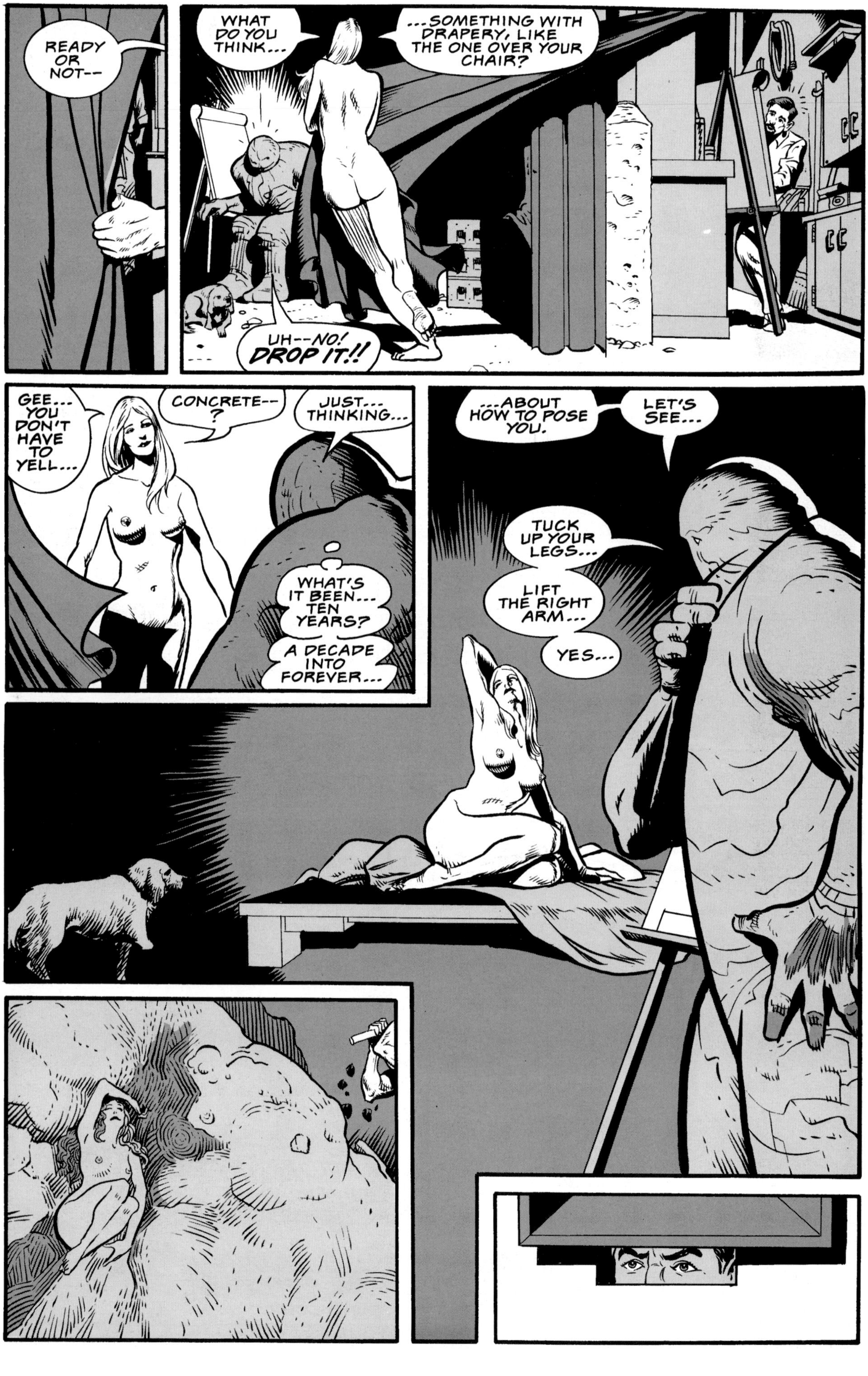
READY OR NOT--
WHAT DO YOU THINK...
...SOMETHING WITH DRAPERY, LIKE THE ONE OVER YOUR CHAIR?
UH--NO! DROP IT!!
GEE... YOU DON'T HAVE TO YELL...
CONCRETE-- ?
JUST... THINKING...
WHAT'S IT BEEN... TEN YEARS?
A DECADE INTO FOREVER...
...ABOUT HOW TO POSE YOU.
LET'S SEE...
TUCK UP YOUR LEGS...
LIFT THE RIGHT ARM...
YES...

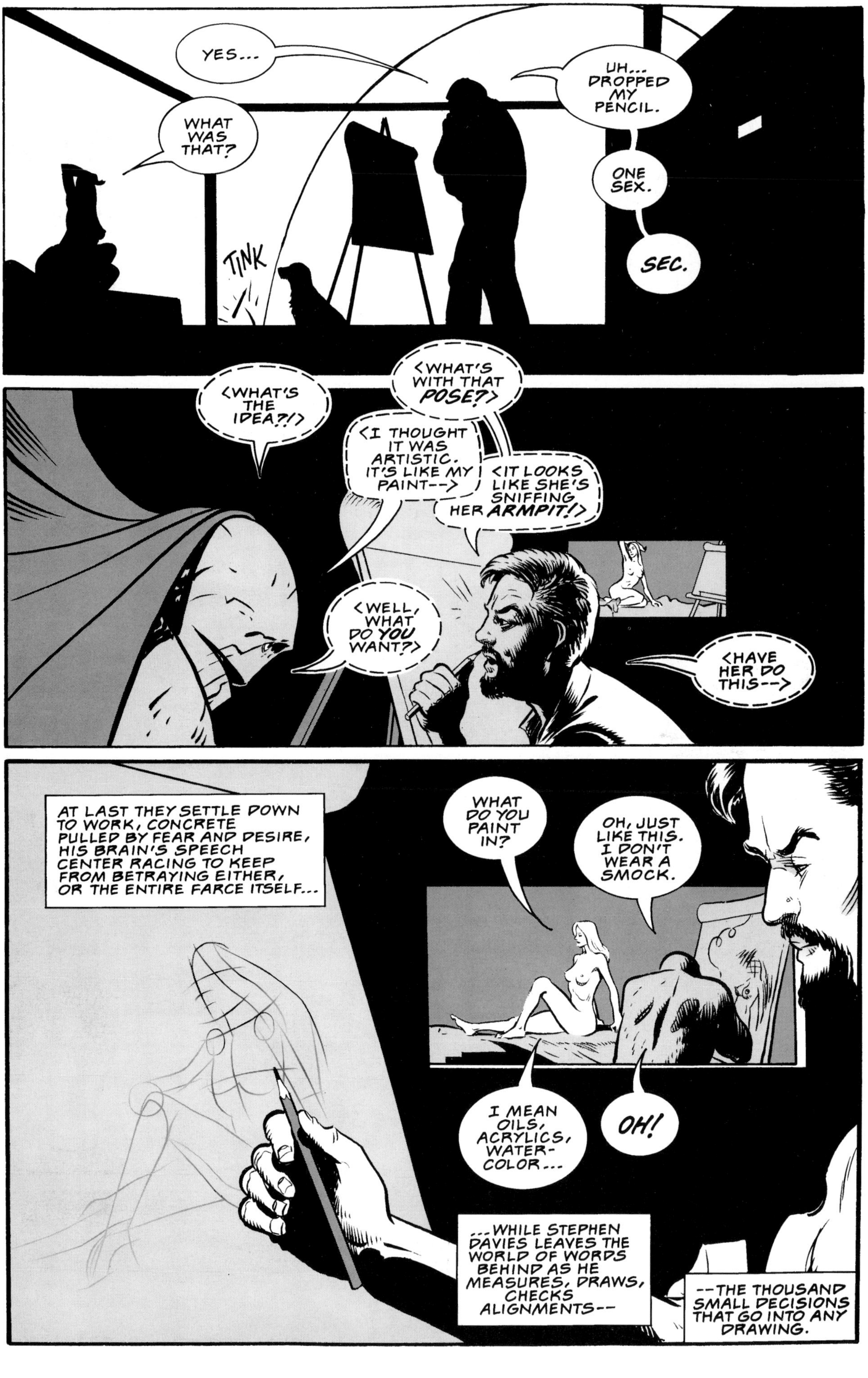
YES...
WHAT WAS THAT?
UH... DROPPED MY PENCIL.
ONE SEX.
SEC.
TINK
<WHAT'S THE IDEA?!>
<WHAT'S WITH THAT POSE?>
<I THOUGHT IT WAS ARTISTIC. IT'S LIKE MY PAINT-->
<IT LOOKS LIKE SHE'S SNIFFING HER ARMPIT!>
<WELL, WHAT DO YOU WANT?>
<HAVE HER DO THIS-->
AT LAST THEY SETTLE DOWN TO WORK, CONCRETE PULLED BY FEAR AND DESIRE, HIS BRAIN'S SPEECH CENTER RACING TO KEEP FROM BETRAYING EITHER, OR THE ENTIRE FARCE ITSELF...
WHAT DO YOU PAINT IN?
OH, JUST LIKE THIS. I DON'T WEAR A SMOCK.
I MEAN OILS, ACRYLICS, WATER-COLOR...
OH!
...WHILE STEPHEN DAVIES LEAVES THE WORLD OF WORDS BEHIND AS HE MEASURES, DRAWS, CHECKS ALIGNMENTS--
--THE THOUSAND SMALL DECISIONS THAT GO INTO ANY DRAWING.

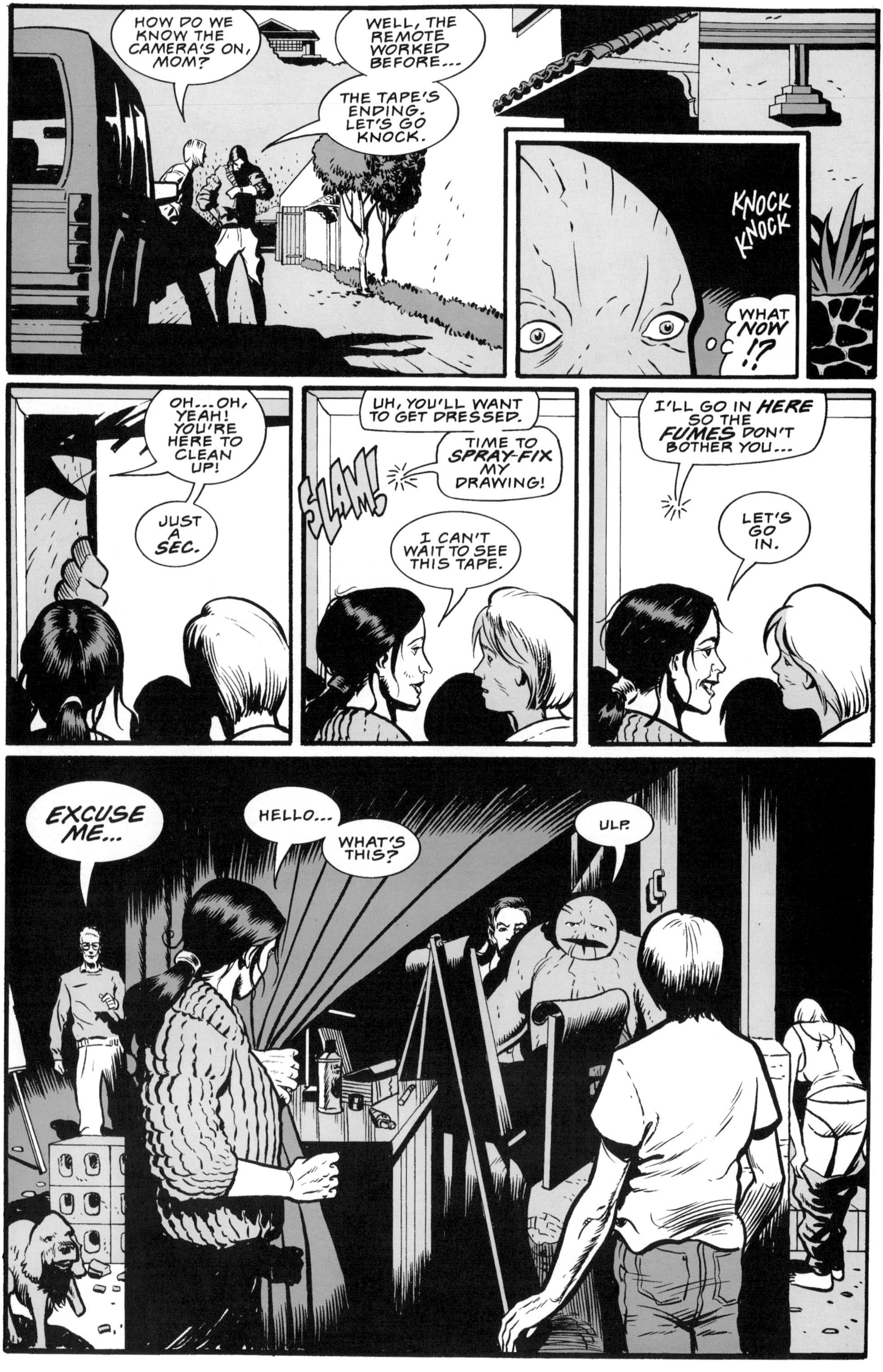
HOW DO WE KNOW THE CAMERA'S ON, MOM?
WELL, THE REMOTE WORKED BEFORE...
THE TAPE'S ENDING. LET'S GO KNOCK.
KNOCK KNOCK
WHAT NOW !?
OH...OH, YEAH! YOU'RE HERE TO CLEAN UP!
JUST A SEC.
UH, YOU'LL WANT TO GET DRESSED.
TIME TO SPRAY-FIX MY DRAWING!
SLAM!
I CAN'T WAIT TO SEE THIS TAPE.
I'LL GO IN HERE SO THE FUMES DON'T BOTHER YOU...
LET'S GO IN.
EXCUSE ME...
HELLO...
WHAT'S THIS?
ULP.

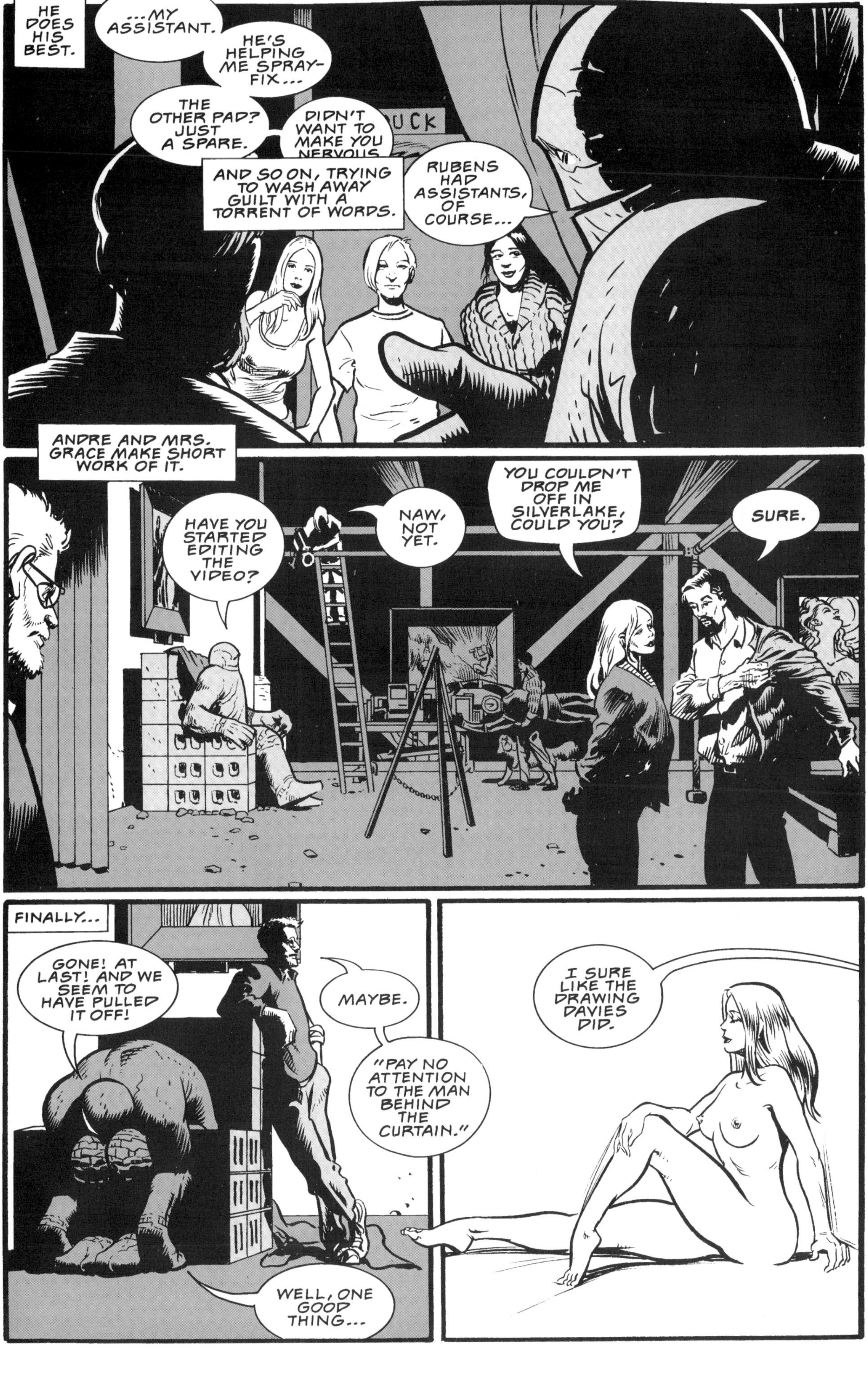

HE DOES HIS BEST.
...MY ASSISTANT.
HE'S HELPING ME SPRAY-FIX...
THE OTHER PAD? JUST A SPARE.
DIDN'T WANT TO MAKE YOU NERVOUS
AND SO ON, TRYING TO WASH AWAY GUILT WITH A TORRENT OF WORDS.
RUBENS HAD ASSISTANTS, OF COURSE...
ANDRE AND MRS. GRACE MAKE SHORT WORK OF IT.
HAVE YOU STARTED EDITING THE VIDEO?
NAW, NOT YET.
YOU COULDN'T DROP ME OFF IN SILVERLAKE, COULD YOU?
SURE.
FINALLY...
GONE! AT LAST! AND WE SEEM TO HAVE PULLED IT OFF!
MAYBE.
"PAY NO ATTENTION TO THE MAN BEHIND THE CURTAIN."
WELL, ONE GOOD THING...
I SURE LIKE THE DRAWING DAVIES DID.

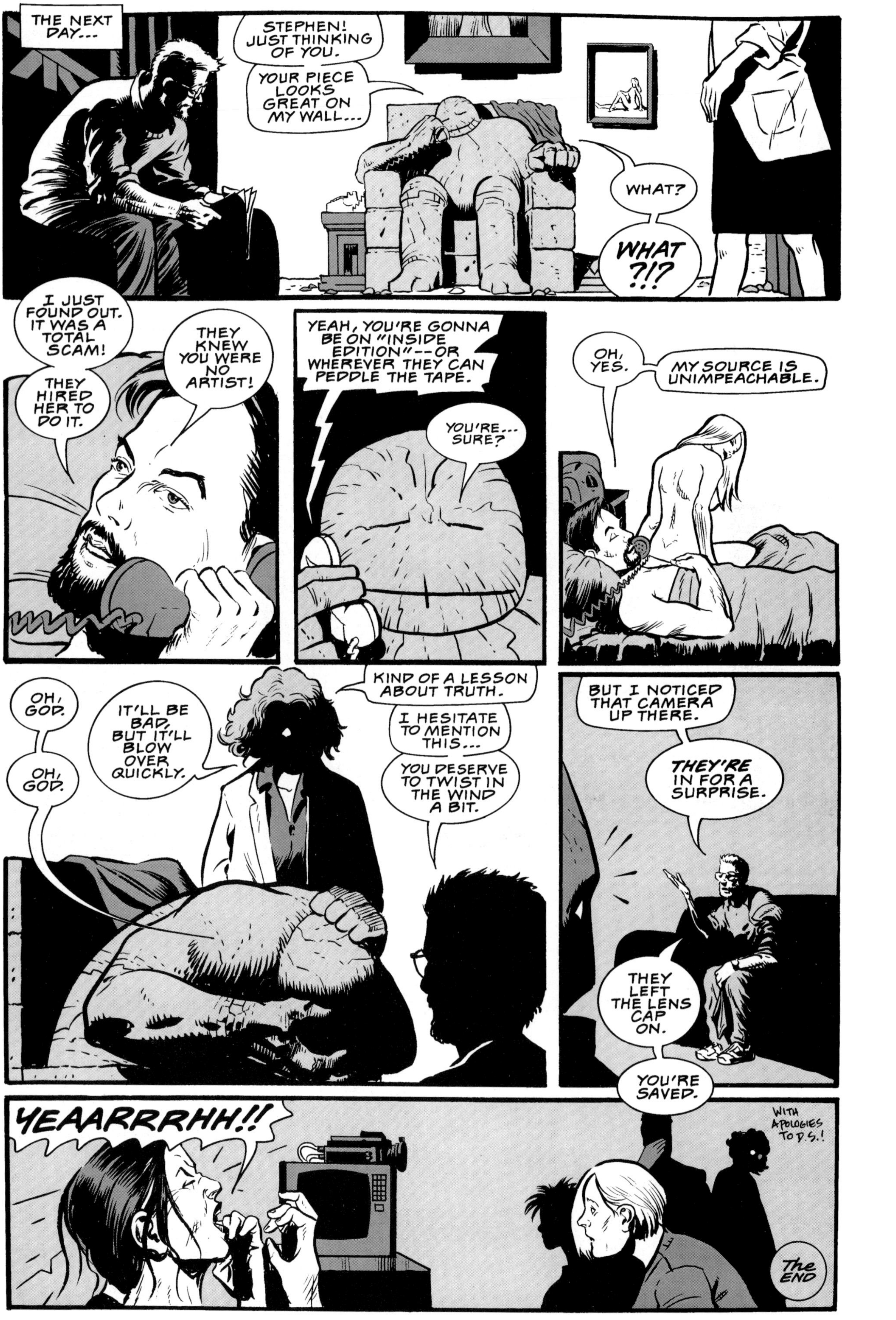
THE NEXT DAY...
STEPHEN! JUST THINKING OF YOU.
YOUR PIECE LOOKS GREAT ON MY WALL...
WHAT?
WHAT ?!?
I JUST FOUND OUT. IT WAS A TOTAL SCAM!
THEY HIRED HER TO DO IT.
THEY KNEW YOU WERE NO ARTIST!
YEAH, YOU'RE GONNA BE ON "INSIDE EDITION"--OR WHEREVER THEY CAN PEDDLE THE TAPE.
YOU'RE... SURE?
OH, YES.
MY SOURCE IS UNIMPEACHABLE.
OH, GOD.
OH, GOD.
IT'LL BE BAD, BUT IT'LL BLOW OVER QUICKLY.
KIND OF A LESSON ABOUT TRUTH.
I HESITATE TO MENTION THIS...
YOU DESERVE TO TWIST IN THE WIND A BIT.
BUT I NOTICED THAT CAMERA UP THERE.
THEY'RE IN FOR A SURPRISE.
THEY LEFT THE LENS CAP ON.
YOU'RE SAVED.
YEAARRRRHH!!
WITH APOLOGIES TO D.S.!
The END

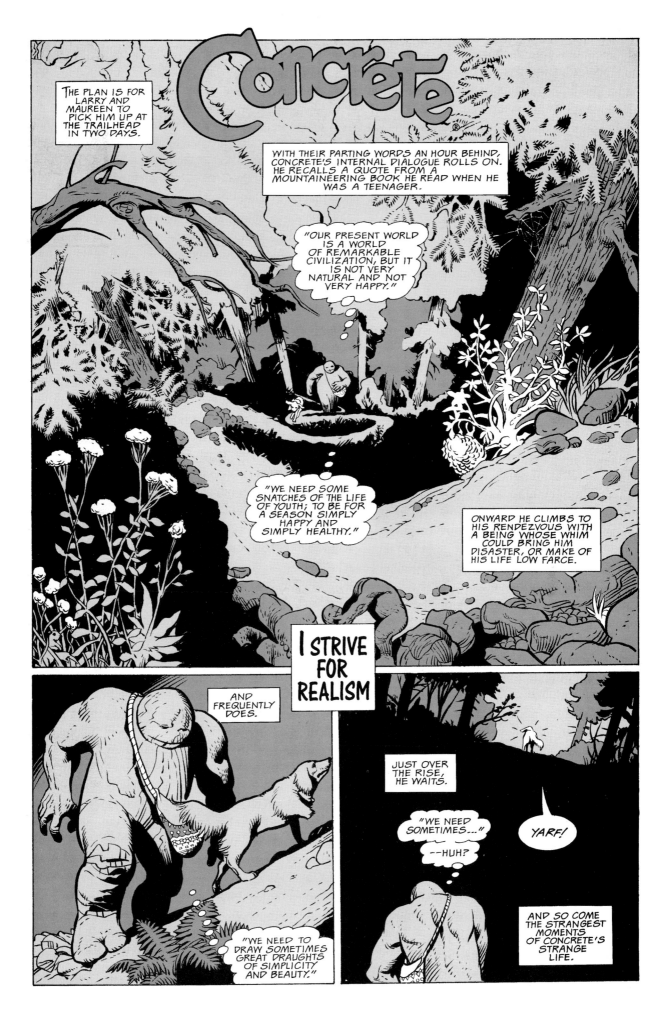

Concrete

THE PLAN IS FOR LARRY AND MAUREEN TO PICK HIM UP AT THE TRAILHEAD IN TWO DAYS.

WITH THEIR PARTING WORDS AN HOUR BEHIND, CONCRETE'S INTERNAL DIALOGUE ROLLS ON. HE RECALLS A QUOTE FROM A MOUNTAINEERING BOOK HE READ WHEN HE WAS A TEENAGER.

"OUR PRESENT WORLD IS A WORLD OF REMARKABLE CIVILIZATION, BUT IT IS NOT VERY NATURAL AND NOT VERY HAPPY."

"WE NEED SOME SNATCHES OF THE LIFE OF YOUTH; TO BE FOR A SEASON SIMPLY HAPPY AND SIMPLY HEALTHY."

ONWARD HE CLIMBS TO HIS RENDEZVOUS WITH A BEING WHOSE WHIM COULD BRING HIM DISASTER, OR MAKE OF HIS LIFE LOW FARCE.

I STRIVE FOR REALISM

AND FREQUENTLY DOES.

"WE NEED TO DRAW SOMETIMES GREAT DRAUGHTS OF SIMPLICITY AND BEAUTY."

JUST OVER THE RISE, HE WAITS.

"WE NEED SOMETIMES..."

--HUH?

YARF!

AND SO COME THE STRANGEST MOMENTS OF CONCRETE'S STRANGE LIFE.

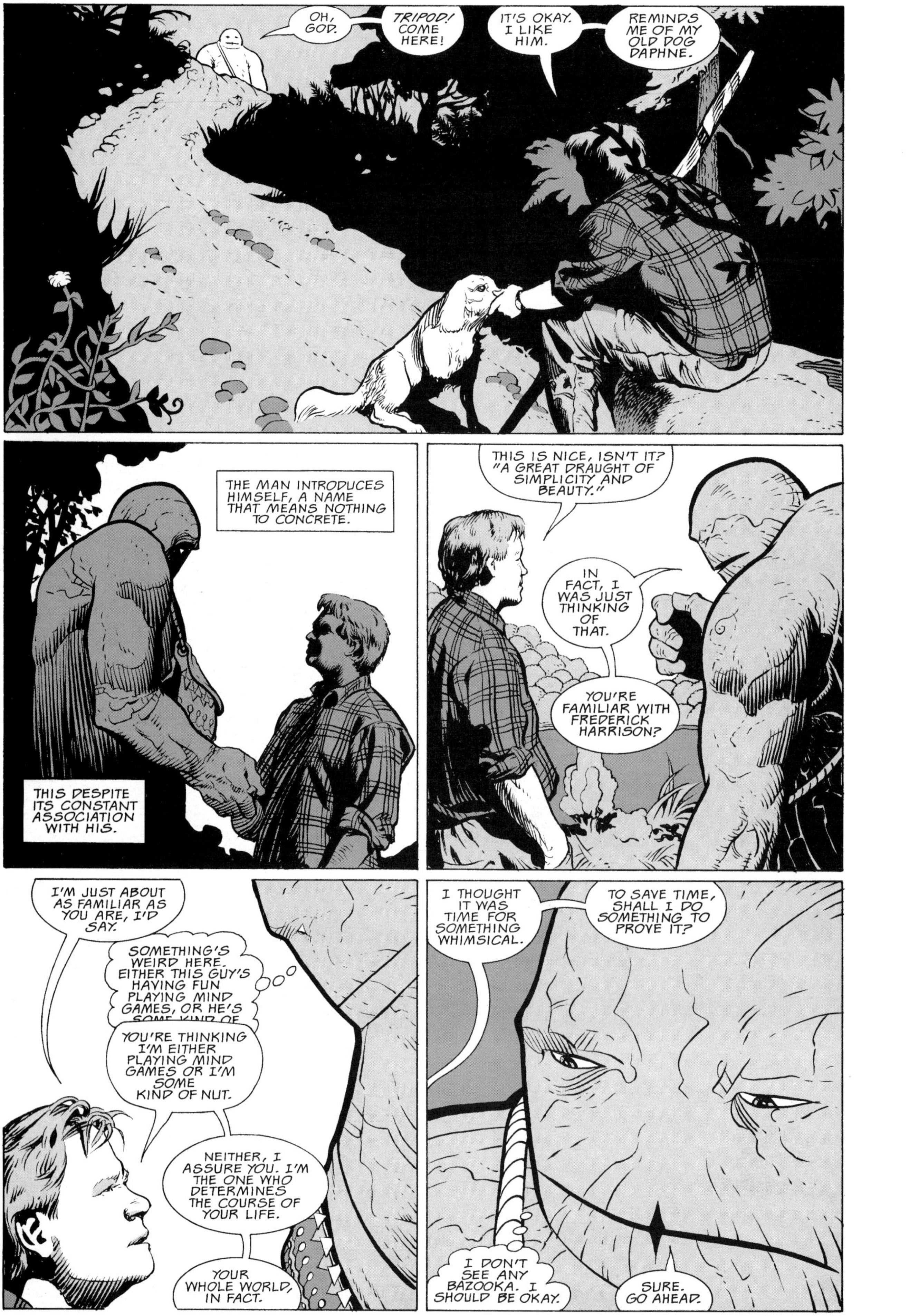
OH, GOD.
TRIPOD! COME HERE!
IT'S OKAY. I LIKE HIM.
REMINDS ME OF MY OLD DOG DAPHNE.
THE MAN INTRODUCES HIMSELF, A NAME THAT MEANS NOTHING TO CONCRETE.
THIS DESPITE ITS CONSTANT ASSOCIATION WITH HIS.
THIS IS NICE, ISN'T IT? "A GREAT DRAUGHT OF SIMPLICITY AND BEAUTY."
IN FACT, I WAS JUST THINKING OF THAT.
YOU'RE FAMILIAR WITH FREDERICK HARRISON?
I'M JUST ABOUT AS FAMILIAR AS YOU ARE, I'D SAY.
SOMETHING'S WEIRD HERE. EITHER THIS GUY'S HAVING FUN PLAYING MIND GAMES, OR HE'S
YOU'RE THINKING I'M EITHER PLAYING MIND GAMES OR I'M SOME KIND OF NUT.
NEITHER, I ASSURE YOU. I'M THE ONE WHO DETERMINES THE COURSE OF YOUR LIFE.
YOUR WHOLE WORLD, IN FACT.
I THOUGHT IT WAS TIME FOR SOMETHING WHIMSICAL.
TO SAVE TIME, SHALL I DO SOMETHING TO PROVE IT?
I DON'T SEE ANY BAZOOKA. I SHOULD BE OKAY.
SURE. GO AHEAD.

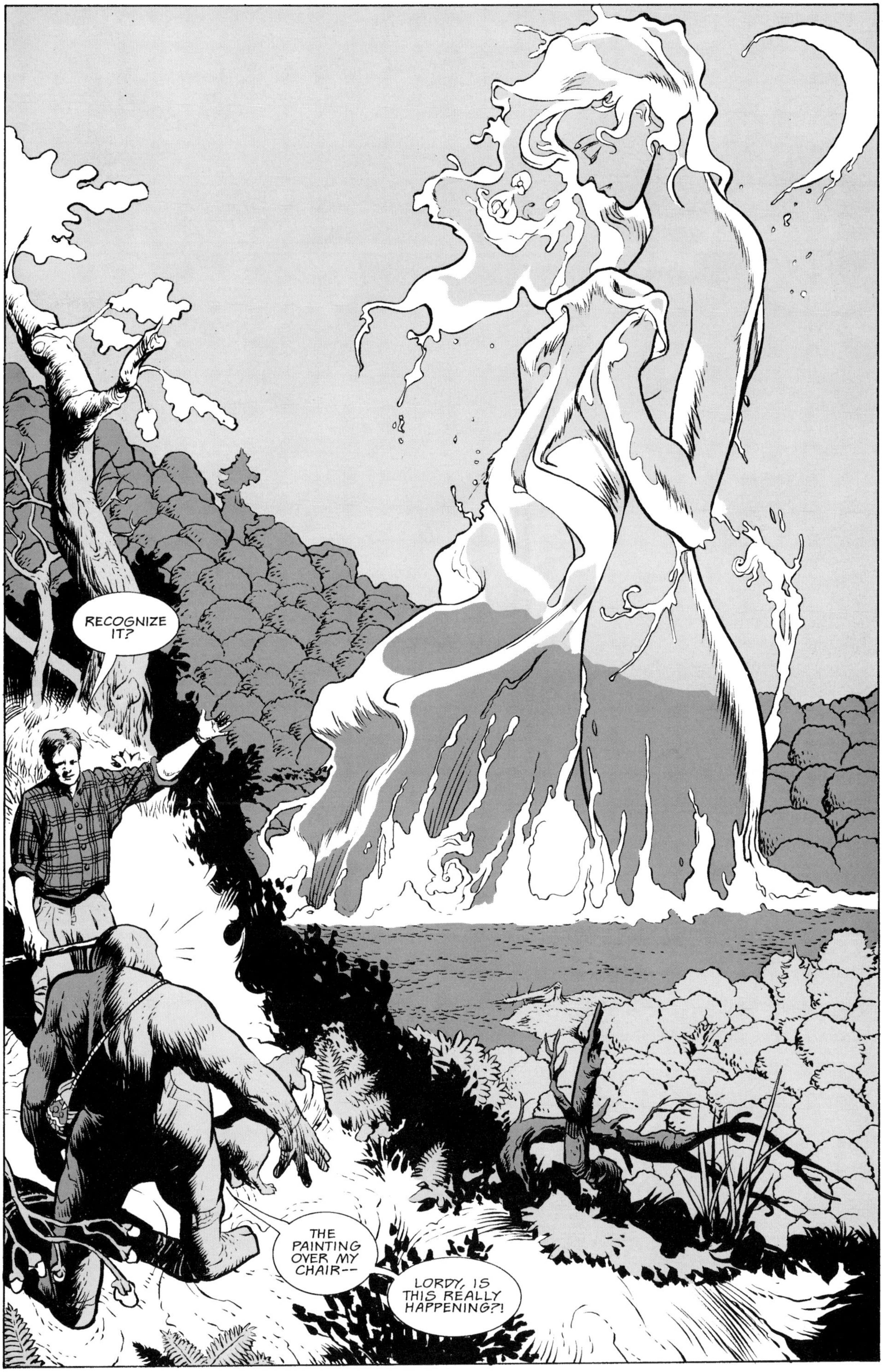
RECOGNIZE IT?
THE PAINTING OVER MY CHAIR--
LORDY, IS THIS REALLY HAPPENING?!

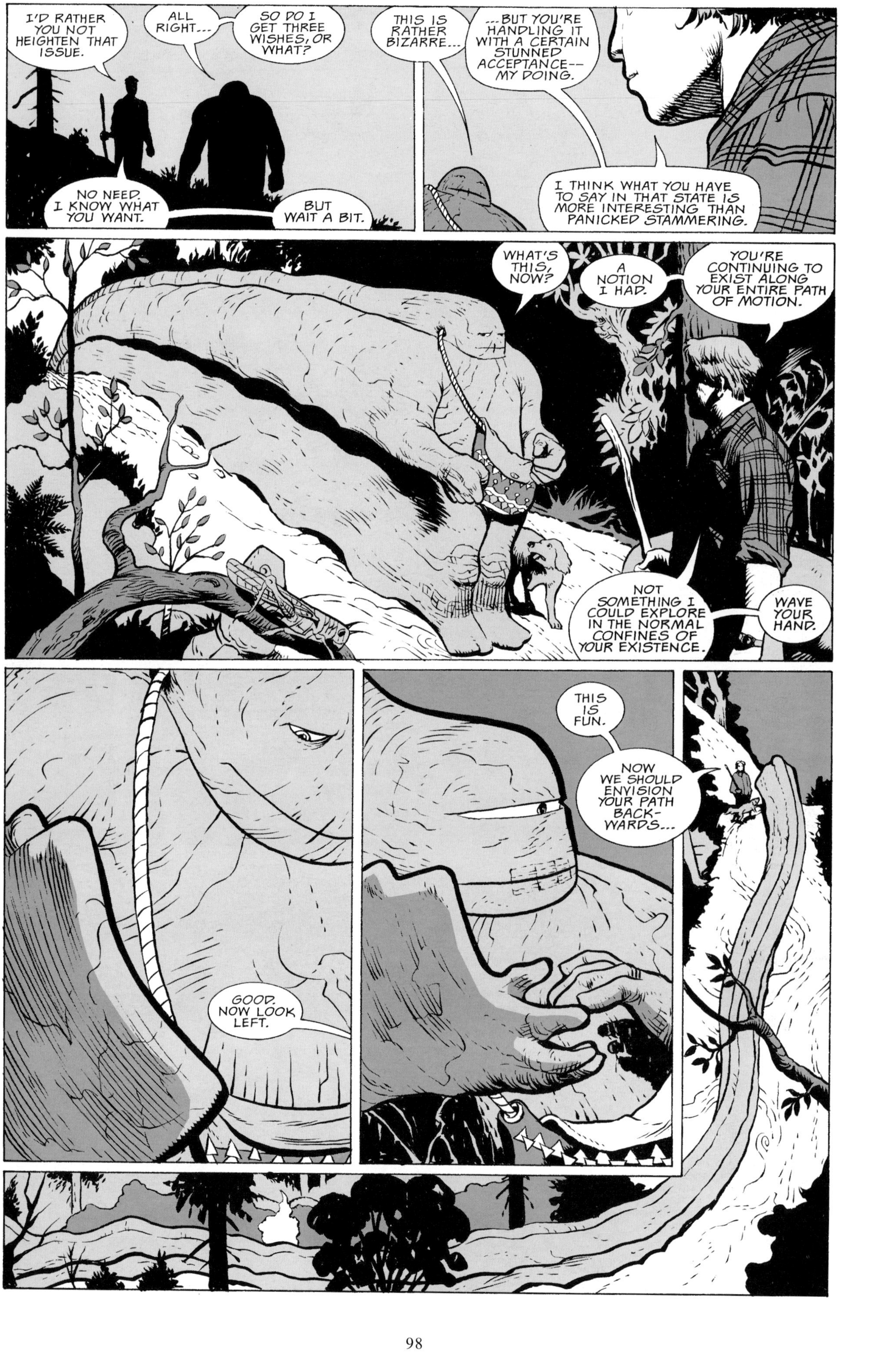
I'D RATHER YOU NOT HEIGHTEN THAT ISSUE.
ALL RIGHT...
SO DO I GET THREE WISHES, OR WHAT?
NO NEED. I KNOW WHAT YOU WANT.
BUT WAIT A BIT.
THIS IS RATHER BIZARRE...
...BUT YOU'RE HANDLING IT WITH A CERTAIN STUNNED ACCEPTANCE-- MY DOING.
I THINK WHAT YOU HAVE TO SAY IN THAT STATE IS MORE INTERESTING THAN PANICKED STAMMERING.
WHAT'S THIS, NOW?
A NOTION I HAD.
YOU'RE CONTINUING TO EXIST ALONG YOUR ENTIRE PATH OF MOTION.
NOT SOMETHING I COULD EXPLORE IN THE NORMAL CONFINES OF YOUR EXISTENCE.
WAVE YOUR HAND.
THIS IS FUN.
NOW WE SHOULD ENVISION YOUR PATH BACK-WARDS...
GOOD. NOW LOOK LEFT.

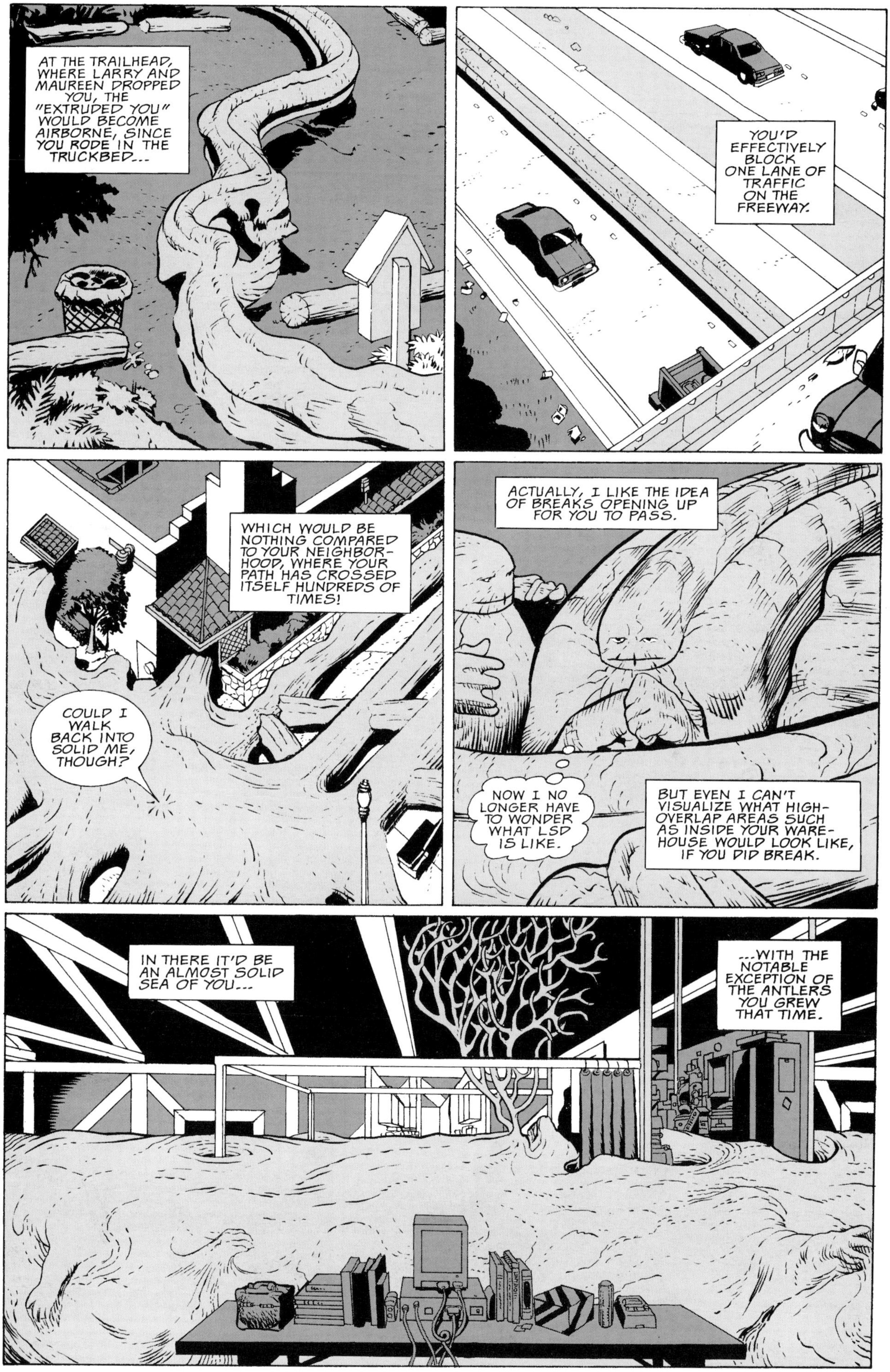
AT THE TRAILHEAD, WHERE LARRY AND MAUREEN DROPPED YOU, THE "EXTRUDED YOU" WOULD BECOME AIRBORNE, SINCE YOU RODE IN THE TRUCKBED...
YOU'D EFFECTIVELY BLOCK ONE LANE OF TRAFFIC ON THE FREEWAY.
WHICH WOULD BE NOTHING COMPARED TO YOUR NEIGHBORHOOD, WHERE YOUR PATH HAS CROSSED ITSELF HUNDREDS OF TIMES!
COULD I WALK BACK INTO SOLID ME, THOUGH?
ACTUALLY, I LIKE THE IDEA OF BREAKS OPENING UP FOR YOU TO PASS.
NOW I NO LONGER HAVE TO WONDER WHAT LSD IS LIKE.
BUT EVEN I CAN'T VISUALIZE WHAT HIGH-OVERLAP AREAS SUCH AS INSIDE YOUR WAREHOUSE WOULD LOOK LIKE, IF YOU DID BREAK.
IN THERE IT'D BE AN ALMOST SOLID SEA OF YOU...
...WITH THE NOTABLE EXCEPTION OF THE ANTLERS YOU GREW THAT TIME.

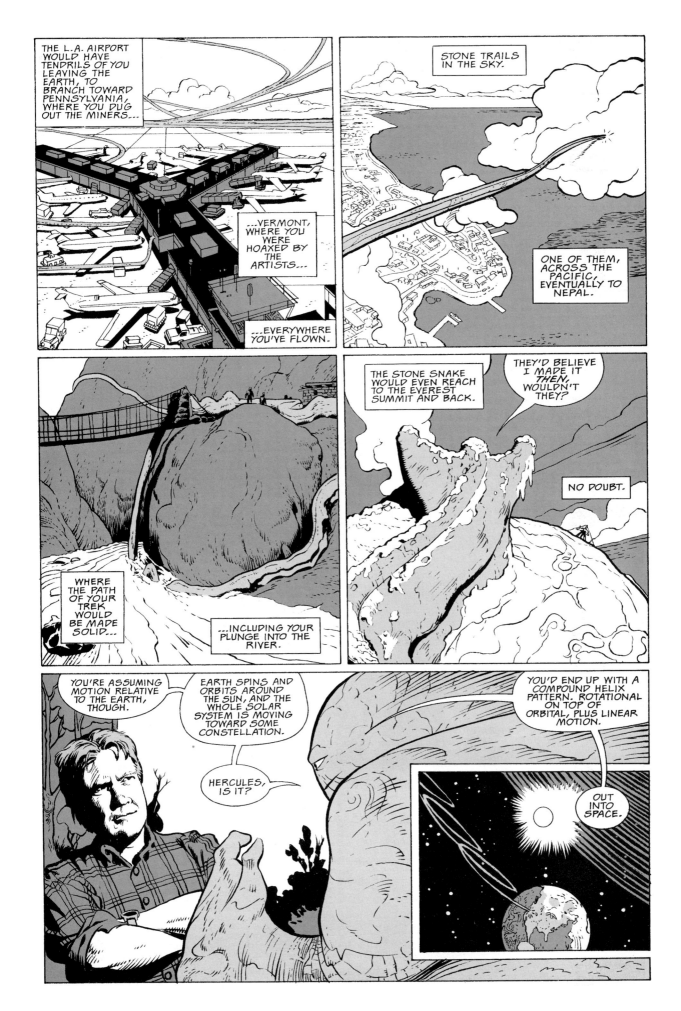

THE L.A. AIRPORT WOULD HAVE TENDRILS OF YOU LEAVING THE EARTH, TO BRANCH TOWARD PENNSYLVANIA, WHERE YOU DUG OUT THE MINERS...

...VERMONT, WHERE YOU WERE HOAXED BY THE ARTISTS...

...EVERYWHERE YOU'VE FLOWN.

STONE TRAILS IN THE SKY.

ONE OF THEM, ACROSS THE PACIFIC, EVENTUALLY TO NEPAL.

WHERE THE PATH OF YOUR TREK WOULD BE MADE SOLID...

...INCLUDING YOUR PLUNGE INTO THE RIVER.

THE STONE SNAKE WOULD EVEN REACH TO THE EVEREST SUMMIT AND BACK.

THEY'D BELIEVE I MADE IT THEN, WOULDN'T THEY?

NO DOUBT.

YOU'RE ASSUMING MOTION RELATIVE TO THE EARTH, THOUGH.

EARTH SPINS AND ORBITS AROUND THE SUN, AND THE WHOLE SOLAR SYSTEM IS MOVING TOWARD SOME CONSTELLATION.

HERCULES, IS IT?

YOU'D END UP WITH A COMPOUND HELIX PATTERN. ROTATIONAL ON TOP OF ORBITAL, PLUS LINEAR MOTION.

OUT INTO SPACE.

100

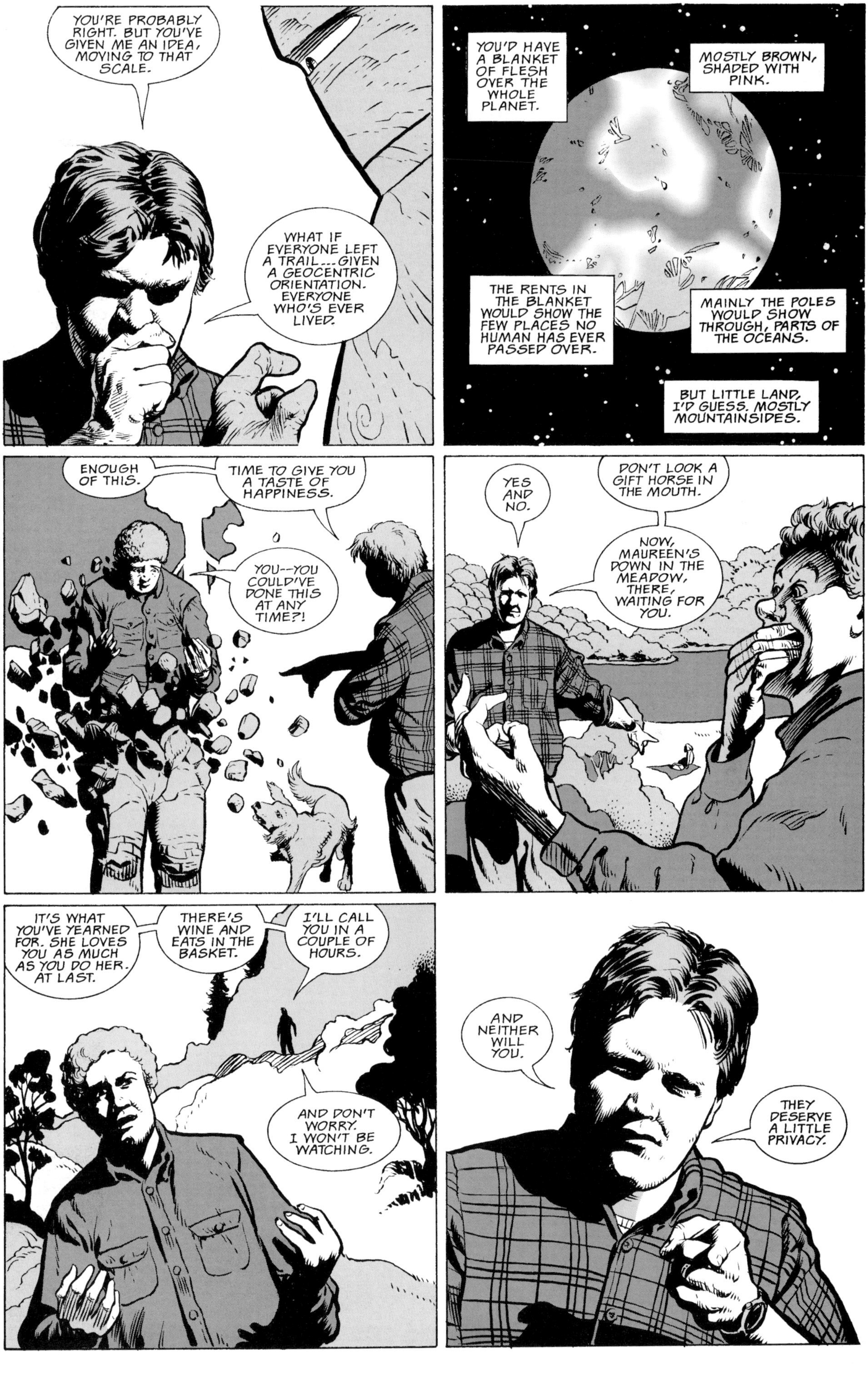
YOU'RE PROBABLY RIGHT. BUT YOU'VE GIVEN ME AN IDEA, MOVING TO THAT SCALE.
WHAT IF EVERYONE LEFT A TRAIL... GIVEN A GEOCENTRIC ORIENTATION. EVERYONE WHO'S EVER LIVED.
YOU'D HAVE A BLANKET OF FLESH OVER THE WHOLE PLANET.
MOSTLY BROWN, SHADED WITH PINK.
THE RENTS IN THE BLANKET WOULD SHOW THE FEW PLACES NO HUMAN HAS EVER PASSED OVER.
MAINLY THE POLES WOULD SHOW THROUGH, PARTS OF THE OCEANS.
BUT LITTLE LAND, I'D GUESS. MOSTLY MOUNTAINSIDES.
ENOUGH OF THIS.
TIME TO GIVE YOU A TASTE OF HAPPINESS.
YOU--YOU COULD'VE DONE THIS AT ANY TIME?!
YES AND NO.
DON'T LOOK A GIFT HORSE IN THE MOUTH.
NOW, MAUREEN'S DOWN IN THE MEADOW, THERE, WAITING FOR YOU.
IT'S WHAT YOU'VE YEARNED FOR. SHE LOVES YOU AS MUCH AS YOU DO HER. AT LAST.
THERE'S WINE AND EATS IN THE BASKET.
I'LL CALL YOU IN A COUPLE OF HOURS.
AND DON'T WORRY. I WON'T BE WATCHING.
AND NEITHER WILL YOU.
THEY DESERVE A LITTLE PRIVACY.

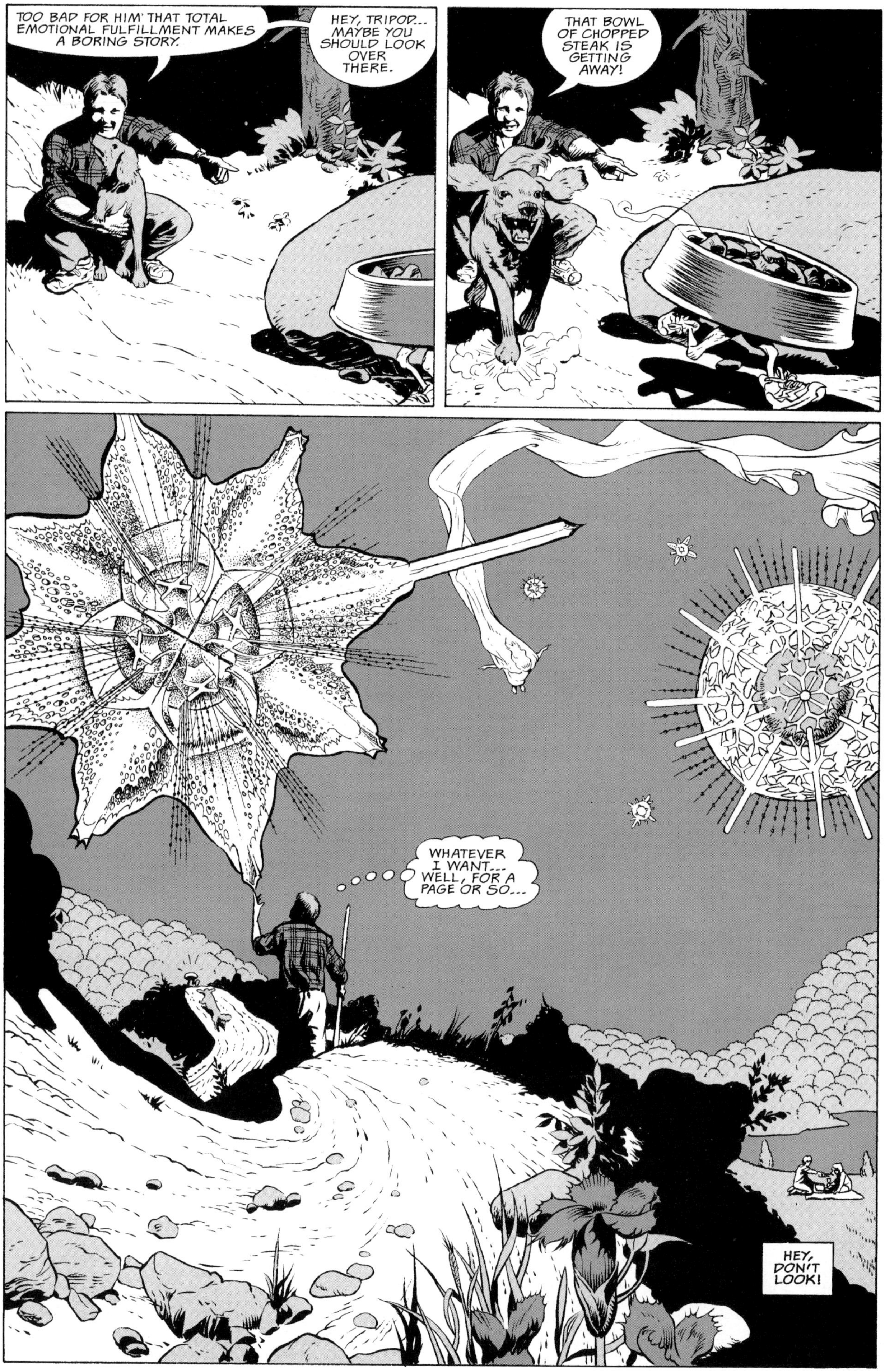
TOO BAD FOR HIM THAT TOTAL EMOTIONAL FULFILLMENT MAKES A BORING STORY.
HEY, TRIPOD... MAYBE YOU SHOULD LOOK OVER THERE.
THAT BOWL OF CHOPPED STEAK IS GETTING AWAY!
WHATEVER I WANT... WELL, FOR A PAGE OR SO...
HEY, DON'T LOOK!

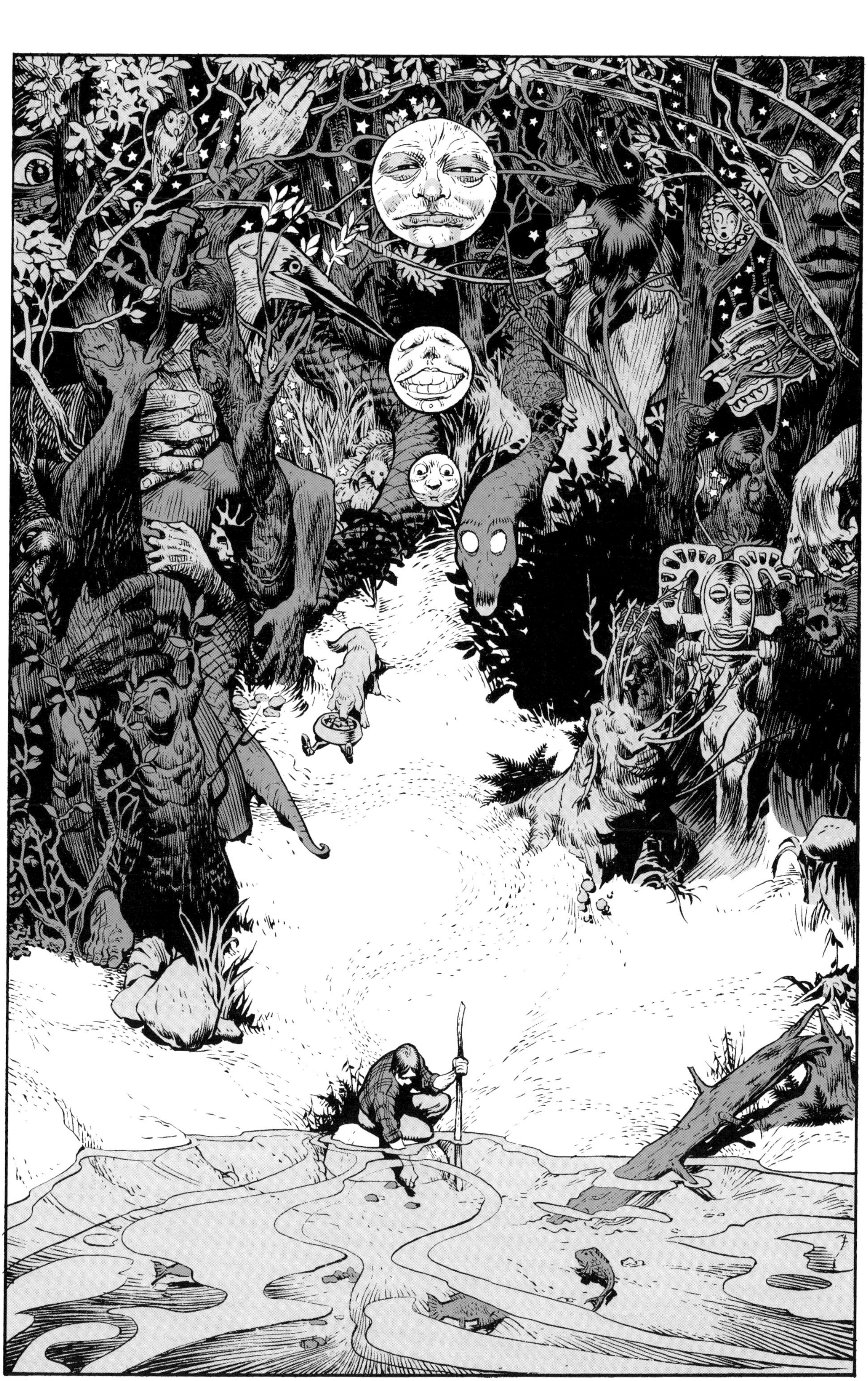

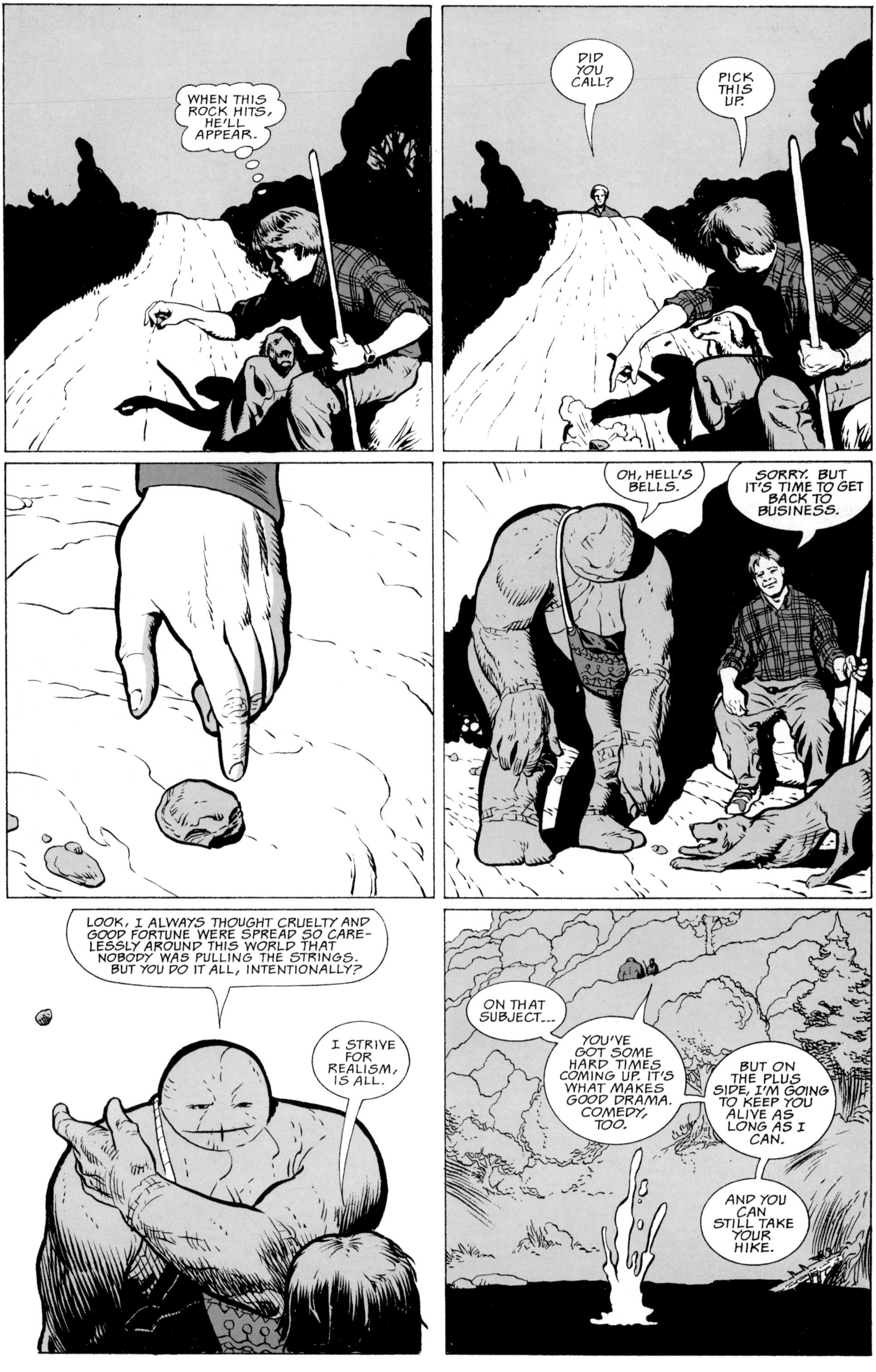

WHEN THIS ROCK HITS, HE'LL APPEAR.
DID YOU CALL?
PICK THIS UP.
OH, HELL'S BELLS.
SORRY. BUT IT'S TIME TO GET BACK TO BUSINESS.
LOOK, I ALWAYS THOUGHT CRUELTY AND GOOD FORTUNE WERE SPREAD SO CARELESSLY AROUND THIS WORLD THAT NOBODY WAS PULLING THE STRINGS. BUT YOU DO IT ALL, INTENTIONALLY?
I STRIVE FOR REALISM, IS ALL.
ON THAT SUBJECT...
YOU'VE GOT SOME HARD TIMES COMING UP. IT'S WHAT MAKES GOOD DRAMA. COMEDY, TOO.
BUT ON THE PLUS SIDE, I'M GOING TO KEEP YOU ALIVE AS LONG AS I CAN.
AND YOU CAN STILL TAKE YOUR HIKE.

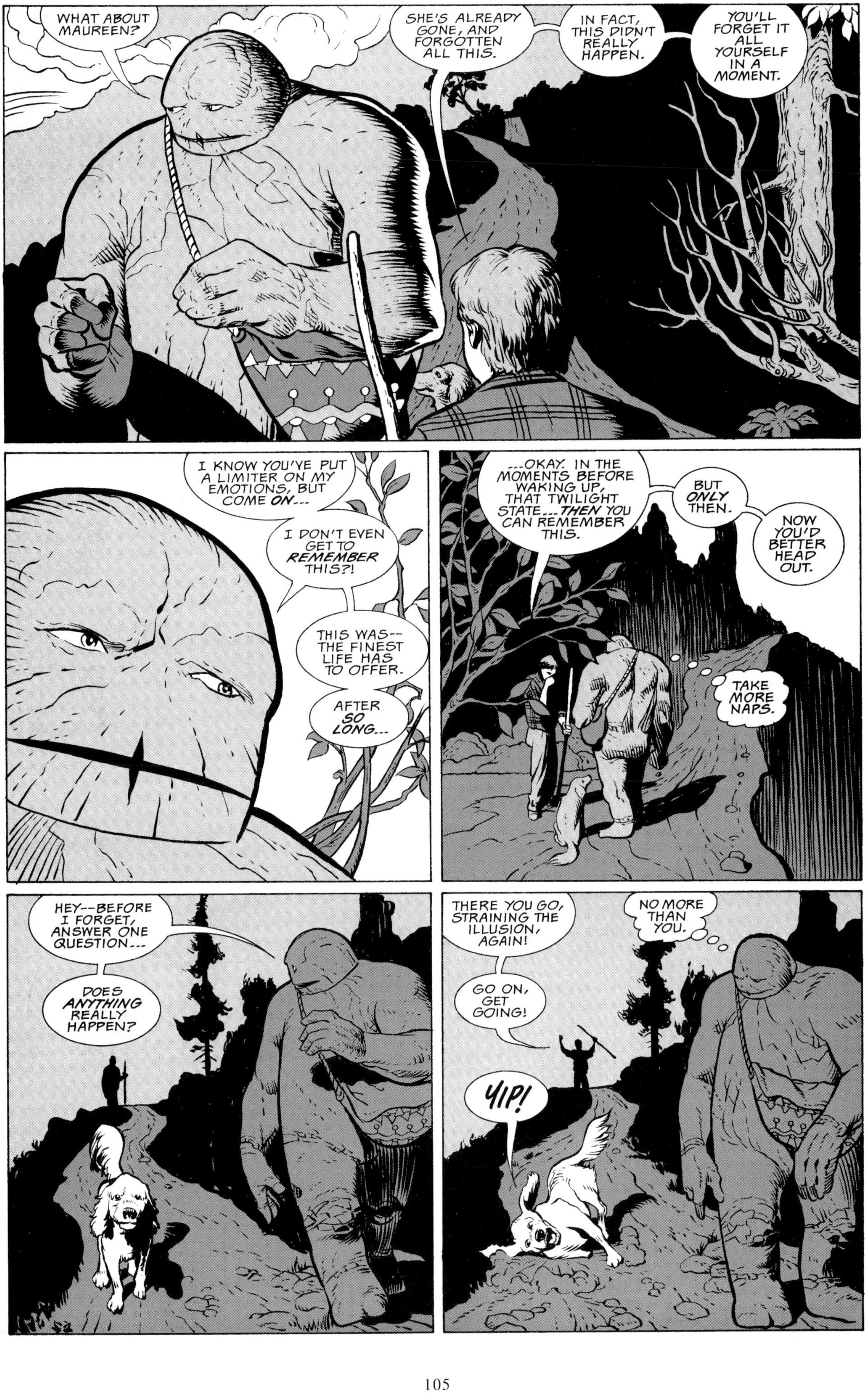
WHAT ABOUT MAUREEN?
SHE'S ALREADY GONE, AND FORGOTTEN ALL THIS.
IN FACT, THIS DIDN'T REALLY HAPPEN.
YOU'LL FORGET IT ALL YOURSELF IN A MOMENT.
I KNOW YOU'VE PUT A LIMITER ON MY EMOTIONS, BUT COME ON---
I DON'T EVEN GET TO REMEMBER THIS?!
THIS WAS-- THE FINEST LIFE HAS TO OFFER.
AFTER SO LONG...
...OKAY. IN THE MOMENTS BEFORE WAKING UP, THAT TWILIGHT STATE...THEN YOU CAN REMEMBER THIS.
BUT ONLY THEN.
NOW YOU'D BETTER HEAD OUT.
TAKE MORE NAPS.
HEY--BEFORE I FORGET, ANSWER ONE QUESTION...
DOES ANYTHING REALLY HAPPEN?
THERE YOU GO, STRAINING THE ILLUSION, AGAIN!
NO MORE THAN YOU.
GO ON, GET GOING!
YIP!

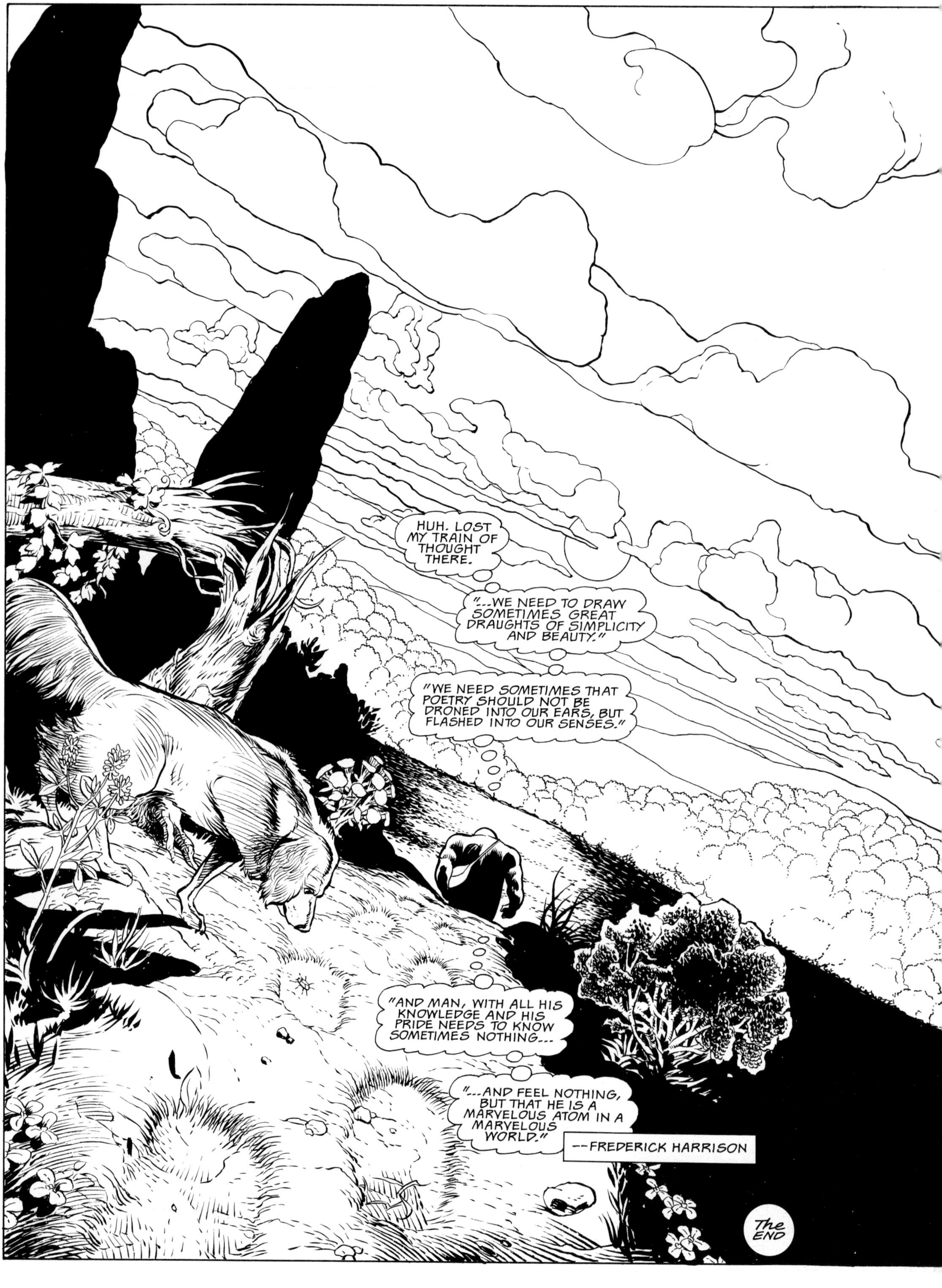
HUH. LOST MY TRAIN OF THOUGHT THERE.
"...WE NEED TO DRAW SOMETIMES GREAT DRAUGHTS OF SIMPLICITY AND BEAUTY."
"WE NEED SOMETIMES THAT POETRY SHOULD NOT BE DRONED INTO OUR EARS, BUT FLASHED INTO OUR SENSES."
"AND MAN, WITH ALL HIS KNOWLEDGE AND HIS PRIDE NEEDS TO KNOW SOMETIMES NOTHING...
"...AND FEEL NOTHING, BUT THAT HE IS A MARVELOUS ATOM IN A MARVELOUS WORLD."
--FREDERICK HARRISON
The END

A BRIEF GEOLOGICAL HISTORY

An intelligent and thoughtful child, Ron Lithgow dreamed of being an adventurer like Richard Burton, exploring the world and doing heroic deeds. As an adult, he never thought he'd be more than a senatorial speech writer . . . and then everything changed. This brief timeline details the events leading up to and following Ron Lithgow's transformation into Concrete.

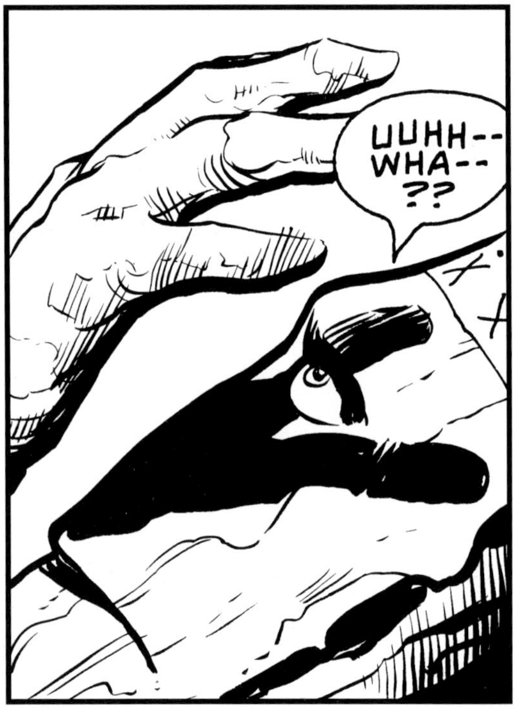
UUHH--
WHA--
??

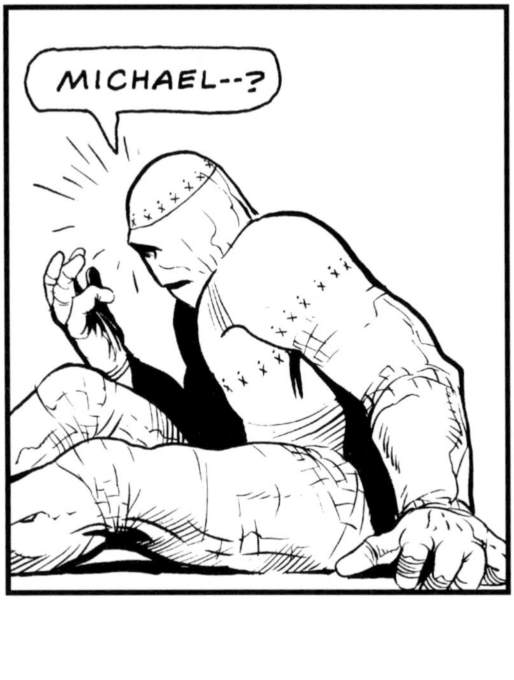
MICHAEL--?

LEGEND

▲ ***The Complete Concrete***
★ ***Concrete Celebrates Earth Day***
● ***Concrete: Complete Short Stories 1986-1989***
■ ***Concrete Color Special***
◆ ***Concrete: Fragile Creature***
+ ***Concrete: Killer Smile***
▼***Dark Horse Presents* #66**
****Dark Horse Presents* #100-3**

1984

▲ Ron Lithgow and his wife, Lisa, split up.

1985

▲ Nursing his wounds from the divorce, Ron goes on a camping trip with his friend and confidant, Michael Maynard. On their first night out, Michael spots a strange light coming from a distant mountain. The pair decide to investigate the area the next day.

▲ Having ascended the mountain to the cave, Ron and Michael are attacked by unseen assailants.

▲ **Ron wakes up in a strange room. He is greeted by Michael, who is now imprisoned in a body that appears to be made out of rock. Michael informs Ron that he is in a similar body. They share the room with two other rock creatures, whom they have named Fang (due to its growling and animal-like behavior) and Shrinking Violet (due to its timid nature).**

▲ Ron and Michael discover they are captives of an enclave of rock-like people. They are drugged and forced to undergo rigorous experiments. It is apparent that their new bodies possess a strength and resiliency far beyond their human capabilities.

▲ Ron and Michael encounter their original bodies, which they believe are now housing the brains of the previous inhabitants of their new bodies. With them are a bear and a deer, which are most likely Fang's and Violet's bodies. They are all evidently subjects in a brain-transplant experiment.

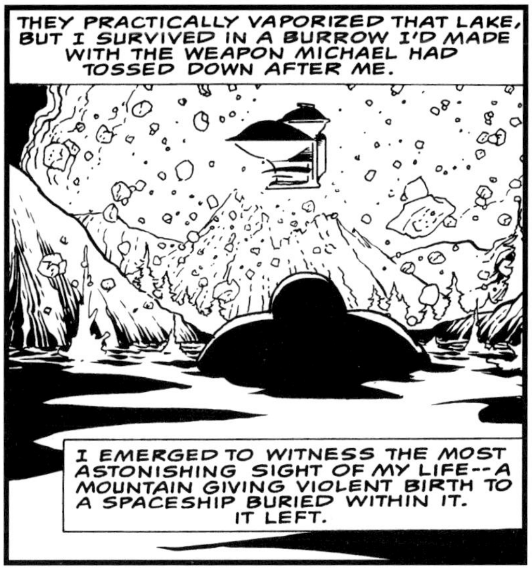
THEY PRACTICALLY VAPORIZED THAT LAKE, BUT I SURVIVED IN A BURROW I'D MADE WITH THE WEAPON MICHAEL HAD TOSSED DOWN AFTER ME.
I EMERGED TO WITNESS THE MOST ASTONISHING SIGHT OF MY LIFE--A MOUNTAIN GIVING VIOLENT BIRTH TO A SPACESHIP BURIED WITHIN IT. IT LEFT.

▲ Ron convinces Michael that they must escape and warn the world. At the last minute, Michael decides to stay, determined to get his human body back. He forces Ron to go without him.

▲ **A massive spacecraft erupts from the mountain, decimating it. It disappears into the sky, taking Michael with it.**

▲ Unsure of what to do, Ron goes to the home of his boss, Senator Mark Douglas. Senator Douglas connects Ron with the National Science Agency, who they hope can explain what Ron has experienced and help him understand his new body.

▲ **All traces of Ron Lithgow are erased. Dubbed "John Doe," he is subjected to a continuous series of tests that will measure the capabilities and explore the make-up of the rock body. Ron becomes enamored with one of the researchers, Dr. Maureen Vonnegut.**

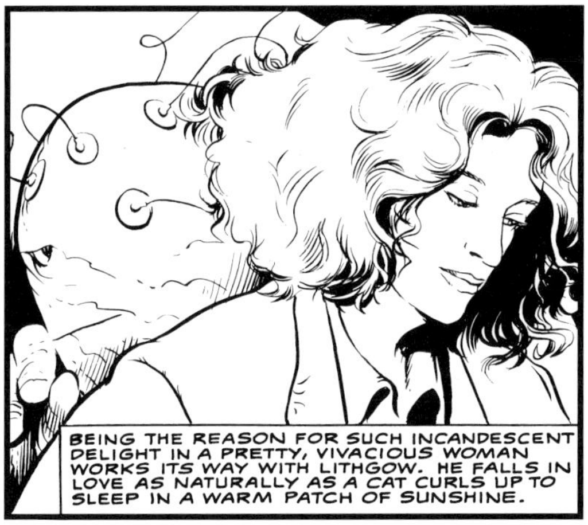
BEING THE REASON FOR SUCH INCANDESCENT DELIGHT IN A PRETTY, VIVACIOUS WOMAN WORKS ITS WAY WITH LITHGOW. HE FALLS IN LOVE AS NATURALLY AS A CAT CURLS UP TO SLEEP IN A WARM PATCH OF SUNSHINE.

▲ Some of the test results are that the rock-coated body: has an extremely high natural temperature; features eyes that can see fine details at a long distance under any condition; can digest just about anything; possesses amazing strength; and has a very low fatigue rate.

▲ Frustrated with the government's failure to find a way to return him to normal life, Ron attempts escape. He is detained with violence. In the aftermath, it is discovered that his body regenerates and heals itself.

▲ The government offers a deal. They will release Ron if he presents himself as "Concrete," sole survivor of an effort to create cyborgs, and submit to more testing. Ron agrees, so long as Maureen is the one testing him. A publicity campaign is launched in hopes of quickly exhausting public

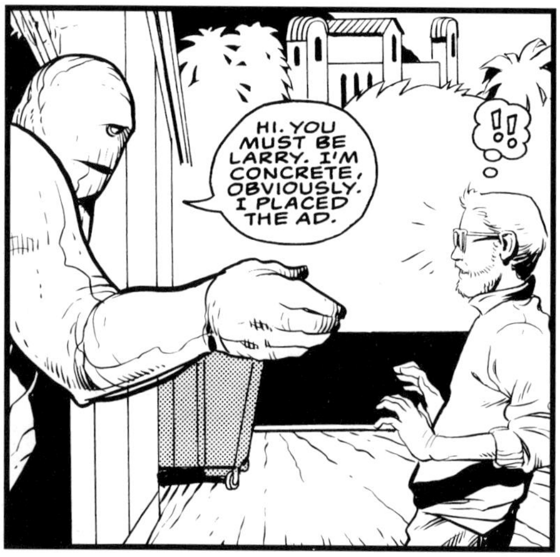
HI. YOU MUST BE LARRY. I'M CONCRETE, OBVIOUSLY. I PLACED THE AD.
!!

curiosity about this ubiquitous, but unforthcoming, new celebrity.

1986

▲ Concrete settles in Eagle Rock, California, near his Hollywood obligations.

▲ Concrete decides he wants to live out his childhood dream of being an adventurer. He appears on "The Tonight Show with Johnny Carson" and asks the viewers to contact him with possible uses of his extraordinary skills.

▲ Larry Munro, a grad student and aspiring novelist, answers Concrete's ad for a personal assistant. He will record details and take photographs of Concrete's adventures. This will aid Concrete when he writes about his exploits.

▲ Senator Douglas enlists Concrete's help to rescue trapped miners. While the rescue is partially successful, the press attacks Concrete when some of the miners are found dead.

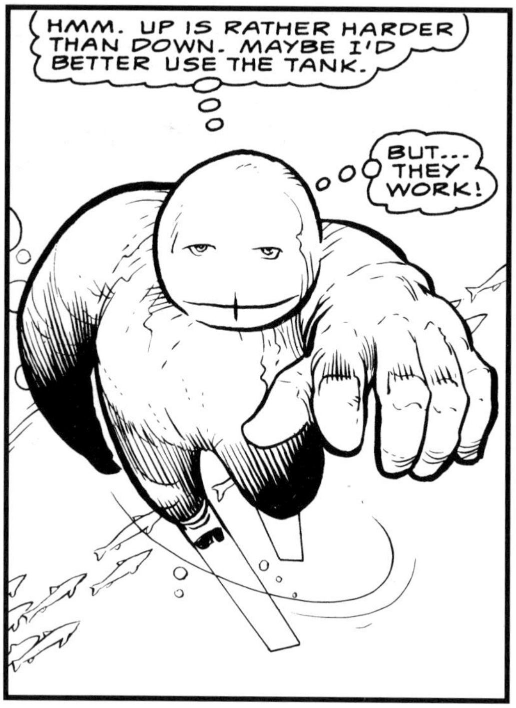
HMM. UP IS RATHER HARDER THAN DOWN. MAYBE I'D BETTER USE THE TANK.
BUT... THEY WORK!

• Concrete is inundated with letters in response to his "Tonight Show" appearance. As a result, he accepts an invitation to entertain some children at a birthday party. The hostess promises $1,500, which will help fund his expeditions. Unfortunately, the child's mother lied about the money.

• Melissa Strangehands, a Los Angeles-based artist, decides to devote her career to painting Concrete. He politely declines her many requests to sit for her.

▲ Hoping to set a world record, Concrete attempts to swim the Atlantic Ocean. During a storm, Maureen, Larry, and the representative from the record-book company, are thrown from the pacer boat. Concrete expeds all of his energies to keep them alive, and after many days adrift, they are finally rescued.

▲ Larry's actions during the ordeal on the Atlantic prove his loyalty to Concrete. In turn, Concrete takes Larry into his confidence, revealing his true origins.

● Concrete rescues Larry's brother, Adam, who has crashed his plane in the Montana wilderness.

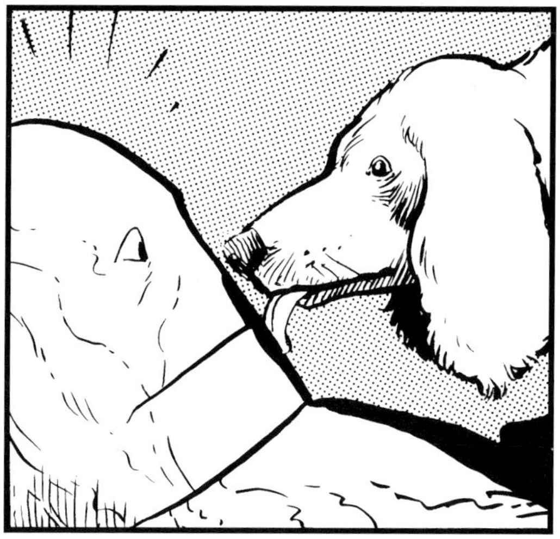

1987

▲ Concrete works as the bodyguard for a deranged rock star named Duke, whose life he ultimately saves from a would-be assassin, the blood brother Duke betrayed.

▲ **Concrete spends the summer helping a struggling farm get back on its feet. He becomes close to the family, but discovers they have a terrible secret — the eldest boy killed their abusive father. Believing this was not the boy's intentions, he helps the family bury the secret for good. In gratitude, the family gives Concrete Tripod, the three-legged dog that will become his companion.**

▲ **Maureen's estranged husband comes to Eagle Rock to win her back. As a result, Concrete is jealous. At the same time, he begins to grow antler-like appendages from his forehead. Whether the two events are connected or not is never exactly clear.**

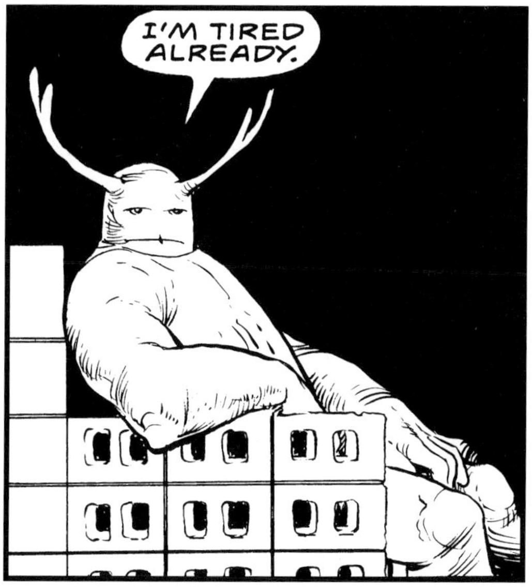
I'M TIRED ALREADY.

▲ Concrete goes to Nepal with Kent Taylor, a filmmaker who wants to make a documentary about Concrete's travels. After helping build a bridge for a remote community, Concrete fulfills his dream of climbing Mount Everest, solo. On Concrete's way down, a Communist spy attempts to capture him for his government, and — unfortunately — destroys Concrete's evidence of reaching the peak.

▲ **Elaine Lithgow, Ron's mother, becomes terminally ill. Concrete goes to her house, revealing that he is Ron and is not dead as the government has led her to believe. It is the last time he sees her.**

1989

■ Artists Ben Storey and Diedre Low lure Concrete to Vermont to investigate UFO sightings. Concrete hopes he will find information on the aliens who captured him and Michael Maynard. Instead, armed with Maureen's insights,he exposes the sightings as a hoax.

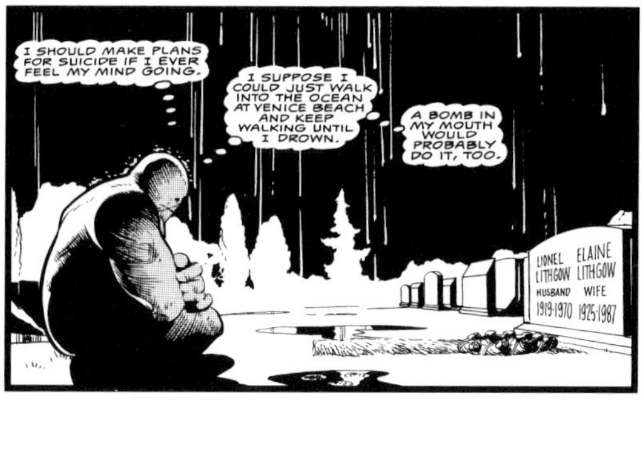
I SHOULD MAKE PLANS FOR SUICIDE IF I EVER FEEL MY MIND GOING.
I SUPPOSE I COULD JUST WALK INTO THE OCEAN AT VENICE BEACH AND KEEP WALKING UNTIL I DROWN.
A BOMB IN MY MOUTH WOULD PROBABLY DO IT, TOO.
LIONEL LITHGOW HUSBAND 1919-1970
ELAINE LITHGOW WIFE 1925-1987

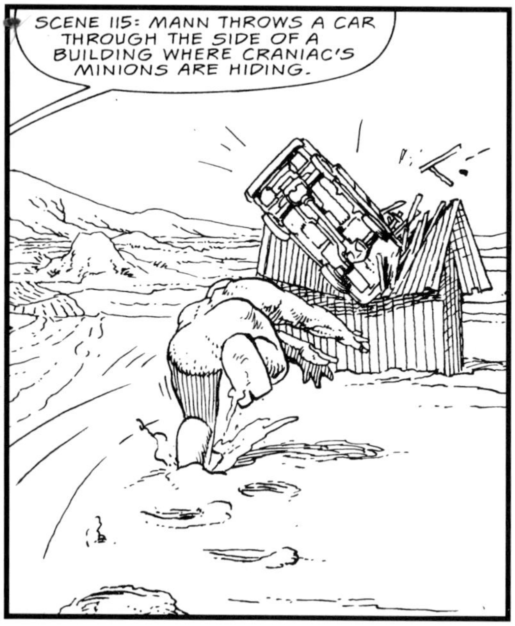
SCENE 115: MANN THROWS A CAR THROUGH THE SIDE OF A BUILDING WHERE CRANIAC'S MINIONS ARE HIDING.

1990

⋆ Concrete gives a speech commemorating Earth Day.

1992

◆ **Kent Taylor contacts Concrete about working on stunts and special effects for a small film based on a line of toys. Though a troubled production, *Rulers of the Omniverse* finally gets finished.**

◆ Against the CIA's orders, Maureen strikes up a professional and romantic relationship with Ed Buchner, an expert on biological transmutation known for his activism. Maureen hopes that his research can aid her in learning how Concrete's outer crust regenerates. The relationship is halted (at least, officially) before any answers can be found.

▾ Concrete meets Dwayne Byrd, the noted author who wrote the original draft for the *Rulers of the Omniverse* screenplay. Byrd owns a Melissa Strangehands original — an erotic painting inspired by Concrete. For the first time, he is intrigued by the woman's abilities.

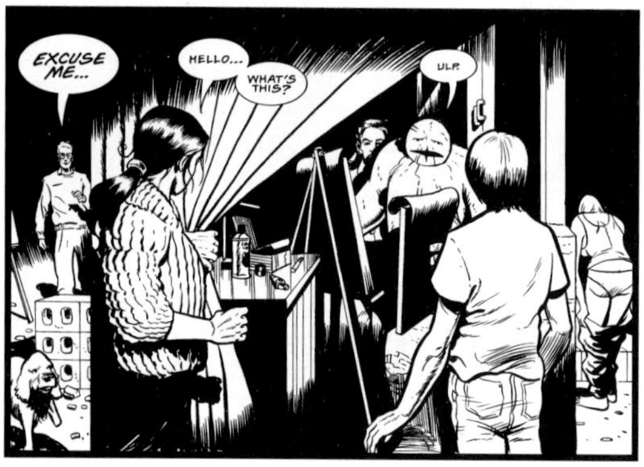
EXCUSE ME...
HELLO...
WHAT'S THIS?
ULP.

1994

+ Larry Munro is kidnapped by Rick Pratt, a fugitive of justice. The four-hour trial is resolved without Larry being hurt but not before both Larry and Concrete's capabilities are pushed to their limits.

1995

* **Concrete is reunited with Andre, the birthday boy whose party at which Concrete had entertained. Andre's mother attempts to swindle Concrete again, luring him into a *faux* sex scandal and taping it for a tabloid TV show. Thankfully, Andre's mother's amateur video efforts thwart her own plans.**